Good Food
Great Medicine

Recipes & Ruminations

*Making better use of food and your kitchen
in the battle against type 2 diabetes, high blood pressure,
heart disease, stroke, and cancer.*

First Edition: Third Printing

ISBN 978-0-9796339-0-4

To our mother, Jane Hartt Hassell,
Who says that when you get to be her age
You get to choose your photo.
Here she is with her first car.

…and with profound gratitude to Lisa Uchytil, who works so hard with us on the movement forward of the cookbooking journey, and whose clarity, patience, and inexplicable confidence is of inestimable value; to our sister Marcia McCoy and our friend Marcia Watkins for their editing help; to our colleague Angela Hahn, M.D. for her help; and to Sheila Hanson, Kathleen Mullane, Kay Thompson, Katherine Knight, Sandy Leavitt, Dave Pattillo, and the many others who have encouraged us.

Contents

Miles Hassell, MD

Internist

Director, Comprehensive Risk Reduction Clinic

Director, Integrative Medicine Program

Providence St. Vincent Medical Center

Miles Hassell is an internist in private practice at St. Vincent Hospital in Portland. He was born in Seattle, Washington, and grew up in Perth, Western Australia. Miles received his medical degree from the University of Western Australia, and then moved back to the United States where he completed his residency in Internal Medicine in Portland, Oregon.

Miles' medical practice emphasizes a combination of conventional and complementary approaches to the treatment and prevention of disease. In particular he encourages the vigorous application of evidence based nutritional and exercise interventions.

He established the Integrative Medicine Program at Providence Cancer Center in Portland, Oregon, and lectures widely to physician groups regarding the appropriate use of nutritional medicine. Miles is also a clinical instructor in the training of Internal Medicine residents, twice receiving "Outstanding Teacher of the Year" award. He is board certified by the American Board of Internal Medicine.

He has been selected by his peers for the "Portland Top Doctors" list in *Portland Monthly* magazine.

Introduction

This book had its beginning in the office of Miles' medical practice. He poked his head out of an exam room and said, "Hey, Mea, we need some brown rice recipes in here." So *Good Food, Great Medicine* was conceived.

My brother Miles and I started working together in his internal medicine practice in 1996. Since that time Miles has been tirelessly and passionately arguing the case for good food. "But you can't get people to change the way they eat," people would tell him. That response helped motivate Miles to develop a series of patient education handouts, the first of which was *Fat Is Good, Bagels Are Bad*, as seen in chapter one. As he sees it, *he* can't change the way people eat, but he can give them the information that can help *them* decide to make changes themselves. This book deals with ways to translate that information into practical day-to-day living and eating.

My background is notable for food, both in and out of the kitchen; working with restaurants and natural food stores as well as writing about food and teaching cooking classes. For that matter, both Miles and I have been involved in the food business all our lives, beginning with a country inn as a family business in Western Australia and continuing with natural food stores in Seattle, Pennsylvania, and Perth, Western Australia.

Miles and I were raised in Western Australia and have eaten the way we talk about in this book all our lives. Our mother always understood the importance of whole food, and we didn't realize then how ahead of the curve she was. These days, most of what is known about food and health sounds a lot like instructions from our mother. *Eat your vegetables. Beans are good for you. Finish your oatmeal. If you're still hungry, eat an apple. Clean up your plate before you have dessert. Go outside and play.*

The approach to eating in this book is just as uncomplicated. *Choose good food. Food is medicine.* It only gets complicated when good sense collides with personal tastes and tolerances. The issue is our willingness to make the changes necessary for the food-as-medicine strategy to work.

Then there's the business of cooking. There is no avoiding the fact that it takes a certain amount of time to fix your own food. We don't assume that you are in the kitchen because you love to cook or have plenty of disposable time. Chapter one reminds you of *why* you are standing in your kitchen with a knife in one hand and an onion in the other. Chapter two talks more about things like knives and onions themselves — a sort of kitchen starter kit.

The recipes reflect our personal tastes as much as our philosophy. Most of the recipes are very simply constructed and designed for speed, but the agenda also calls for maximum vegetable, whole grain, and bean per square inch of plate whenever possible. And Miles assures me that my affection for extra virgin olive oil, onions, and garlic is fully supported by epidemiological evidence.

Mea and Miles

What Is So Important About Good Food?

Miles Hassell, M.D.

Most people have in their own hands the most important tools for the prevention and treatment of heart disease, cancer, type 2 diabetes, stroke, dementia, osteoarthritis, obesity, and high blood pressure. These tools are food, exercise, and sleep. The thoughtful use of these is the strongest predictor of good health for most people, and their real power is generally under-appreciated.

Good food, daily exercise, and adequate sleep are all critical in the fight against chronic disease and disability. The decisions *we* make about our diet, weight, and habits are more important than the decisions our physician will make.

Also, the impact of those decisions can reach well beyond the goal of risk reduction, and may actually help *reverse* disease.

For example, someone who already has heart disease can reduce the risk of future events such as a heart attack by 70% or more with diet alone, and 60% or more with exercise. That's better than we see from our best drugs and medical procedures! And we find that the combination of conventional medicine added to diet and exercise seems to give even better results.

The Mediterranean Factor

The food choices we recommend in this book for the best possible results are all part of the traditional Mediterranean diet. This means eating food mostly from plant sources, like whole grains, beans, raw nuts, fruits, and vegetables. The diet includes moderate-to-high levels of 'healthy' fat (such as extra virgin olive oil and nuts) and fish, variable amounts of cheese and yogurt, and small amounts of meat.

In fact, the Mediterranean diet guidelines that have been shown to improve health in medical trials allow for almost all minimally processed naturally occurring foods.

The Fine Print

Most whole, minimally processed food is good for you, but there are some foods to be avoided. We've expanded on this list and the reasons for it in *Fat Is Good, Bagels Are Bad* in chapter one. The good news is that the list of food to avoid is pretty short.

- Hydrogenated/partially hydrogenated oil
- Preserved meats
- White flour and white rice
- Refined sugars
- Fake foods

Most foods *not* on the list appear to be relatively healthy *when eaten as part of a varied diet*. For example, raw nuts, caffeine, dark chocolate, aged cheese, real butter, eggs, meat, and modest amounts of alcohol can all be part of a healthy diet that already includes plenty of fruits, vegetables, beans, and whole grains.

I tell my patients that any food commonly eaten for more than 150 years should be innocent until proven guilty, and any food created by man in the last century is guilty until proven innocent.

Diet and Exercise: A Brief Review

Miles Hassell, M.D.

You can find impressive results from all kinds of traditional diets. The Masai in Africa have thrived on milk, blood, and beef. The Eskimos have flourished on a diet of pretty much unlimited fat from the fish and animals they killed. The Japanese used to do very well when they ate the traditional low fat diet.

From the evidence we have today it seems clear that pockets of people within primitive populations all over the world — Japan, China, Russia, Greece, India, Africa — with dramatically different diets have enjoyed good health and long life. *And* all without the help of modern medicine and cookbooks, it should be added.

In our Western societies, heart disease and cancer are the most common causes of death. Much of the blame for these premature deaths is likely to be attributed to a sedentary lifestyle and overly processed foods, typically part of a high-tech low-fat diet. In contrast, some of the healthiest modern societies have a diet characterized by whole foods and fairly high fat content. In this regard, Ansel Key's Seven Countries Study gives us valuable insights. For example, the traditional Greek or Mediterranean diet eaten on the island of Crete is very high in fat, about 40 percent, mostly as nuts, olives and olive oil, fish and cheese. Yet despite this high fat diet, the people of Crete had the lowest rate of heart disease in the entire study. And they enjoy their food!

What is the Mediterranean Diet?

There is no precise definition of the Mediterranean diet. However, it is safe to say that there is a general pattern common with most Mediterranean regions, and consistent with what has been found in the published studies. It is pretty simple.

- Food mainly from plant sources: fruits and vegetables, breads and grains, beans, nuts, and seeds. Vegetables, fresh and cooked, as part of every meal, and fresh fruit as a typical dessert

- Plenty of complex carbohydrates in the form of whole grains and beans daily

- Olive oil as the main fat, replacing other oils and fats, including butter

- Animal protein in the form of fish, poultry, and eggs, and small amounts of red meat

- Dairy food in the form of cultured products, such as yogurt and high fat, full-flavored cheeses, rather than milk

- Moderate consumption of wine, generally with meals

In this book — and in my practice — we recommend what we call the *whole food* Mediterranean diet. For example, we would suggest our patients did not eat white rice, white bread, or regular pasta, even though the contemporary Mediterranean diet includes all three.

Not surprisingly, most of my patients have some aspect of their health compromised when they come to see me, so we are dealing with a reduced margin of error from the start. I tell them what kind of improvement we can expect to see in their symptoms, and suggest as aggressive an approach as can be tolerated.

Heart Disease, Cancer, and the Mediterranean Diet

Recent studies confirm the impression gained over the last thousand years that diet and exercise play a large part in whether people develop these diseases prematurely. These same studies show us how we can use diet and exercise to prevent or reverse many of these diseases. We'll review some of the recent key studies here.

HALE (Healthy Aging: a Longitudinal Study in Europe)[1]

The HALE project looked at the effects of a Mediterranean diet, alcohol use, nonsmoking, and physical activity on the health of seventy-to-ninety-year-old men and women throughout eleven European countries over twelve years.

In this population, the Mediterranean diet reduced deaths by 23 percent. Moderate alcohol use (such as one alcoholic drink daily) reduced deaths by 22 percent. Regular physical activity reduced deaths by 27 percent.

To summarize: if you were a nonsmoker who ate well, *and* exercised for 30 minutes or more daily, *and* drank a small amount of alcohol, *your risk of dying from any cause was reduced by 65 percent.* The reductions were similar for cancer, heart disease, and other cardiovascular disease such as stroke.

Nurses Health Study

Other studies have shown that if you are younger than seventy years old, this approach can be expected to work even better. For example, in the Nurses Health Study [2], studying women in North America, reductions of about 90 percent for diabetes and 80 percent for heart disease were seen in association with similar diet and exercise choices as described in the HALE study.

Studies such as these show that *nothing* your doctor can do for any chronic disease you may have can equal the degree of benefit you can achieve with sensible daily diet, exercise and lifestyle choices. *And* not smoking. Under most conditions, you determine your health outcomes to a far greater degree than your doctor does. Of course, the combination of good medical care and sensible lifestyle choices is going to give even better results.

The Lyon Study

One of the most successful diet/health trials was the Lyon Diet Heart Study. The Lyon study stands out in being one of a handful of high quality randomized controlled prospective studies examining diet and disease with a method considered the gold standard for health research. The Lyon study followed men who had already had a heart attack, and who were randomized to either an American Heart Association Diet, or a Mediterranean diet and followed for four years.

After four years, those following the Mediterranean diet had 72 percent fewer major cardiac events, 56 percent fewer deaths[3] and 61 percent fewer cancers.

Those numbers may be difficult to absorb, so I'll repeat them: *72 percent fewer major cardiac events, 56 percent fewer deaths, and 61 percent fewer cancers*[4]. We know of *no* drug trials that can give such results.

(The Mediterranean diet used in this trial emphasized more root vegetables and green vegetables, fresh fruits, beans and legumes, breads and fiber, and fish. The main fats in the diet were to be olive or canola oil, and study participants were to eat

[1] Knoops, K. et al. JAMA 2004;292:1433-39
[2] Rimm, E and Stampfer, M. JAMA 2004;292:1490-1492
[3] Circulation 1999;99;779-785
[4] Archives of Internal Medicine 1998;158;1181-1187

less meat, butter, and cream. Moderate alcohol consumption was allowed.)

The Greek EPIC study
Supporting the results of the Lyon study are the findings from the Greek EPIC study, which compared the health outcomes of Greeks who eat a Mediterranean-type diet compared to Greeks who do not, and found similar reductions in heart disease and cancer risk as in the Lyon study. [1]

The Mediterranean Diet and Conventional Medicine for Heart Disease
One agreeable side effect of the Mediterranean diet is that patients find it leads to improvements in many of the risk factors for heart disease and other diseases, so they can sometimes reduce the dose or eliminate some medications altogether.

The benefits most commonly seen among my patients are improvements in cholesterol, weight, blood pressure, blood sugar, esophageal reflux (heartburn), and measurements of inflammation such as C - reactive protein (CRP). This has also been seen in many prospective randomized controlled trials.

One of the most instructive of these studies is PREDIMED, which compared a prudent low fat diet with a Mediterranean diet, and found significant benefits for the Mediterranean diet in blood pressure, blood sugar, cholesterol, and C - reactive protein.[2]

In another study, the use of the Mediterranean diet combined with conventional cholesterol lowering medicine led to a further drop in cholesterol.

Of course, because a Mediterranean type of diet allows a far more liberal use of certain fats, it is much more pleasant for most of us than a low fat diet, and we are

more likely to stick to the program. This is a particularly significant factor when we are talking about a *lifetime* program, not a temporary diet.

Weight Loss and the Mediterranean Diet
The moderate-fat Mediterranean Diet, when followed intelligently, will help with weight reduction as well as risk reduction. Many people who need to lose weight have been taught that they need to follow a low fat diet, and certainly there are many healthy low-fat approaches to weight loss.

The key question is this: which eating plan for weight loss is most likely to be continued for the long term? It is not the weight loss program that works for six months that is important; you should choose the weight loss program that works for the *long term.* For most of us this means it should allow for a wide variety of enjoyable foods and blend with a 'normal' life.

As an example of this, take a look at the weight loss study in which a fairly high fat Mediterranean diet, with 35 percent of the energy from fat, was compared to a low fat diet, with 20 percent of the calories from fat. In this study the Mediterranean diet group was instructed to eat more nuts, olive oil, and vegetables.

After eighteen months, the group eating the higher fat Mediterranean diet had significantly better participation, weight loss, and smaller waists. The low fat diet group _gained_ weight at eighteen months, probably not because the diet was bad, but because they had a lot more trouble following the low fat diet compared to the tastier and more satisfying Mediterranean diet.[3]

As a postscript on the subject of losing weight on the Mediterranean diet, the importance of daily physical activity,

---

[1] Trichopoulou et al. NEJM 2003;348:2599-608
[2] Estruch et al. Annals of Internal Medicine 2006;145:1-11

---

[3] McManus. Int J Obesity 2001;25:1503-11

portion control, and common sense can't be overstated. Also, it makes sense to keep the otherwise healthy but very starchy and high-calorie vegetables like potatoes and corn to a minimum.

Diabetes and the Mediterranean Diet

The Mediterranean Diet can substantially reduce your risk of adult onset diabetes (type 2 diabetes) and can reverse the metabolic syndrome.

Diabetes is responsible for a large proportion of the heart attacks, strokes, blindness, and kidney failure seen in our society. Not only is it a bad disease, but it is becoming much more common, tripling in frequency in our society over the last twenty years.

It used to be that children with type 2 diabetes were rare. Now, children and teenagers with type 2 diabetes are the fastest growing subgroup of this disease! Yet it is completely preventable, and probably reversible in many patients.

Two groups of studies demonstrate the use of the Mediterranean diet to prevent diabetes. One group shows that a Mediterranean-style diet can prevent the metabolic syndrome, a constellation of findings (high blood pressure, central obesity, high triglycerides, low HDL cholesterol, and elevated blood sugar levels) that are precursors to most cases of type 2 diabetes.[1]

The other studies show that diet and exercise can prevent the development of type 2 diabetes in those who already have the metabolic syndrome. One program instructed at-risk patients to exercise for thirty minutes daily, eat *more* monounsaturated fat (like olive oil and nuts), whole grains, fruit, and vegetables, as well as more low fat milk and meat products

and less saturated fat. Another goal was to lose 5 percent of their weight.

Overall, this program resulted in 58 percent less diabetes developing compared to the control group. If the patients who were particularly careful to follow all the instructions were studied, they found that *none* of those patients developed diabetes![2]

In our medical practice we take this one step farther, applying the same instructions vigorously to those patients who already have type 2 diabetes. *Some of those patients who are able to do the hard work this approach requires are able to completely obliterate any evidence of diabetes, and get off all of their diabetes medication and insulin.*

(A cautionary note: Never stop your diabetes medication without the supervision of your physician.)

Aging, Dementia, and the Mediterranean Diet

Good food and exercise reduce the chances that bad medical events will occur in your life…events like heart attacks, strokes, cancer, dementia, surgery, and death.

When I talk to patients about reducing risk of death, some get confused. After all, don't we all have to die sometime? Of course, for the most part that is true, right along with paying taxes. But we don't need to die prematurely — or live miserably, for that matter.

In my practice, those in their seventies, eighties, and nineties who don't give in to the aging process have taught me a lot. They stay physically active every day. They walk, climb stairs instead of ride the elevator, play tennis, work out at the gym, go fishing, or paddle a kayak.

They keep their minds active, turn off their television, read widely, get enough sleep, and spend time with others interested in good conversation and interesting

---

[1] Esposito et al. JAMA 2004;1440-46

[2] Tuomilehto NEJM 2001;344:1343-50

activities. Some stay employed, some run businesses, and some do volunteer work.

Their joints feel pretty good, their prescriptions are few, they can breathe just fine…and it is no accident! They've made sensible decisions about what they eat and how they spend their time. They don't only live longer, they live better. They say things like, "You know, Miles, I may be eighty but I really feel as good as I ever have!"

Adhering to a Mediterranean diet pattern lowers the risk of developing dementia by 40%, with vegetable consumption being found to be one of the most important components.[1] In addition, there are many factors apart from diet that help prevent dementia. For example, staying physically fit, keeping up a high level of mental activity, and drinking small amounts of alcohol can help.

Other Diets

Consider some other diets you may wish to follow: Atkins, Ornish, Pritikin, South Beach, Zone, Eat Right For Your Blood Type, Macrobiotic, vegetarian, vegan, and so on. Compare them to what we know about the Mediterranean diet.

- The Mediterranean diet has been studied prospectively in large numbers of people, in various parts of the world, with individual studies of over 4 to 12 years duration.
- It has been associated with reduced deaths from the common causes found in our society such as cancer, heart disease and stroke.
- It has successfully treated obesity over extended periods of time.
- It can reduce the risk of developing type 2 diabetes, cancer, high blood pressure, and dementia.

- It has prevented deaths in patients with heart disease.
- It can be adapted to the various tastes in almost every household.

While each of the diet patterns mentioned earlier has something to recommend it, nothing can compete with the Mediterranean-style diet for verifiable benefit in large populations.

Whether or not we are dealing with ongoing disease or remote family history, none of us can afford to dismiss the importance of food. If you are going to trust your health to any diet, it seems to me an easy decision to make the whole food Mediterranean diet the model to follow. It is safe to say that people who develop healthy habits (as opposed to making an occasional effort) lower their risk factors for most diseases and raise the probability of a better and longer life. As outcomes go, that's a jolly good one, I'd say.

Stay Open Minded!
Question all diet dogma, including ours. Ask for evidence. Consider good nutrition as non-negotiable as seatbelts and bicycle helmets – and remember that the evidence of benefit for nutrition is stronger.

Historically stable ideas that are well grounded in solid research will generally be the ones to depend on. For example, highly refined foods such as white rice and white flour have been associated with poor health outcomes for a hundred years, and that is not likely to change any time soon. But stay alert for those new ideas and fresh research that come along to keep us all humble.

And above all, *better is a dinner of herbs where love is, than a stalled ox and hatred therewith.* (Proverbs 15:17)

---

[1] Scarmeas Annals of Neurology 2006 59:912-921

1   Practical Eating

Fat Is Good, Bagels Are Bad
So, What Can We Eat?
Notes on Some Foods and Supplements
Transition Tips
Healthy Habits
Suggestions for Feeding Children and Other People
Recommended Reading

Fat is Good, Bagels are Bad

Some Rules to Eat By

Many of us accept that food is our best medicine. It can be harder to agree upon *which* food. However, if we have health problems, are overweight, or have a family history of heart disease or cancer, here are six dietary dangers we should take seriously.

The extent to which we take these seriously would naturally depend on our own risk factors, but these guidelines work for most of us. (Special occasions like birthday parties are exceptions: it may be appropriate, and arguably even therapeutic, to see how many of these rules we can break at one sitting.)

Foods to Avoid

- Hydrogenated and partially hydrogenated oils (like margarine and vegetable shortening)
- White flour (called 'unbleached' and/or 'enriched wheat flour') and white rice
- Refined sugars (white or brown, high fructose corn syrup, and so on)
- Preserved meats (like deli meats, bacon, ham, cured sausages, and hot dogs)
- Fake foods (like egg substitutes, non-dairy creamer, and sugar substitutes)
- Commercially fried foods (mostly foods you don't fry yourself)

Empty Calories

One of the first things you may notice about the preceding list is that, with the exception of preserved meats and some fried foods, these are all essentially nutritionally bankrupt foods. They supply calories, but do not provide significant vitamins, minerals, oils, nucleic acids, phenolics or the thousands of other nutrients that build strong tissues, clean arteries, and cancer-fighting immune systems.

Hydrogenated Oils

Hydrogenated and partially hydrogenated oils are the main sources of the chemically altered fats known as trans fats. Even as a small proportion of the diet trans fats are bad for us. They raise "bad cholesterol" (LDL), lower "good cholesterol" (HDL), raise total cholesterol, and seem to contribute to arterial disease and diabetes risk.

You'll find partially hydrogenated oils in most margarine, shortening, fast food, most processed snack food, crackers, fried food, and most commercially baked food. Pay no attention to claims like *No Saturated Fat!* or *Cholesterol Free!* or *Zero Trans Fat!* Go straight to the fine print on the ingredient list, and if you see the words *hydrogenated* or *partially hydrogenated*, avoid that product. Even products that claim to have no trans fat are actually allowed to have what many of us would consider a significant amount of trans fat, due to the way the labeling rules are written. So, in my opinion, a food with hydrogenated oil should be considered suspect even if it says *'no trans fats'*.

White Flour

Two of the most popular foods in this country are made from mostly white flour: bagels (white bread with attitude) and pasta (white bread with sauce). Bagels and pasta have inexplicably come to be seen as part of a healthy diet. Both are low in fiber and nutrition, and should be avoided along with any other foods containing mainly white flour or white sugar, like muffins, cookies, and crackers.

Read ingredient lists regardless of any promises on labels. Hundreds of products claim to be whole-wheat or whole grain but in most cases it just means the product contains a proportion (generally small) of whole-wheat flour or whole grains.

Beware the term *wheat flour,* which is just another name for white flour. If it is a true 100 percent whole grain product, it will say so. (Remember that the more plentiful ingredients are listed first.)

Cold breakfast cereals should be treated with suspicion. Even when made from whole grain, they appear to be much more likely to adversely raise blood sugars. They also create less satiety — a sense of having eaten enough — than their cooked whole grain equivalents, such as cooked oatmeal.

A general rule of thumb that works well is, the coarser the whole grain food, and the longer it takes to cook or chew, the better it is for us.

White Rice

White rice, which is brown rice with most of the vitamins, minerals, amino acids, and fiber polished off, is similarly a source of empty calories. Brown rice is a superb food full of valuable nutrients, and it is worth making a serious effort to integrate it into your regular diet. There are many varieties of brown rice, but try starting with brown basmati rice, cooked to fluffy perfection. (See *Brown Rice* page 124.)

Commercially Fried Foods

Obvious examples of this group includes deep fried potatoes ('chips' in the British world, 'French fries' in North America) and fried meat products like corn dogs. The main problem here is the type of long-life

fats (what we uncharitably call 'bad fat') used in any viable commercial frying operation. Another problem is the likelihood of there being unstated preservatives in the food, along with the relative lack of nutrients. Instead of going to a fast food place, why not go home and fry up some toasted cheese and tomato sandwiches at home? Mmm-mm!

Refined Sugar

It is interesting that while Americans have substantially reduced their fat intake, there has been a simultaneous rise in the per-capita intake of refined sugar accompanied by a rise in the incidence of obesity.

Fat — good and bad fat — has been demonized while refined sugars and other refined carbohydrates have been given little attention, which is ridiculous. Sugar has no nutritional value apart from empty calories, and it contributes to obesity as much or more than fat.

Refined sugars may also suppress our body's immune response. Cutting refined sugar from your diet is a splendid first step toward better health and ideal weight.

Avoid sodas of any kind, and keep in mind that just two ounces of soda per day will increase your weight by about three pounds per year. (See *Fake Food* on page 14 for more information about diet sodas.)

Even 100 percent fruit juice should be considered borderline junk food, for children with poor or picky appetites especially. There is nothing natural about removing and discarding the most valuable part of the fruit. It would make more sense to eat the fiber and discard the juice, which is comparatively low in nutrients and high in simple sugars.

Avoid most packaged foods: often they contain three or four types of sugar so that it won't show up so high on the list of ingredients. Some examples of sugars are sucrose, fructose, glucose, dextrose, maltose, maltodextrin, evaporated organic cane sugar, turbinado sugar, and high fructose corn syrup. *Read ingredient labels!* All packaged food is guilty until proven innocent!

Preserved Meats

Preserved meats (bacon, ham, sausages, deli meats, bologna, and so forth) seem to be much more identified with ill health than other animal products in general. In addition to preservatives, they generally contain excessive salt and often-excessive sugar.

It is unclear what it is in preserved meat that tends to be associated with diseases like cancer, heart disease, and diabetes. Nitrates and nitrites have been on the short list of suspects, but we may never be sure. What *is* sure is that we will be taking one less chance with our health by avoiding them most of the time. And finding tasty alternatives is not difficult.

Traditionally aged meats like prosciutto (Italian ham which has been salt-cured and air-dried) may be exceptions. Many natural food stores carry fresh sausages without additives, and these would appear to be perfectly healthy.

On those special occasions when you indulge in preserved meats, a prudent step would be to eat antioxidant-rich vegetables (like spinach and broccoli) and fruits (like berries and apples) to help combat some of the adverse effects. For example, if you are going to have bacon, fry some fat slices of tomato to eat at the same time.

Fake Food

If a product has been made using ingredients that don't appear in nature, avoid it. Fake food would include egg substitutes, non-dairy creamer, fake fats like olestra, and artificial sweeteners like aspartame (*Nutrasweet* and *Equal*) and sucralose (Splenda) commonly found in diet sodas and other 'diet' foods.

As well as having the problem of being nutritionally worthless, the health effects of these additives are somewhat controversial, and they are usually markers of food products that are of dubious value.

Most junk foods include artificial colors and flavors in their ingredient lists. Lots of junk food would qualify as fake food. The flagrant examples (like Twinkies) don't pretend to be anything else, but most junk food is presented as positively as possible in order to make it into our grocery cart.

An additional problem with artificial sweeteners is that they maintain your sweet tooth, which obstructs what the rest of this book is going to try to do. Our palate can be trained, and by gradually decreasing the sweets in our lives, the less we'll desire them. It won't happen overnight, of course. So start now!

It is unfortunate that the ingredients we should be trying to avoid take up so much of the shelf space in the average supermarket. They occupy most of the deli counter, most of the cookie, cracker, and snack food aisles, and bakery cases. They are in sodas (both sugared and calorie-free), fruit drinks, and cold breakfast cereals.

In general, and at the very least, avoid products with ingredient lists that include two or more of the following: partially hydrogenated oils, white flour, refined sugar, and artificial additives. This means almost all fast foods, deep-fried foods, most prepared dishes from deli counters, processed deli meats, and "lite" cheeses. And the bottom line? If you are serious about pursuing optimal health, the best defense against junk food is simply not to have it within reach.

So, What Can We Eat?

That is an easy question. Simply emphasize foods that have been minimally processed. The more recently the food has been attached to the plant or animal it came from, the better.

Fiber!

By avoiding refined grains and hydrogenated fats we automatically increase our fiber intake. Fiber is an amazing entity. Increased fiber is associated with *reduced* cancers, *reduced* heart disease, *reduced* diabetes, *reduced* obesity, *reduced* cholesterol … and it comes as a no-added-cost bonus with most of the food we should be eating anyway.

Beans are a great source of fiber, as are whole grains, vegetables and fruits. *Unprocessed* whole grains (like minimally sweetened muesli or granola, or cooked whole grain cereal like oatmeal) should replace refined cold breakfast cereals, which are not nearly as beneficial despite their "high fiber" claims.

Good, 100 percent whole grain bread is available if you search, but it can be expensive; consider making it yourself. (See *Bread and Baking* on page 161.) As a rule of thumb, the heavier and coarser the whole grain — the longer it takes to chew — the better it is for you.

Flavor!

Eating food that is good for you doesn't mean giving up enjoying food that *tastes* good. By allowing yourself the liberty of using healthy fats and seasonings, you can easily find a wide range of delicious meals from simple whole foods.

Being too strict about food can defeat the purpose if it means the food doesn't get eaten. The presence of enough fat, salt, and sometimes sweetening can make all the difference. Something as plain as an egg can be memorable when it's scrambled in olive oil or butter with salt and a splash of Tabasco sauce.

A simple bowl of beans and rice is transformed when you toss it with a rich sauté of olive oil, onion, garlic, cumin, lemon juice, salt, and pepper. Remember that most of us don't need to worry when we add salt to our food as long as we get rid of the hidden salt in prepared foods and fast foods.

Vegetables and Fruit

Include a *minimum* of five servings (with a goal of nine servings) of vegetables and fruit in meals and snacks each day. This means *whole* fruits and vegetables, not juiced. Fiber is king, and with it come more vitamins, minerals, phenolics, and so on.

Eat as wide a variety as you can — red, orange, yellow, gold, green, blue, purple, and white. Fresh and raw is good, but cooked is fine and even preferable in some cases. (A well-known example of the benefits of cooking is the tomato, which needs to be cooked for the antioxidant called lycopene to be available to your body.) Frozen can be almost as good as fresh, but read the labels of canned vegetables and fruit carefully.

A serving could be one piece of fruit, a medium carrot or tomato, maybe two six-inch stalks of celery, a half-cup of broccoli florets, a scoop of coleslaw, or a two-inch chunk of cucumber. Depending on how dense (like squash) or fluffy (like spinach salad) the item, a serving could be considered as one half to one cup.

No amount of iceberg lettuce should be counted as a serving. With lettuce, consider the possibility that the deeper green the leaf, the higher the nutritional value.

Whole Grains

Choose brown rice instead of white rice, for example, or 100 percent whole-wheat flour instead of white (also known as 'enriched wheat') flour. The more intact or coarsely ground the grains you eat, the more slowly and steadily they raise the blood sugar as they are digested.

Most of us eat too much wheat, so try to introduce as many non-wheat options as you can. Get to know alternatives grains like polenta (corn meal) and quinoa (pages 132-133). Experiment with polenta as an alternative for pasta and potatoes. Try pasta made with whole wheat, brown rice, spelt, or corn. Find one you enjoy.

Finding 100 percent whole-grain bread that you like can be difficult, but it is important *if you want bread to be a daily part of your diet.* The key here is naturally occurring fiber. Don't be fooled by bread made with enriched wheat flour but with added purified fiber to give the impression of being a whole grain product.

It doesn't matter *how* "enriched" and "unbleached" and "organic" the bread, or if it's a nice brown color with a grain speckled crust: if the first ingredient mentioned is not 100 percent *whole* grain (wheat or some other whole grain), it's a compromise.

Fragrant, chewy, European-style artisan loaves may be simple, honest, and rustic, but if the first ingredient is white flour (organic and enriched notwithstanding) they still count as white bread and should be considered special-occasion food.

Making your own bread can be practical if you keep it simple and make it often. A bread machine or food processor can take care of all the kneading. (See chapter eight on *Bread and Baking*.)

Beans (and Legumes)

Beans tend to be neglected but they have a remarkable nutritional profile (vitamins, minerals, fiber, protein, and antioxidants) and are easy to slip into any kind of diet and adjust to any kind of taste. You don't even have to cook them yourself, thanks to the convenience of canned cooked beans. (See *Beans* chapter starting on page 107.)

Beans and whole grains historically have a warm relationship, and their compatibility is useful in one-dish meals. Recipes that combine the two are useful when one is trying to ease away from being too dependent on meat as a main feature of a meal. Beans enjoy being served cold or at room temperature in salads, which makes them particularly heroic in last-minute meal scenarios.

Protein

Meat is a good source of protein but in our society it is served too often and too generously. You'll find it easier to cut back on meat when your meals are rich in good fats, beans, and whole grains.

Meals should frequently feature fish rich in omega-3 fatty acids, like tuna and wild salmon. (However, mild-flavored white fish like halibut is a good option when anti-salmon/tuna sentiment is a factor.)

Canned tuna is easy to work with and can form the basis of some delicious dishes, especially with the help of brown rice and whole grain pasta. (See index for tuna fish recipes.) We favor 'light' tuna over the more expensive white tuna. 'Light' tuna tends to have less mercury than 'white' tuna, and the light tuna also has more of the healthy oils. (See page 142 for more on tuna.)

Beans, whole grains, tofu, and nuts are good protein alternatives, too. If you get into the habit of leaving meat out of your meals, you will be more likely to explore the world of beans and grains to a greater degree. Remember that small quantities of meat, cheese, and eggs included in dishes made primarily with beans and whole grains can improve the flavor immensely.

Eggs are rich sources of protein and have some "good fat", and are valuable as the basis for some simple and satisfying meatless main dishes with vegetables, grains, and cheese. Buying true 'free range' eggs from a farmer, or 'omega 3' eggs may have some small added benefit.

If you like eggs, consider getting a few hens. Aside from the miracle of each perfect egg, chickens are marvelous entertainment, with natural comic timing. They are always delighted to see you, yet independent enough to keep busy all day while you are gone. Hens do tend to raise their voices when they lay eggs but they mostly keep their voices down to a murmur.

Good Fat

We *need* good fat. We need it not only for the health of body parts such as skin, hair, and brains, but also to reduce the risks of diseases like diabetes, heart disease, and cancer. The best fats are probably those found in foods like extra virgin olive oil and foods like fish, raw nuts, seeds, and avocados. For vegetable oils, expeller pressed canola and soy oils are likely a distant second best.

Animal (saturated) fats should not be demonized, but omega-3 fatty acids (found in fish, nuts, and flaxseeds) and extra virgin olive oil (mostly monounsaturated, or omega-9, fats) should be more abundant in the diet than saturated fats. Saturated fat in moderation appears to be fine: modest amounts of eggs (like one or two a day), and aged cheese and small amounts of butter are reasonable. Small servings of meat appear to be perfectly healthy. One piece of advice is to keep servings of animal protein to no more than twenty five percent of your plate.

Cholesterol

It does not appear that eating whole, traditional foods containing cholesterol and saturated fat causes heart disease. Some populations known to eat the largest amounts of saturated fat and cholesterol have among the lowest levels of heart disease, while other population groups with similar dietary fat intake have very high levels of heart disease. This is why we recommend a broad based diet with a high intake of vegetables, fruit, beans, whole grains, and *good* fat, and worry less about your saturated fat and cholesterol intake.

Can a thoughtful argument be made against eating eggs, for example? Nope. Eggs contain cholesterol but little saturated fat, and they also contain dozens of other valuable nutrients, including protein, and do not appear to be associated with increased risk of disease. This is an important area, and reading *The Cholesterol Myths* (see *Recommended Reading* on page 30) can be instructive. A very useful analysis is also found in British Medical Journal.[1]

Adding dietary cholesterol to a diet very low in cholesterol, without changing other dietary factors, will typically raise your total cholesterol by a fairly small degree. Adding further dietary cholesterol to a diet with moderate cholesterol will typically have very little effect on total cholesterol level. It has not been shown, despite decades of research, that dietary cholesterol increases risk of heart disease.

For practical purposes, of course, when you eat a diet emphasizing fruits, vegetables, beans, and grains, your consumption of saturated fat and cholesterol will tend to fall naturally. But we would hate to see people avoiding good food simply because of the saturated fat. Finally, avoiding dietary fats and cholesterol will have the adverse effect of lowering HDL (good) cholesterol.

---

[1] British Medical Journal 2001;322:757-63

Notes on Some Foods and Supplements

For each of us there may be individual factors which make any particular food, no matter how healthy, a poor choice. The following are recommendations that apply to the majority of people. Most of these are based on clinical studies in humans with evidence for better health outcomes. Only some of the more common foods are covered here.

Whole-Wheat Bread

When you're shopping for a loaf you can trust, first look for the words '100% whole wheat'. Next, check the ingredient list. The first and only flour mentioned should be whole-wheat flour. Remember that the term *wheat flour* means *white flour.*

The heavier and coarser the loaf, the better: the best bread may be the heavy, moist pumpernickel style bread (also called "European style"). If a loaf claims to be 100 percent whole wheat but feels light when you heft it, chances are it contains a large proportion of something called *gluten flour*, a highly refined product made from mostly wheat gluten. (Gluten is the protein in wheat that provides the elasticity that develops when you knead dough.)

When you do find a good honest specimen — *Great Harvest Bread Company* makes a fine honey whole-wheat loaf, for example — consider buying two and freezing one of them. For more information about bread, as well as recipes and tips on making your own, see *Bread and Baking* starting on page 161.

Crackers

Most crackers are junk, and have no redeeming nutritional characteristics. Saltines, for example, could be described as white flour and salt held together with hydrogenated oil. The only way to find a good cracker is to read the ingredient label: if it says 'partially hydrogenated oil' (as most do), then leave it alone.

Old-fashioned rye krisp and rye vita are good choices, and so is *Ak-mak,* a good tasting whole-wheat cracker sold in many stores. Whole grain toasted brown rice cakes come in a variety of types; most people should be able to find one that suits them. Remember to read ingredient labels.

Cheese

Arguably the healthiest people in the world live in Southern Europe and eat generous amounts of cheese. The best evidence would favor using aged, drier cheese, like sharp cheddar and authentic Italian Parmesan (Parmigiano-Reggiano.) You are less likely to over-indulge with the stronger flavored cheeses than mild cheeses like mozzarella and jack, or the popular string cheese. Minimize soft, creamy cheeses, saving them for special occasions.

Milk

In contrast to cheese, the evidence for benefit for milk is less clear cut, so we recommend minimizing fresh milk consumption. It may be better to choose cultured dairy products like cheese, yogurt, and kefir over fresh milk products.

Yogurt and Kefir

The process of turning milk into cheese, yogurt, or kefir seems to do something to milk to make it better for adult humans: research is under way to try to find out why there is a difference. A plain yogurt or kefir with live cultures is anti-bacterial, immune boosting, and has high available calcium content.

Most commercial frozen yogurt and sweetened packaged yogurts have little or no live cultures. To get the value from the yogurt you eat, choose plain yogurt or kefir and add your own fruit or sweetening. (See page 57 for more on yogurt.)

Nuts

Raw nuts are good food; they're full of healthy fats and associated with better cholesterol profiles and lower rates of heart disease and diabetes.

Avoid roasted nuts for three reasons: the fats are damaged by heating, nuts are higher in calories if they are roasted in oil, and the quality of oil used in the roasting process is unknown. Raw nuts are also easier to eat in moderation. Raw walnuts, almonds, Brazil nuts, pecans, and hazelnuts (filberts), are probably your most sensible choices.

To help avoid the problem of overeating raw nuts, keep a bowl of nuts in the shell handy, and crack them yourself. Make sure to buy them from a dependable source – old nuts taste awful.

Nuts are undeniably fattening, so keep that in mind if you have any problem with weight. If you are adding nuts to your diet, remove calories from somewhere else.

Remember that delectations like trail mixes, especially the ones with bits of chocolate and whatnot in them, are strictly for trail use, and preferably for the *uphill* portions of the trail.

Peanuts and Nut Butters

Peanuts are not true nuts: strictly speaking, they are legumes, like soybeans. Optimally speaking, peanuts may be on shaky ground because of the mold (aflotoxin) associated with them, although it doesn't seem to be a problem in North America. Also, the fatty acid profile of peanuts is not as favorable as the omega-3-rich nuts such as walnuts.

If you eat peanut butter, we recommend that you grind it yourself using dry roasted nuts at a health food store. You can also replace peanut butter with freshly ground roasted almond butter. But don't forget that whole raw nuts are still better than any kind of nut butters.

Seafood

Fish is *great* food. For the purpose of treating heart disease and diabetes, oily fish appears to be the best choice. These are generally darker, more highly flavored fish like salmon, mackerel, and trout. Some other readily available and ready-to-eat examples are canned tuna, sardines, salmon, and raw pickled herring. (For more on canned tuna, see page 142.)

Shellfish and white, mild fish such as cod and halibut may not be quite as beneficial as the oily fish, but are still good food, and great sources of protein.

Meat

It is hard to be sure that any one type of meat, red or white, is nutritionally superior to others. In any case, keep portions of meat smallish — like no more than one quarter of your total plate area — and fill the rest of your plate with beans, whole grains, and vegetables.

Think of meat as a condiment, not the main part of the meal. Large servings of meat will decrease your appetite for the most important items – vegetables, beans, and whole grains. Avoid preserved meats, like ham, bacon, sausages, bologna, and the sandwich meats found in the deli case of your supermarket. These seem to be associated with more heart disease, diabetes, and cancer. (See page 14 for note on preserved meat.)

Chocolate

Many studies over the past ten years have associated eating chocolate with health benefits, such as less heart disease[1], better cholesterol, and lower blood pressure. Much of the benefit probably is associated with a group of chemicals in chocolate called phenols, which are also present in tea, extra virgin olive oil, and many other foods.

Choose dark chocolate with a cocoa percentage of 70 percent or more. Up to one or two ounces per day is probably reasonable. (If you prefer your chocolate in a liquid form, see recipe for *Hot Chocolate* on page 187.) However, when you add something like chocolate to your diet, remember to remove calories somewhere else. Gaining weight on chocolate would tend to defeat the purpose.

Sugar

White and brown sugars should be used only limitedly. I know of no evidence of benefit for artificial sweeteners, and my observation is that people do better when they stick to natural sweeteners.

The sugar you add to food is not as much a problem as the sugar you consume in prepared foods from the store or fast foods so don't fret over whether or not to put a spoonful of brown sugar on your oatmeal. For general sweeteners, honey (naturally occurring and rich in antioxidants) and even pure maple syrup are probably your best choices.

You will avoid a lot of excess sugar simply by avoiding packaged foods: often they contain three or four types of sugar (like sucrose, fructose, dextrose, glucose, maltose, maltodextrin, and so on) so sugar won't appear as high on the ingredient lists. *Read labels.* Don't be fooled by romantic descriptions like "organic evaporated sugar cane extract".

Sugar alcohols like sorbitol and mannitol are probably fine, but they can cause diarrhea if you eat much of them.

Caffeine-Containing Foods

If someone you know insists that caffeine in any form is harmful, ask to see the data. Tea, coffee, and dark chocolate (which contain caffeine-like compounds) appear to be part of a healthy lifestyle and are seemingly associated with lower rates of heart disease, diabetes[2], and maybe even some cancers.

Of course, caffeine doesn't work for everybody. Even in small amounts, it causes some people to have abnormalities of their heart rhythm or other problems. As with most of the advice in this book, the use of caffeine needs to be modified depending on your particular health situation.

In general, tea is lower in caffeine than coffee and may be better tolerated. Tea not only is associated with less heart disease, but also less osteoporosis. Green tea generally has less caffeine than black tea, but it is unclear whether it is 'healthier' than black tea. It is also uncertain whether decaffeinated coffee and tea have the same benefits as their full-strength versions.

Definitely *not* part of a healthy lifestyle is caffeine that comes attached to sodas, or in boutique espressos combined with steamed milk, flavored syrups and sweetened whipped cream look-alikes.

Alcohol

Beverages with alcohol, such as wine and beer, have been used and abused throughout recorded history, with spirits having arrived slightly more recently. The bottom line is this: people who drink a small amount of alcohol have lower death rates, mainly due to less heart disease. [3] A little alcohol is also

---

[1] Buijsse Arch Int Med 2006;166:411-417

[2] Salazar-Martinez et al. Ann Intern Med 2004;140:1-8 and Arnlov et al JAMA 2004;291:1199-1201
[3] J Am Geriat Soc 2006;54:30-7

associated with less incidence of type 2 diabetes, stroke, and dementia.

The trouble is that excessive alcohol is toxic, and for some, any alcohol *at all* is too much. For those who have no philosophical or medical reason to avoid alcohol, such as alcoholism, consuming a small amount of alcohol may be wise.

Reasonable maximums are one drink daily for women and two for men. (A drink is twelve ounces of beer, five ounces of wine, or one ounce of spirits.)

Fruit juice

Fruit juices are associated with increased obesity and should not be an everyday food. Juice has limited nutritional value, with most of the precious fiber, vitamins, and minerals removed, but with the sugar and calories retained.

Keep fruit juices to a minimum and remember that even 100 percent fruit juice should not count as a serving of fruit. This includes juice you squeeze yourself. Juices are a wonderful 'special occasion' food. (Unsweetened and naturally flavored sparkling mineral water is a pleasant alternative to juice for some who would like something cold and refreshing in the refrigerator.)

Nutritional Supplements

When we examine the evidence connecting nutrition and good health in real people in the real world, something should jump out at you. Almost all of that evidence shows that good food improves health, while controlled prospective studies using nutritional supplements generally show no benefit. Some nutritional supplements have even been shown to cause harm, such as higher doses of Vitamin E and beta carotene.

The more we study food and its components, the more evidence we see for the benefit of the *whole* food rather than extracts or supplements. We simply don't know enough about what it is in any given food that makes it work. It may even be that there is something in the combination of foods that creates some of the benefit.

Choose whole food as your source of nutrients and fiber, as close to the original formula as possible. Don't trust your health to man's ingenuity or extraction processes. Too much may be lost in the translation. Supplements cannot replace good food, adequate sleep, and daily exercise.

In our medical practice we use supplements only when there is a good reason. We treat nutritional deficiencies with supplements when we can't achieve adequate levels with food. We use supplements in the absence of documented deficiency when there is reasonable evidence for benefit, and only on a case-by-case basis.

We always remind patients that most nutritional supplements are very unnatural, and should be considered as mild drugs with potential for both benefit and harm, and not as food substitutes. When thought of in that way, nutritional supplements get used with much more discretion.

Be equally cautious of using nutritional supplements based on results of obscure blood tests or other controversial testing methods. Always be ready to ask for the evidence behind the recommendation, and *examine that evidence* to see if taking the supplement can be expected to lead to a clear-cut benefit.

Multivitamins

Multivitamins are hard to recommend for most people, based on the currently available data on lack of benefit in most populations. Be particularly cautious when using supplements that are sold by the same health care provider who happens to be recommending them. Such conflicts of interest are troublesome.

Transition Tips

Whether you are dealing with your own dietary changes or someone else's, the transition does not need to be traumatic or dreary. You will more likely be in for some pleasant surprises. What if you find out that you actually *like* lima beans? (Fresh baby limas, anyway — see *Luscious Lima Beans* on page 115.)

Following are some observations and suggestions that may help those who are just beginning to take health seriously and could use a few tips.

- Don't be overwhelmed by the journey ahead of you or frustrated when progress seems too slow. Just break it down to steps you can easily handle. The one-step-at-a-time method works for most of us, although some may find change easier when it's dramatic.

- No improvement is too small. Eliminating one cookie a day, one burger a week, one fast food meal a month … these are all significant steps.

- You may be surprised to find your tastes changing along with your diet, so don't give up on any healthy foods too quickly. Likes and dislikes are not necessarily something we are born with; they are learned.

- An obvious but underrated fact is that any food tastes a lot better when you're hungry. If you're learning to like something, wait until you're hungry before you eat it. And if you have to learn to like just about *everything*, only eat when you're hungry.

- …but don't go shopping hungry. Go with a list and a firm hand, and don't let anything but good food make it into your cart. Choose *whole* foods, not juiced, powdered, dried, or instant. Buy fresh fruit that you really *are* going to eat and vegetables that you really *will* find time to prepare. While you are transitioning to a better eating pattern, it makes sense to stick to vegetables you know and like.

- Read ingredient labels and stoutly resist products admitting to sugar, white flour, artificial flavors, and hydrogenated fat. This means avoiding items like packaged cookies, snack foods, sodas, refined breakfast cereals, and most bakery items… but you will be delighted at the amount of good food to add to your shopping cart. It is because of sensible choices made by brave and smart people like you that most supermarkets now have healthy options in every department.

- A transition trick that worked well for at least one former diet junkie was to divide all food into 3 categories — Toxic Treats, Treats, and Food. In the toxic category she puts things like non-dairy creamer and sodas, to be avoided almost completely. Treats are things like white bread, cookies, and fast food, to be eaten on special occasions. In the Food category she includes all unrefined whole foods (like whole grains, beans, vegetables, fruit, meat, eggs, and cheese) which she eats without restriction. She said it was easier to resist or cut back on the wrong foods when she identified them clearly in her mind first.

- It helps some of us to keep a list of good snacks on the front of the fridge. Then, if you're not thinking clearly due to an acute deficiency of refined carbohydrates, the list can help you through the crisis by thinking for you. Soon you'll have built up such good habits that you won't need the list anymore.

- For most of us, it's best to clear the house of the junk we love. Sadly, this may even include ice cream, which should only have access to your freezer on birthdays. (And only birthdays of people you actually know personally.) Limit fast foods and junk food to special occasions.

- It helps to identify food triggers. For example if you crave a sweet treat when you stop for a latté, then don't stop for a latté. Brutal, but it works.

- Daily routine works well for many of us: an orange at breakfast, half of a banana for the mid-morning hungries, an apple before bedtime …three servings of three different fruits without trying. (Our stomach will probably remember even if we don't.)

- If you run into resistance making the transition from white bread, you don't need to move directly to 100 percent whole wheat. Find some decent compromise, like a loaf with at least half whole-wheat flour, and then move on to the good stuff when the fuss dies down.

- Sandwiches made with whole-wheat bread are not always interchangeable with white bread sandwiches: the heavier bread can easily overwhelm the filling. Slice bread as thinly as possible or switch to whole-wheat pita bread.

- Homemade whole grain muffins or oatmeal cookies are compromises worth considering. In fact, just about *anything* you make yourself is generally better than any ready-made commercially prepared stuff you can buy. (See *Bread and Baking* on page 161.)

- Don't feel compelled to replace white rice with brown rice on every occasion. Brown rice has a more assertive taste and texture and – at least in the beginning – should perhaps be presented in recipes that particularly suit brown rice. (See pages 126 – 131 and 147.)

- In your effort to increase your intake of whole grains, experiment with different kinds. (See *Whole Grains,* beginning on page 123.) Variety is the ideal. If you don't care for one, move on.

- Increasing your vegetable consumption can be almost effortless. Salads can be as easy as opening bags of pre-washed bite-sized greens, or even a selection of vegetables custom-cut for anything from party trays to stir-fries. Mushrooms are sliced and packed in neat little cartons for you. English (hothouse) cucumbers are shrink-wrapped individually and need no peeling or seeding. And so on.

- There are many commercially prepared dressings and dips with impeccable ingredients and enough variety to suit anyone available in good food stores, but they really are easy to make yourself. (See *Favorite Bits & Pieces*, chapter 3.)

- Raising your omega-3 fatty acid level can be pleasant and convenient if you shop around for something to suit your tastes. For example, tuna fish comes in all forms including appetizing-looking slices in easy-open serving-sized cans.

Sardines are available in all kinds of sizes and flavors with handy peel-back lids like their tasty smoked counterparts, kippered snacks. Experiment.

- If you are new to the world of whole foods, remember to *make it taste good*! Eating well doesn't mean compromising on taste. Think rich, spicy, hot, sweet, and sour, and adjust your recipe accordingly. Think *good* fat, not *low* fat.

- Remind yourself that the enemy is not salt and butter and cheese and meat. Mankind has been enjoying these since the beginning of recorded history. The problem is generally user error. We are guilty of eating too much.

- Drinking plenty of water is important when you increase your fiber intake and decrease your calorie intake. Happily, increasing your liquids and fiber effortlessly in the form of whole fruits and vegetables is a pleasant bonus that comes with the Mediterranean approach.

- If you're trying to cut back or eliminate soda pop, a good strategy is to keep sparkling mineral water chilled in your refrigerator. (Lemon lime flavor is spunky without being distractingly fruity.) You can mix it with a bit of frozen fruit juice concentrate to make a sort of punch, or add lemon or lime wedges. Sparkling mineral water can also help you resist a second glass of wine.

Question any nutrition advice to avoid falling for some nutty ideas. Get an opinion from a qualified, objective professional. Stay open minded and ask for the evidence. It's too easy to accept something just because it sounds sensible at the time.

Healthy Habits

We all battle habits, preconceptions, and our own perceptions of what tastes good, but it's amazing how easily we can slide into new habits and tastes once we come to know all our options. New habits can be formed. There is nothing complicated about eating well but it *does* require attitude and discipline. You will probably constantly fine-tune your own rules, but the most important principle will keep floating to the top: food really *is* your best medicine.

Making intelligent food choices has never been easier or more enjoyable than it is these days – mainly because nutrition is so much more of a marketable commodity than it used to be. The average person is alert to the importance of diet and exercise, so restaurants and supermarkets are scrambling to keep ahead of the demand.

Change
Eating well is a privilege and not a sentence to serve, but that's not always obvious at first. Not only is change difficult for most of us, giving up food we love can be pretty painful.

If faced with family resistant to change, don't nag! Just make sure there is plenty of good food available. After a while of being exposed to better food, tastes can gradually adjust. However, it certainly does not make any sense to sacrifice any relationship on the altar of good food.

The whole food approach to eating is not a temporary program to lose weight or feel better. This is a way of life: a new perspective for some and a return to good sense for others. While you work on improving your diet, make other changes.

Watch TV less. Shut down your computer sooner. Get more sleep. Get more exercise, even if it is just climbing stairs at work and skipping rope at home. Learn all you can about eating sensibly. (Some reading suggestions are on page 28.)

Get a Waist
The weight you carry around your middle is more hazardous for heart disease, diabetes, and some cancers than weight elsewhere on your body. So, losing weight is not as important as losing inches around your waist. This means that when you divide your waist measurement by your hip measurement, your goal is .85 or less for women and .90 or less for men.

Weight Loss
Just about any diet works for short-term weight loss, but what works best for *long term* weight control is a diet of real food that includes healthy fats needed by you *and* your immune system. For anyone trying to control or reduce weight, there are four steps to success that work for everyone.

- Eliminate refined carbohydrates: that is, white flour and sugar. The simplest (not the easiest) way to do this is (1) avoid eating out (2) try to fix your own food (3) skip dessert or eat whole fruit instead and (4) read the ingredient label of every item of prepared food you buy.
- Eat less food: consciously serve yourself smaller portions.
- Exercise daily any way you can.
- Use smaller plates.

Eat Out Less
If your health is at all compromised, whether by excess weight or other risk factors, it would be wise to eat out as little as possible. The degree of strictness would logically depend on your particular health problems and family history. Obviously a lean,

healthy person whose parents are 100 years old and still playing tennis can be less strict than, say, a plump diabetic.

When you do eat out, don't fool yourself. Even a "good" restaurant or deli can't afford to make *your* health a higher priority than *their* survival. This means they will tend to choose methods and ingredients that have the best effect on *their* bottom line, not yours. (For more on eating out, see reference in *Lunch and Dinner Tips* on page 47.)

Exercise
Making a habit of exercise has an obvious benefit of helping to control weight, but that is only a bit of the story. Exercise, even without any help from diet, is a powerful force on many fronts:

- lowers LDL ("bad" cholesterol)
- lowers triglycerides
- raises HDL ("good" cholesterol)
- protects against cancer, stroke, heart disease, and dementia
- protects against (or helps reverse) type 2 diabetes
- protects against osteoporosis and arthritis
- eases symptoms of pain and stiffness
- improves energy
- relieves depression

Exercise can take many forms. Some people do very well with short bursts (minutes) of maximal exercise daily, such as running stairs and skipping rope. Most of the research has concentrated on thirty – sixty minutes of daily moderate-to-brisk walking, which is fine for most people. The most important rule is … do some exercise every day. And if there is any doubt about your ability to perform any particular type of exercise, check with your physician.

Suggestions for Feeding Children and Other People

Children generally like food that tastes good. This means they usually love junk food instantly, of course, and that can be a problem. The later we introduce whole foods to them, the slower they may take to them, but kids are adaptable. Even if they weep and rage and threaten to throw up or stop eating completely, there is a good chance that within a few days or weeks the formerly unacceptable may be the new status quo.

The Bottom Line

Providing good food for our children is a responsibility, not a choice, much like insisting that your child rides in a car seat. There has never been a generation of parents better equipped with the knowledge needed to eat well and stay well. The whole-food concept has finally shed its Birkenstocks and is standing before us in a white coat and stethoscope.

Do It

How do we get children to eat good food? We serve it. That's not just the short answer, it's the *only* answer. It's not an accident that children start off small and helpless: it establishes parents as protectors and providers. But somehow it happens that perfectly sane and loving people, grown-ups who make important decisions about what cars to drive and which houses to buy, become small and helpless when it comes to decisions about maintaining their child's health and well-being. "My child won't eat good food. What can I do? Let him/her

starve?" ***Answer:*** Definitely. Let the kid starve for a few minutes, which is all the time it should take to figure this out.

Sell It!

If you think a junk-free diet is a good concept but not really practical, your child will too. The same psychology of marketing that works in the business world works at home. If we're not enjoying *our* vegetables, why should they? Good food should taste good! Do what it takes to make it taste good to you, and you may find the job of feeding your children much easier.

When a child is very young (say, 0 – 18 months) you can prepare meals without being concerned about flavor. (Think of baby food.) You really only need a blender and some leftover cooked vegetables, beans, brown rice, or whatever.

However, in the case of a child whose palate is already tuned to the fast food frequency, the vegetables, beans, and brown rice have to practically *leap* off the plate with excitement. This simply means making judicious use of things like good fat and salt, which are the ingredients that make fast food so appealing. Rich, spicy, salty, sweet, and sour: it's that simple. Make good food taste seductive, too. This is war.

Strategy

You don't have to say "no". Of course, the most direct solution is to remove the junk you don't want them to eat, but if that isn't practical you can always resort to cunning. You can say "yes, *after* you've eaten your dinner", or "yes, *after* you've eaten this apple."

If they surprise you and actually eat their part of the bargain, make it a little more difficult to meet your terms next time you strike a deal. However, it's important that good food should not be seen as the enemy. Access to junk food is not the critical issue

— the important thing is that we *eat the good food first.*

Mealtime Discipline

Avoid asking young children what they would *like* to eat. Serve them what you know they *need* to eat. However, keep the portions small, and include tiny samples of detested food. Three peas or two carrot matchsticks or one pinto bean is neither unfair nor is it a wasted gesture.

Exposure to a *wide selection* of real food is important for every child — not only for his/her immediate nutritional needs, but also as preparation for a lifetime of eating choices.

Because food is so important, stand firm. "No, we don't have any more of your favorite fiber-free fructose-filled fudge-flavored flim-flams. How about a banana?" If your child refuses to eat and chooses to go to bed hungry it should be seen as the child's choice, not punishment. Food is not a reward for good behavior: food is necessary fuel. Mealtime is a good time for teaching good manners, but it also happens to be the best time to make sure children get what they need to thrive.

Battle Plan

Make rules and *stick to them*. Don't get flustered. Once boundaries and expectations are established a certain degree of order will follow, and children do much better in order than in chaos. So do you. Everyone wins.

Don't forget the battle plan! The weapons are *good* fat and *real* flavor and the strategy is *reasonable* compromise and incremental progress. Also, commitment and personal resolve are probably the most decisive factors in the victory.

Lead your family into a diabetes-free future, striding with clean hearts, strong bones, shiny hair, clear skin, good hip-to-waist ratios, and plump, healthy brains.

Smoothies for Littlies

- The smoothie strategy is possibly the easiest way to significantly boost a small child's daily nutritional intake, especially on a hectic day when an instant infusion of good calories is called for. And when you have to pack a child in the car and go somewhere, few things are as convenient as a cup or two of smoothie to feed him on the road.

- Colored plastic cups with solid and spouted lids make wonderful smoothie receptacles—just switch to the spouted lid when you're ready to hand over the smoothie to the child. You may find that the spout narrows too much at the top to allow the free flow of a thick smoothie, so just cut down the plastic mouthpiece about ¼-inch with a sharp knife; they virtually never get clogged that way.

- Children generally aren't as conflicted by preconceptions about textures and flavors as adults, so they can be a lot more satisfying to feed. A child's smoothie can be more basic and sensible, while still tasty. A child who is started on fiber-packed smoothies very young has no expectations, and will cheerfully suck down a smoothie fortified with his leftover breakfast oatmeal, or even a half-cup of yesterday's brown rice. If you must make the smoothie more like a milkshake for any reason, simply leave out the cereal … but you may be amazed at the adaptability of a child in the hands of a cunning and confident parent. *(See page 43 for more on smoothies.)*

Recommended Reading

There will always be some disagreement between the various authors, but that shows the degree of uncertainty existing in this field. Stay flexible and keep reading. You will be constantly fine-tuning your own rules, but the most important principle will keep floating to the top: good food is great medicine.

Eat, Drink, and Be Healthy; The Harvard Medical School Guide to Healthy Eating
(Walter C. Willett, MD, Dr. P.H., ©2001)
An enjoyable read as well as a valuable source of information on the science and common sense of eating well. His chapter on calcium is worth the price of the book. The book lays out the evidence and conclusions for healthy eating and includes a large section on "the practical translation of nutritional science to food selection and preparation".

The Omega Diet
(Artemis P. Simopoulos, M.D., and Jo Robinson, ©1999)
Explores both theoretical and practical applications of a Mediterranean-type diet. Focuses on maintaining a balance of essential fatty acids, and offers a nutritional program based on the traditional diet of the Greek island of Crete. Lots of science as well as menus, recipes, and useful tips.

The Mediterranean Diet Cookbook
(Nancy Harmon Jenkins, ©1994)
One of the best reasons to buy this book (or check it out from the library) is the 9-page Introduction: The Mediterranean Diet and Health written by Antonia Trichopoulou, M.D. and Dimitrios Trichopoulos, M.D. As a cookbook, it is for the serious Mediterranophile.

The Mediterranean Diet
(Marissa Cloutier, MS, RD and Eve Adamson, ©2001)
An unpretentious little paperback with tiny print, but a thorough and enthusiastic presentation of the cultural and nutritional aspects of the Mediterranean way of eating. The authors are a little too opposed to saturated fat, in our opinion, but a good book nonetheless.

The Food Pharmacy Guide to Good Eating (Jean Carper, ©1991)
Food — Your Miracle Medicine
(Jean Carper, ©1993)
Both of these books by Jean Carper have lots of good information in brightly-written and easily read formats. Scientific substance is not the first reason to pick these up, but the wealth of practical information and motivation are rewarding.

Passionate Vegetarian
(Crescent Dragonwagon, ©2002)
Whether or not you are a vegetarian, this is a woman we could all use in our kitchens. There are over 1000 exuberant pages of recipes and food-talk. The sheer mass of ideas alone is likely to inspire even reluctant cooks.

The New American Plate Cookbook
(American Institute for Cancer Research © 2005)

This book is the work of a team of cooks, writers, and scientists working with the American Institute for Cancer Research (AICR). Their mission was to produce a cookbook that would "satisfy your conscience while it dazzles your palate", and at the same time helping to reduce our risk of serious health problems like cancer and heart disease as well as maintain a healthy weight. The photographs are glorious.

The Schwarzbein Principle: The Truth About Losing Weight, Being Healthy and Feeling Younger
(Diana Schwarzbein, M.D. and Nancy Deville, © 1999)

This is an excellent book to acquaint the reader with the concept of using a whole foods diet to minimize insulin resistance, a metabolic problem that is related to the majority of cases of obesity, type 2 diabetes, heart disease, stroke, and some cancers.

On Food and Cooking: The Science and Lore of the Kitchen (Harold McGee, © 2004)

One of the best books on food ever written. Not surprisingly, the author is fascinating, too. He was enthralled by chemistry and physics growing up and decided to study astronomy, then switched to English literature. Harold McGee wrote the first edition of this book in 1984, but as he points out, "A lot has changed in twenty years! It turned out that *On Food and Cooking* was riding a rising wave of general interest in food, a wave that grew and grew, and knocked down the barriers between science and cooking, especially in the last decade."

What to Eat
(Marion Nestle © 2006)

Marion Nestle is one of the greats of contemporary academic nutrition but she is also a food lover and consumer. These aspects come together well in this easily-read yet powerful book which takes you on a tour of a North American supermarket. In each section there is a discussion of the food's origin, what has gone on during its production to affect the food, and her recommendations for the consumer.

The breadth of material she covers is vast; production methods, historical comparisons, political and environmental controversies, federal government and special interest group influences, and practical applications of nutrition research are all blended into a very useful set of realistic and humbly presented recommendations. The assumptions and thought processes she uses are laid out clearly to help the reader see whether her conclusion is something they can share. Often her conclusions are amusingly simple: "Milk is just a food. There is nothing special about it. Cow's milk is not necessary and it is not perfect (at least not for humans). But cow's milk is also not a poison."

We do not always share her concerns or solutions. A couple of areas of disagreement would be her position on saturated fats, and her 'Taking Action' conclusions that seem to encourage the imposition of centralized controls over which foods the consumer can buy.

However, excellent tools are given to allow the consumer to practice personal responsibility and take control of their own food environment, and the disagreements we may have are far outweighed by the rich store of practical knowledge you will gain from reading this book.

> *In the interests of open-minded and healthy intellectual hiking, we are also including books that test confrontational waters on some of the controversial nutritional issues.*

The Cholesterol Myths (Exposing the Fallacy That Saturated Fat and Cholesterol Cause Heart Disease)
(Uffe Ravnskov, MD, Ph.D., © 2000)
Dr. Ravnskov is a cheerful Swede who addresses the flaws in the argument that dietary fat and cholesterol are responsible for heart disease. This book is only for the genuinely open minded, and those who want to read a contrarian but evidence-based view. It is probably only helpful for those who already have a reasonable knowledge of the evidence underpinning contemporary dietary recommendations.

The Fat Fallacy: The French Diet Secrets to Weight Loss
(William Clower, Ph.D., © 2003)
A lively, funny, well-written book contrasting the American obsession with low fat dogma and the French disregard for fat and carbohydrate restrictions. The author points out the much higher rate of obesity and heart disease in this country and tries to show how the prudent use of chocolate, butter, eggs, and cheese can help you lose weight and gain health.

French Women Don't Get Fat
(Mireille Guiliano © 2005)
Yet it was precisely the experience of getting fat, albeit as an exchange student in the U.S. that inspired the author – who is French – to write this book! Regardless of the accuracy of the title, the book is full of practical advice, real-life case histories, and recipes. She says the book is for women who need to lose up to thirty pounds, but anyone would benefit from her message.

Nourishing Traditions; The Cookbook that Challenges Politically Correct Nutrition and the Diet Dictocrats
(Sally Fallon with Mary G. Enig, Ph.D., ©1999, 2001)
This book delivers *exactly* what the title promises, and does so with the efficiency of a machine gun and the firmness of an Italian grandmother. It is an encyclopedic blend of old-fashioned liver-and-onions and Adele Davis at her most radical. Each page is crowded with recipes as well as often-fascinating facts on diet, history, religion, sociology, and medicine. This is a book to read on a desert island even if you disagree with something on every page. It may be the only place you'll find a recipe for Brain Omelet.

Eating Well Magazine
This is a self-described "intelligent magazine bringing together food and health." It also does a decent job of presenting evidence-based information, although we are hoping they will stop tip-toeing around the good-fat-versus-low-fat issue and stop recommending stuff like egg substitute and low fat cheese.

www.eatingwell.com

Subscribe online or call toll-free (800) 337-0402

2 Kitchen Strategy

Pantry Basics

If you have the basic ingredients on hand it's much easier to put together meals without any planning and with little effort. When we're tired and wanting to do anything but cook or even *think* about cooking, the right inventory can make the difference between preparing a truly delicious meal or succumbing to the temptation to eat out or order in.

With this kind of selection of mix-and-match whole foods (and the absence of junk food) it's also easier to stay on the wagon where food choices are concerned.

These are the foods I can generally count on having in my refrigerator, freezer, or cupboards at any given time. Of course, the recipes I use most often in this book lean heavily on this list. You can prepare most of the recipes in this book from these supplies without any need to shop. I would consider this a sort of master shopping list.

Refrigerated Food

- ❑ butter
- ❑ milk
- ❑ plain unsweetened yogurt
- ❑ *sharp* cheddar cheese
- ❑ Parmesan (Parmigiano-Reggiano)
- ❑ mild feta cheese
- ❑ eggs
- ❑ mayonnaise (see page 56)
- ❑ whole grain mustard
- ❑ tahini (sesame seed paste)
- ❑ flaxseed meal
- ❑ extra-firm tofu
- ❑ raw almonds, walnuts, pecans
- ❑ raw sesame and sunflower seeds
- ❑ dry active baking yeast

Frozen Food

- ❑ corn
- ❑ baby lima beans
- ❑ green soy beans (in and out of the pod)
- ❑ chopped spinach
- ❑ baby green beans
- ❑ strawberries, blueberries, raspberries

Fresh Vegetables

- ❑ onions
- ❑ garlic
- ❑ carrots
- ❑ celery
- ❑ napa cabbage
- ❑ butternut squash
- ❑ russet and Yukon gold potatoes
- ❑ bell peppers
- ❑ tomatoes
- ❑ fresh ginger

Fresh Fruit

- ❑ apples
- ❑ oranges
- ❑ bananas
- ❑ lemons/limes

Grains

- ❑ brown rice
- ❑ polenta
- ❑ Scottish oatmeal
- ❑ old-fashioned rolled oats
- ❑ oat bran
- ❑ unbleached white bread flour
- ❑ stone ground whole-wheat flour
- ❑ whole grain pastas
- ❑ millet
- ❑ bulgur
- ❑ quinoa
- ❑ toasted buckwheat
- ❑ whole wheat couscous

Dry Beans

- brown and red lentils
- anasazi or pinto beans
- small white beans

Canned Food

- 15-ounce black beans
- 15-ounce chickpeas
- 15-ounce red kidney beans
- 15- and 32-ounce chicken broth
- 5- and 12-ounce evaporated whole milk
- 14- and 28-ounce diced tomatoes
- 14- and 28-ounce crushed tomatoes
- 6-ounce light solid tuna in olive oil
- 12-ounce solid white tuna in water
- 4-ounce whole mild green chiles
- 14-ounce coconut milk (not *lite*)

General Supplies

- extra-virgin olive oil
- apple cider vinegar
- cold pressed canola oil
- non-stick canola spray
- raisins
- currants
- honey
- pure maple syrup
- brown sugar
- baking powder
- baking soda (*see note*)

Special Effects

- fresh cilantro
- fresh parsley
- green onions
- salsa
- soy sauce
- fish sauce
- toasted sesame oil
- almond essence
- dried unsweetened shredded coconut

> *Note:*
> *Baking soda is the best cleaner I've found for just about everything from coffee stained mugs to the kitchen sink – literally. It cleans stainless steel or porcelain, and improves (if not removes) the baked-on residue from non-stick spray that collects on baking sheets and pans. You can even use it to brush your teeth.*

Seasonings

- salt (kosher and table)
- peppercorns (for grinder)
- Tabasco sauce
- crushed chilies
- chili powder
- basil
- thyme
- oregano
- cinnamon
- ground cumin
- curry powder

Favorite Portland Sources: *including local markets like Fred Meyer and Winco Foods*

Bob's Red Mill Natural Foods
(503) 654-3215
www.bobsredmill.com

Whole Foods Market (downtown location)
(503) 525-4343
www.wholefoodsmarket.com

New Seasons Market
(503) 292-1987
www.newseasonsmarket.com

Trader Joe's
(800) 746-7857
www.traderjoes.com

Important Ingredients

There are some fundamental ingredients that are nonnegotiable essentials in my kitchen, like extra virgin olive oil, apple cider vinegar, salt, peppercorns, and honey.

Other ingredients, like Parmesan cheese, lemons or limes, cilantro, and parsley, fall somewhere between necessities and luxuries. These are necessary for their contribution to certain recipes but not always in the kitchen when I need them. (Onions and garlic are dealt with in the *Vegetable* chapter starting on page 71.)

Extra virgin olive oil

Our kitchen has two kinds of oil: canola oil for making mayonnaise (see recipe on page 56) and a 3-liter tin of extra virgin olive oil for everything else, including frying eggs, popping popcorn, and sautéing vegetables. Extra virgin olive oil is remarkably versatile oil, considering its distinctive flavor. In terms of health benefits, extra virgin olive oil (the oil from the first pressing of the olives) is the richest and least processed of the grades of olive oil.

As for choosing from the dozen or more brands you are faced with in most stores, my suggestion is to buy the best selling extra virgin olive oil from any serious food store: it will be moderately priced and it may be their house brand. The turnover of lower-priced oil in a busy food store is far more assured than with any of the expensive imported brands, regardless of how magnificent they were when they left Italy, Greece, or Spain. (Store away from light and heat.)

You can use extra virgin olive oil for almost any recipe where oil is used. I use extra virgin olive oil in all my Asian and Mexican recipes, too. If your sensibilities are not too offended, you should try it yourself. The only recipes where I *don't* use exclusively olive oil are the few times when flavor is an issue: for example, we prefer mayonnaise made with about 30 percent extra virgin olive oil and 70 percent canola oil. (See recipe on page 56.) Also, in the case of the *Soy Ginger Marinade* on page 114, there is no substitute for toasted sesame oil.

Light Olive Oil? If you have been using light or regular olive oil in your kitchen, consider moving it into your bathroom: it is a wonderful moisturizer when used on a just-washed face. Moist skin will absorb the oil and look radiantly healthy, but olive oil applied to a completely dry face, in my experience, gives an oily look and feels itchy. Olive oil is also a skin-friendly treatment to get pine pitch off your skin or hair.

Apple Cider Vinegar

It is the only kind of vinegar I use these days. It's probably more pungent than most types of wine vinegar, but you can use it in place of any vinegar a recipe may call for, in my opinion. A major role for vinegar in my kitchen is in vinaigrette, and my boisterous recipe (see page 55) is no place for exotic or nuanced varieties.

Apple cider vinegar is also a hero in the field of folk medicine. Some find that drinking a glass of water mixed with a couple of tablespoons of cider vinegar can settle a roiling tummy, and sipping a mixture of equal proportions of cider vinegar and honey can ease a cough.

Honey

Honey is a whole food. Use the mildest tasting, lightest colored honey you can find, which will probably be clover honey. For most of my cooking purposes — bread dough, vinaigrette, marinades, and sauces, to name a few — honey is the perfect sweetener. It does take a bit more mixing to dissolve than sugar when making something like vinaigrette, but an extra 30 seconds of whisking is hardly an issue.

Salt

Salt is the difference between food and feast. It's more than a condiment: without salt, the other big flavors like hot, sweet, and sour, are wasted. Salt is also part of a healthy lifestyle. If you get rid of all hidden salt in your diet, which means avoiding most prepared foods, you probably don't need to be concerned about adding salt to your food. I tend to call for more salt (and freshly ground pepper) in my recipes than most, but it is no accident.

For most baking purposes table salt works fine. (I also use it to clean my wok instead of using water.) For stovetop cooking and for salting vegetables and meat before roasting, I prefer the coarser textured kosher salt.

Pepper(corns)

The sweet heat and potent richness of freshly ground pepper make a tremendously important contribution to food, in my opinion. I happen to use black peppercorns rather than pink or red or green or white: the important issue is not the color but whether or not it is freshly ground.

Also important is whether you have a grinder that works well. (See *Some Useful Cooking Tools* on page 37.) A cheap, poorly designed pepper mill with a fitful grinder that spits out a mixture of powdered and cracked pepper at the same time is almost — but not quite — worse than the alternatives.

Parmesan

Freshly grated Parmesan cheese turns up quite a bit in these pages: it generally means *Parmigiano-Reggiano*, the imported Italian original. An acceptable alternative (and about half the price) is another imported Italian cheese called *Grana Padano*. You may find domestic Parmesan that you like as well, but I haven't yet.

Should you have doubts as to what the fuss is about, just do a side-by-side taste comparison between Parmigiano-Reggiano and one of the pre-packed or pre-grated Parmesan cheeses. Shop around for the best price (avoid high-end delicatessens) and buy chunks with the least rind. Check cut edges for freshness; if they don't give at all when you press them and don't look as creamily opaque as the rest of the cheese, keep looking.

Also, random cut and hand wrapped Parmigiano-Reggiano from serious food stores is generally superior to the commercially packaged wedges in the supermarket.

It is usually recommended to grate Parmesan as needed, but it is useful and perfectly acceptable to keep a cup or so of grated Parmesan tightly sealed in a glass jar in the refrigerator. The quantities in my recipes are for Parmesan grated on the ⅛-inch teardrop-shaped holes of my box grater. If you use a Microplane grater, which creates a much fluffier pile of Parmesan, you'll need to use more.

A couple of my favorite uses for grated Parmesan is either tossed (about ½ cup) through a green salad dressed with vinaigrette or added (about 1 cup) to hot, barely-drained whole-wheat pasta with extra virgin olive oil, garlic, salt, and freshly ground pepper.

Fresh Lemons (and Limes)

Both lemon and lime juice are invaluable flavor spikes, especially when cooking with confident ingredients like beans, tuna, and whole grains. Sometimes just a tablespoon of lemon or lime juice can make all the difference to a recipe, particularly dips and patés, or the *Béchamel Sauce* on page 69.

Commercially bottled lemon or lime juice (from concentrate) is not a substitute for fresh, in my opinion.

Zest, which is the colored part of the peel, also makes a critical contribution in recipes like *Mother's Brown Rice Pudding*, *Tuna Tetrazzini*, and *Tuscan Bean Salad*.

If you don't have a citrus zesting tool (mine removes 5 delicate strips of zest) you can use a vegetable peeler, but it's important to peel with almost no pressure to remove only the thin yellow or green layer that holds the aromatic oils. The white pith is bitter. Just mince or finely slice the strips that you remove.

I have a general preference for limes because they have no seeds to fuss with and for my purposes are interchangeable with lemons, but price and quality decide the issue. If you buy lemons or limes at a good price, don't let them die before you use them! Extract the juice and store it in the refrigerator, and try to use it within a week.

One average lemon or lime will give you somewhere between ¼ - ½ cup. (They can still give plenty of juice even after the rinds stiffen but watch that your knife doesn't slip when you're slicing a hard-skinned one.)

The juiciest limes or lemons are those with thin skins and a bit of give when you press them. When I shop for any citrus I always avoid hard fruit with deep dimpling. (In the case of oranges and grapefruit, soft fruit with baggy-feeling peels are to be avoided no matter how large and photogenic they may be. Like a good lemon or lime, they should be thin skinned with a bit of give, and should feel heavy for their size.)

Cilantro and Parsley

These are the two most useful of the fresh herbs, in my opinion. Cilantro can be an acquired taste (or possibly never acquired, as in the case of my mother). It has an aggressive flavor I've heard described as "funky" and "musty", but to cilantro lovers the flavor is seductive and evocative. It also has the additional convenience of tender stems that can be chopped along with the leaves. Cilantro enhances most Asian, Mexican, and Middle Eastern dishes, and is a natural partner to the flavors of cumin, chilies, and lime or lemon juice.

Flat leaf (Italian) parsley usually costs more than regular curly parsley but doesn't seem to have any flavor advantage. Parsley is sturdier than cilantro, but both can lose their essential flavor edge after a few days even if they keep their looks.

Clean them in a few changes of cold water as needed and dry them well. (You really need a salad spinner for this, if you don't have one already.) Pack them loosely in a sealed plastic container or bag. Try to avoid any excess water hanging on the leaves and store with a couple of clean, dry paper towels. If you don't use them within a couple of days, check them daily thereafter for any signs of yellowing or pockets of deterioration.

I have been amazed at how long fresh herbs like basil, thyme, and rosemary will stay fresh if I poke them into a glass with a half-inch or so of water and leave loosely covered in plastic in the fridge or uncovered for days on a window sill. They seem to like the feel of water on their feet and wind in their hair.

Some Useful Cooking Tools

Cooking is like gardening in that your choice of tools can make a big difference to your fun. A person can make do (or do without) in many cases, but for me there are a handful of things I use almost every day. Naturally this list is very subjective. Every home cook would have a different list, and may possibly even feel passionate about a different garlic press.

Knives: I use three only: an 8-inch chef's knife, a paring knife with a 3-inch blade, and a serrated bread knife. I also like my oyster knife, with its sturdy blade for jobs that require serious poking or prying, or whenever one is tempted to use a knife but shouldn't.

Cutting board: A heavy hardwood board, at least 15 x 25 inches, is invaluable. Mine lives permanently on the countertop. (Wood is considered safer than plastic boards, as bacteria are thought to be neutralized by the wood.)

Metal dough scraper: The one I reach for is a 4-inch square piece of stiff metal with a round wooden handle, and it is pretty much an extension of my hand. It scrapes dried dough off counters after I've made bread, separates and scoops up chopped vegetables, and is generally indispensable.

Garlic press: For me, the cleanest and most efficient way to extract garlic is the plain old press method. *(See more about crushing garlic on page 79.)* I like the Zyliss brand.

Vegetable peeler: The Oxo brand with the fat black handle and tip designed for digging is comfortable and efficient.

Citrus reamer: This means the simple little all-wooden tool I use to squeeze juice from lemons and limes.

Kitchen scissors: Used mainly to keep me from using knives in ways that may either damage the knives or me.

Pepper grinder: Having come to a serious appreciation for freshly ground pepper, I use and recommend a 12-inch wooden Peugeot pepper grinder.

Salad spinner: An essential for preparing fresh greens as well as parsley and cilantro, and also refreshing bagged greens. I like the pull-string Zyliss model.

Collapsible basket steamer: Best way I've found yet to reheat leftover rice.

Silicone (heatproof) spatulas: Nonnegotiable. I use a large one with a curved head (called a *spoonula*) that holds a handy 2 tablespoons of olive oil as well as regular sized scraping-type spatula.

Pyrex measuring jugs: Clear, solidly built, and invaluable. You need the 1-cup, 2-cup, 4-cup, and 8-cup. The big one doubles as a mixing bowl, and it can be useful to know how much mixture you have.

Immersion blender: Also called a stick blender, this transforms soup making, allowing you to create creamy ready-to-serve soups with minimum fuss. (You can purée a soup or sauce directly in the pot rather than transferring to and from a food processor or regular blender.)

Breakfast Tips

Mornings arrive at an uncivilized hour and leave too soon. If there are strong opinions about what is and what is not an acceptable food choice, this is not the time to argue. One effective way to avoid an argument with yourself or anyone else is to simply stop buying poor food choices. Whether it's hot oatmeal or coffee and toast, figure out something you can enjoy even if you wake up on the wrong side of the bed.

Avoid Fruit Juice

Or have a *very* small glass. If possible, remove fruit juices from your refrigerator and your life completely. Even if freshly squeezed, juice is low in nutrition and fiber and high in sugar and calories. It is safe to say that most of us *can't afford* extra calories. Juice takes the place of the whole fruit we *should* be eating instead. So, consider juice as a treat rather than a staple.

Include Whole Fruit

As long as our goal is to eat 5 – 9 servings of fruit and vegetables every day, why not start here? An orange or grapefruit is particularly welcome in the morning, especially if you have been used to a glass of orange juice. A banana works well for some people sliced and added to yogurt or eaten on toast with some sort of nut butter.

Avoid Commercial Cold Cereals

Keep in mind that even seemingly honest breakfast cereals that claim whole grain status are still refined carbohydrates. Even if technically made from whole grain, conventional breakfast cereals have been processed to such a degree that the structure of the starch molecule has been changed from gelatinous to crystalline, and acts more like sugar in your body. If you are a cold-breakfast-cereal eater, try replacing it with something like raw, unsweetened muesli, which you can buy ready made or construct yourself. (See page 41.) Whole grain cooked cereals are probably better.

Include Whole Grain Cereals

For cold cereal you can try rolled oats, muesli, or granola served with milk, fresh fruit, or dried fruit. For hot cereal there are options like oatmeal, barley, cornmeal (polenta), brown rice, toasted buckwheat, or millet. Serve with milk or butter, honey or brown sugar. Muesli is delicious as a cooked cereal, too.

Avoid Refined Carbohydrates

This includes foods like traditional bagels, store-bought muffins, pastries, biscuits, white flour pancakes and waffles, cream-of-wheat-type cereals, and all cold breakfast cereals. Try to include as wide a spectrum of whole grains as you can, whether in the form of bread, muffins, or cereals. Custom-built, whole grain, fiber-packed nutrient-dense muffins are actually practical to make yourself. (See *Bread and Baking* on page 161.)

Include Whole Grain Bread

When you are reading ingredient labels remember that *wheat flour* means white flour, and *enriched flour* means that first the flour is stripped of all nutrients, and then about 10 percent is added back. What a deal! Don't compromise: if you don't have the real thing in genuine whole-wheat, spend your breakfast calories on something else.

(***Note:*** *one has to sympathize with those who question the validity of a 100 percent whole-wheat bagel. When is a bagel not a bagel? Is it enough just to look like a bagel?*)

Include (Real) Eggs

Eating an egg a day is a reasonable choice for most of us. Don't eat fake eggs, which are neither food nor medicine. Eggs are rich in protein, folic acid, and other B vitamins and cook quickly. They can be fried, scrambled, poached, boiled, or used in omelets or frittatas. Try cooking your eggs in olive oil, instead of butter. Butter is fine but olive oil is optimal.

Omelets or *frittata* (see page 42) are also tasty ways to sneak extra vegetables into your diet — tomatoes, onions, bell peppers, mushrooms, spinach, and so on. Or just chop a tomato and toss it into the hot pan with your morning egg as it cooks. The tomato is a perfect complement to the egg even if it is just warmed through. (The tomato, not the egg.)

Avoid Preserved Meat

This means bacon, sausages, and ham, of course. They contain added sugar, salt, and preservatives, and should be reserved for special occasions, if possible. Exactly what it is about these processed meats that seems to lead to diseases like cancer, diabetes and heart disease is not clear.

Use Real Butter

Real butter is a legal substance, but use it sparingly. Avoid any butter substitutes or any partially hydrogenated product like margarine. If you want to reduce your butter intake, an option is to make a mixture of 75 percent soft butter and 25 percent olive oil and store in the refrigerator. If you use mild oil like soy or canola you can make the mixture 50-50.

Use Honey

If you want something sweet on your toast or in your cereal, don't forget the perfect sweetener – antioxidant rich honey.

Some Breakfast Suggestions:

- **Eggs:** fried, scrambled, coddled, poached, boiled, or in an omelet or frittata, with whole grain buttered toast.

- **Whole grain toast:** toasted whole-wheat bread, bagels, or English muffins, with nut butter, honey, or 100% fruit spread.

- **Whole grain French toast** with honey, real maple syrup, or a 100% fruit spread.

- **Whole grain fruit-and-nut muffins** with butter. (See page 180.)

- **Whole grain pancakes** with butter and pure maple syrup. (See page 42.)

- **Cold whole grain cereal:** made from whole grains that have not been processed, like muesli, granola, or old fashioned rolled oats served with milk, fresh fruit, or dried fruit. (See page 38.)

- **Hot whole grain cereal:** like oatmeal, barley, cornmeal, brown rice, kasha (toasted buckwheat groats), or millet, and served with milk or butter, honey, or brown sugar. (See pages 40, and 132 - 133.) Muesli is good cooked, too.

- **Plain yogurt or kefir** with live cultures mixed with fresh fruit or canned fruit packed in its own juice. Some even like yogurt mixed with granola or muesli.

- **Smoothies** made with yogurt or kefir, fresh fruit, soft tofu, and any number of other additions. (See page 43.)

- **Fresh fruit,** whole, chopped, or with cereal, yogurt, kefir or cottage cheese.

Oats

Oats are among the best sources of soluble fiber. They reduce cholesterol, stabilize blood sugar, have antioxidant qualities, and even contain psychoactive compounds that may combat nicotine cravings and may even have antidepressant powers! [1]

Rolled Oats as Hot Cereal

Do not use quick-cooking oats! They are too refined and are digested too quickly. They also become gluey when cooked. We recommend old-fashioned rolled oats.

(Makes about 2 cups cooked oatmeal)

> 1 cup old-fashioned rolled oats
> ½ teaspoon salt
> 1¾ cups water

- **Stovetop method**: Bring water to a boil in a small saucepan. Add rolled oats and salt and reduce heat. Cook uncovered on the stove, stirring frequently, until the water is absorbed and the consistency suits you (about 5 – 10 minutes).

- **Microwave method** Place rolled oats and water in 4-cup Pyrex measuring jug. (A 2-cup jug may boil over.) Microwave uncovered for 2 minutes. Stir in salt, and then microwave uncovered for another 1 - 1½ minutes.

- Flavor to taste with honey, brown sugar, butter, more salt, raisins, or fresh fruit. The addition of salt is critical in oatmeal, not only for flavor but to reduce the need for sweetening. I suggest ½ teaspoon of salt per cup of oatmeal.

Scottish and Steel-cut Oatmeal

Scottish oats should not be confused with the much chunkier steel-cut (or Irish) oatmeal. Scottish oats are finely cut oat groats that provide a pleasant variation on rolled oats. They are generally cooked but are even good uncooked. (For an uncooked option try combining ⅓-cup of Scottish oatmeal with ½-cup of milk and let the mixture soak for about 30 minutes, or leave in the refrigerator overnight.)

Steel-cut oats (also called Irish oatmeal) are the coarsest form of oatmeal, made from whole groats that have been cut into two or three pieces. Steel-cut oats make the best porridge, in my opinion, but they are not for the faint-of-heart and will take at least 30 minutes to cook. You can soak the oats and water overnight to reduce the cooking time. Some folks suggest that for the best flavor, first toast the oats in a hot skillet for a few minutes or in a 350-degree oven for about 5 minutes or until fragrant.

(Makes about 3 cups cooked oatmeal)

> 3 cups water
> 1 cup of Scottish or steel-cut oatmeal
> ½ - ¾ teaspoon salt

- Bring liquid to the boil in a 2-quart pot and stir in oats and salt.

- Simmer 10 minutes for Scottish oats *or* 30 minutes for steel cut oats.

---

[1] Jean Carper *Food-Your Miracle Medicine* 1994

Rolled Oats as Cold Cereal

People who don't like hot oatmeal should try the cold version, either in the simplest form or as muesli. Just pour ½ cup of milk over ½ cup of old-fashioned rolled oats. Drizzle some honey over the top or sprinkle with raisins or a chopped banana for sweetness.

Muesli

Muesli is a rolled-oat-based cereal that doesn't need cooking, and is usually eaten with milk. Either buy it ready-made from a reputable local source (like *Bob's Red Mill* in Milwaukie, Oregon) or create your own. The list of ingredients that follows is more suggestion than recipe. The point is to emphasize variety, fiber, and good fat while still enjoying breakfast. (You can also cook the muesli like oatmeal.)

3 cups old-fashioned rolled oats
2 cups rolled rye, barley, triticale, etc.
½ cup toasted buckwheat (kasha)
½ cup raw sesame seeds
1 cup raw sunflower seeds
½ cup flaxseed meal or whole flaxseeds
½ - 1 cup shredded unsweetened coconut
1 cup flaked or slivered almonds
1 cup raisins/currants/chopped dried fruit

- Combine everything and store it in a container in a cool place. (Uncooked whole toasted buckwheat has a surprisingly benign crunch and flavor that we love. For a more frivolous note you could add All Bran cereal.)

Oat Bran

Oat bran is a rich source of soluble fiber. You can add it to breakfast cereal, muffins, or pancakes but don't confuse it with Scottish oatmeal. Oat bran is flaky and can be added directly to cold cereals.

Granola

Granola is a cold cereal alternative that delivers whole grains and good fat. It's so good it tastes like junk food to me. Make it yourself; even with a fine ingredient list commercial granola is guilty until proven innocent. Here is my recipe.

5 cups old-fashioned rolled oats
or blend of rolled oats, rye, barley, etc.
1½ cups flaked almonds
1 cup raw sunflower seeds
½ cup raw sesame seeds
1 cup unsweetened shredded coconut
½ cup honey or pure maple syrup (or both)
½ cup extra virgin olive oil
½ teaspoon salt

Preheat oven to 225 degrees.

- In a large bowl mix together all the dry ingredients. Whisk the honey and/or syrup, oil, and salt until well blended. *(Mix carefully at first — the oil may splash.)* Pour over the dry ingredients and mix until all is pleasantly sticky.

- Spread in your largest baking pan (or two) and bake at 225 degrees for 3 hours. Stir and return to the oven for another hour, then ***turn off oven*** and leave granola in oven for 4 hours or overnight. *The long cooking time at a low temperature is better for the valuable oils in the nuts and grains.*

- When granola is completely cool store in an airtight container in a cool place.

Note:

➢ Some of you may like the addition of raisins or some other dried fruit. If so, add it in the last hour of baking.

Oatmeal Pancakes

(Makes about 20 5-inch pancakes.)

1 cup cold milk
1 cup hot water
½ cup honey
¼ cup extra virgin olive oil
3 cups old-fashioned rolled oats
4 eggs, beaten
1 cup whole-wheat pastry flour
1½ teaspoons salt
1 tablespoon baking powder

- In a mixing bowl combine milk, water, honey, oil, oats, and beaten eggs.

- Combine whole-wheat flour with salt and baking powder. Add to the liquid mixture and whisk until smooth.

- Cook pancakes on hot griddle and flip after bubbles form, but before they pop.

Note:
For my yeast-raised version of these pancakes:

- *Combine milk and water in a large mixing bowl and sprinkle **1 tablespoon of yeast** over the warm mixture. Add oats and flour but don't stir; set aside for 10 minutes, then stir until smooth. Cover and set aside for 30 – 60 minutes or until mixture almost doubles.*

- *In a separate (smaller) bowl, whisk eggs, and then add honey, oil, and salt and whisk until mixed well. Combine yeast mixture with egg mixture and blend thoroughly. That's it — the batter is ready to use. (Follow cooking directions above.)*

Fast Frittata
with Tomato and Onion

The only difficult thing about a frittata is remembering whether to put the two *t*'s in the middle or the end of the word. Frittatas have all the advantages of an omelet but are more like a thick, tender egg pancake.

(Serves 1 – 2)

1 – 2 eggs, lightly beaten with fork
salt and freshly ground pepper
2 teaspoons extra virgin olive oil
1 tomato, diced
¼ cup sliced green onions

- Prepare eggs and set aside. Heat a small skillet over medium heat and add oil. When oil is hot enough it should spit when you add a drop of water. Add green onion. Sauté for 10 seconds, or until sizzling but still bright green.

- Add the tomato. Sauté only long enough to heat the tomato through. Add the egg and distribute it evenly around the vegetables. Cook until the eggs are set, lifting sections of cooked egg to let any uncooked egg flow underneath.

- Flip so the golden-brown underside shows, slice into wedges, and serve.

Note:
➤ You can use diced regular onion instead of green onion; sauté until tender enough for your taste. (I like it a bit crunchy.) Any ingredients you would use for an omelet would work here.

➤ This recipe expands any way you like — just adjust the size of your pan. (See *Zucchini Frittata* on page 157.)

Yogurt Smoothie
Yogurt and Fruit Drink

Often the very people who need the benefits of yogurt the most are the ones who *really hate* yogurt. But a cunningly constructed smoothie can get yogurt into just about anyone — unless they hate fruit, too. (For more about yogurt see page 57.)

- A smoothie is one of the easiest and most pleasant ways to boost daily nutritional intake, especially when the appetite is puny or missing altogether. A smoothie is *especially* useful for those who don't like eating breakfast but know they should.

- If you're not familiar with making smoothies, the following recipe is a safe starting point from which to wander with your own variations. Bananas are virtually always available because you can keep a supply in your freezer.

- Naturally there is enormous scope here for variation as far as fruit is concerned. Just about any fresh or frozen fruit works, but a balance between sweet (like ripe bananas) and tart (like berries) is a good idea. A good blender will have no problem with (edible) skins.

- *Don't forget that smoothies are not milkshakes!* This is no place for ice cream or syrup. Think of them as liquid power bars; a daily hit of immune-boosting enzymes, protein, and all the benefits of yogurt.

- And if you choose to take the concept of a liquid power bar further, you could add a raw egg, soft tofu, soy powder, nutritional yeast, vitamin C powder, and so on.

Smoothie

(Serves 1 – 2)

> 1 cup unsweetened yogurt or kefir
> 1 banana (fresh or frozen) sliced if frozen
> 1 cup (fresh or frozen) strawberries, or
>   any berries

- Combine everything in the blender and whirr until smooth and lump-free.

Note:
- If it isn't sweet enough, add honey or a frozen juice concentrate. However, try to adjust the sweetness by the fruit you choose, rather than adding sweetener or juice of any kind.

- If it's not cold enough, add ice or more frozen fruit.

- Smoothies are a good way to use up overripe or bruised bananas. You can also freeze ripe bananas if you find yourself with too many; peel them and put them into the freezer individually wrapped in plastic, or on a plate or a cookie sheet until they're hard, then transfer them to a plastic bag. It's nice to have back-up smoothie bananas on hand.

- If it's too thick, add more yogurt. *(Yogurt does not thicken smoothies; it breaks down and acts as a liquid in the blender or food processor.)*

Snacking Suggestions

If you make a point of always having a supply of healthy snacks that you like, you will find it a lot easier to maintain good eating habits. Find what you like, and don't obsess over the details. As long as you are eating good food, it's more important to enjoy what you eat than to meet some kind of imagined criteria. (Of course, if you have a weight problem, you would be wise to consider calorie content, as well.) Here are some ideas.

Fruit: Fresh fruit comes in its own skin — ready-to-eat, naturally sweetened serving-sized packages. Apples, oranges, and bananas are always easily available. Frozen grapes or frozen bananas can be snacked on anytime, and make good snacks for kids *and* grown-ups. (Peel and freeze bananas *before* wrapping in plastic.)

Vegetables: Like broccoli with a cheese or bean dip, or carrots with *sharp* cheddar cheese, or celery sticks stuffed with dip or roasted almond butter (grind it yourself at a natural food store).

Raw Nuts: One of our favorite snacks is a handful of raw almonds. A bag of almonds in your desk drawer are useful for times when your mind wanders toward food. Keep a bowl of uncracked nuts handy. You may eat less if you have to crack them first.

Raw Seeds: ¼ cup raw sunflower or pumpkin seeds are a sensible and satisfying snack. Buy them from a good source; they can be awful if they're not fresh. Roasted and salted seeds are not a good choice

Yogurt: Avoid the sweetened versions. Buy plain full-fat or low fat yogurt and stir in whatever makes it taste good — fresh fruit or honey, for example. (See *Yogurt*, page 57.)

Cottage Cheese: A natural cottage cheese (read the label) is wonderfully compatible with fresh fruit, vegetable sticks, or green salads.

Green Soybeans (*Edamame*): (See page 113.) In or out of the pod, these are good freshly cooked or cold from the refrigerator — in a car, at a picnic, as an appetizer, or anytime.

Boiled Egg or Scrambled Egg: A boiled egg can wait until you're ready to eat it (with salt and pepper, I hope) and a scrambled egg is a quickly made hot snack.

Whole Grain Muffin: Whole grain muffins with fruit and nuts are nutrition dense yet sweet enough to satisfy the need for a treat. (See *Muffins*, starting on page 180.)

Brown Rice Cakes: You can find quite a variety of sweet and savory crispy brown rice cakes in most supermarkets. For a plain rice cake, a scraping of roasted nut butter is tasty.

Popcorn Popped in Olive Oil: Popcorn is a great snack. Our favorite popper is the *Stir Crazy* popcorn popper. Pop a cup of popcorn in 1/3 cup of extra virgin olive oil (don't shake your head until you've tried it), salt, and serve. The best we've had and even good the next day.

Also see *Marinated Tofu (page 114), Brown Rice Power Patties (page 128)*, and *Scottish Oatcakes (page 179.)*

Lunch and Dinner Tips

The prescription for maximum health and minimum risk calls for most of our daily intake to consist of whole foods like fruits and vegetables, beans, unrefined grains, and good fats. However, reality may be a full schedule and an empty kitchen. Working away from home can make lunch and dinner a challenge. Packing a lunch and limiting fast foods to special occasions are two important steps.

Avoid Fast Food
Picking up something on the way home can be a compelling argument hard to resist when you're hungry and tired, but don't give in too soon. Fast food doesn't have to compromise your eat-smarter-feel-better goals. Consider the many ready-to-eat and heat-and-serve options you can find at serious food retailers like Whole Foods Market, New Seasons Market, and Trader Joe's. In the history of civilization there has never been less excuse to eat well. Still, the value of preparing food from scratch can't be overstated in terms of health and financial benefits.

Start Cooking
If you're new to cooking it may be helpful to refer to *Pantry Basics* (pages 32-33) and *Some Useful Cooking Tools* (page 37). A few practical recipes to start with would be *Quick Little Black Bean Chili* (page 121*),* *Tuna & Broccoli Pasta* (page 144*),* and *Green Eggs and Rice* (page 127*).* These are easy and make great leftovers. From a recipe like *Basic Baked Brown Basmati Rice* you can make any of the seven recipes for rice in the *Whole Grains* section (starting on page 123) and any others you may feel like

inventing. For an especially tasty way to increase your vegetable consumption check out the section on *Roasted Vegetables* (pages 83 – 87).

Eat More Leftovers
Packed lunches don't have to be made to order. For cooks like me, leftovers are part of a grand strategy. Properly orchestrated leftovers take a lot of the work out of planning and cooking meals. Things like soup, casseroles, and chili can be reheated, and taste as good or better the next day.

Leftover polenta can be sliced and reheated, and served topped with chili, or fried and eaten as a snack or appetizer. Leftover bean or grain salads are ready to eat straight from the refrigerator or at room temperature for days after they are made. A dish like *Tuna & Broccoli Pasta* (page 144) is great the next day at any temperature.

Three favorite leftovers for me are plain brown rice (tremendous versatility), polenta (most everyone likes fried polenta) and beans (taste the same leftover as fresh). Whether you deliberately or accidentally end up with leftovers, they will save you planning and kitchen time.

Discover Whole Grain Salads
Salads made with grains or whole grain pasta are happy to go with you to work and hang around until lunch. They combine complex carbohydrates with vegetables, and can be made in advance, languishing happily at room temperature. (There's generally no need to refrigerate a grain salad when you make it on the same day that you eat it.)

Find a recipe you like or invent your own. One of my favorites is leftover brown rice with a diced tomato, a chopped hard-boiled egg, and either *Faux Ranch Dressing* (page 59) or one of the vinaigrettes (page 55), or leftover *Tuna Salad* (page 64), and enough salt and pepper to make it lively.

… and Whole Grain Pasta

All kinds of whole grain pastas are available from natural food stores and supermarkets. There are pastas made from grains like corn, quinoa, soy, spelt, and brown rice as well as wheat. There is even sprouted wheat pasta, which got high marks from our tasters, although it broke up easily. I especially like brown rice pasta. It is a bit fragile but the flavor is mild and delicious and the texture is tender. Don't give up on whole grain pasta until you have found one or two that you like. Many people say they hardly notice a difference when they transition to whole-wheat pasta.

Avoid the Sandwich Trap

The brutal truth is that the difference between white bread and most so-called whole-wheat bread is color rather than fiber. It is even safe to say that the term "whole grain bread" is meaningless without some clarification like "100 %".

As a general rule, deli sandwiches should be a rare indulgence. White bread is not legitimized by any amount of lettuce or tomato, but if you really must eat your sardine and onion sandwich on white bread, a loophole clause may be found.

… and Preserved Meats

This means the sliced deli meats that are so popular and convenient. If you can't lay your hands on sliced home-cooked meat, consider sandwich alternatives like cheese, chicken, tuna salad, or egg salad. You will get the same amount of protein but in a far better form. There is absolutely nothing good about modern preserved meats, but there is a lot that is worrisome.

Eat More Beans

Beans with vinaigrette are a natural match, and it's unlikely any of us are too busy to drain a can of beans and toss them with vinegar, olive oil, salt and pepper. Even better, with some added diced onion and bell peppers and cilantro. Fresh frozen beans can be almost as spontaneous; baby lima beans cook in 7 minutes straight from the freezer. (*Luscious Lima Beans*, page 115) Home cooked beans are shockingly easy; you can cook up a different color and size every couple of weeks and prepare them in a dizzying number of ways. (See *Beans* chapter starting on page 107.)

On the subject of canned beans, *hummus* is an easy dip made with chickpeas, and a great lunch option with raw vegetables or in pita pocket sandwiches stuffed with grated carrot, cucumber, and tomato slices. (See *Hasty Tasty Hummus* on page 62.)

I should add that this hummus does have a significant garlic presence that may affect the atmosphere in the workplace. Bring enough to go around. It's surprisingly popular once people actually try it. Ready-made hummus and all its variations are everywhere, as are recipes for hummus — but I hope you try my recipe.

Both beans and grains can be cooked ahead and stored in the refrigerator, and used in all kinds of combinations as you feel like it. They generally reheat with no effect on their texture or flavor, or can be served cold or at room temperature when transformed into salads. This makes them particularly heroic in last-minute meal scenarios.

Eat More Tuna

You can buy single-portion rip-top cans of tuna that are perfect for snacks or meals, eaten just as is, or with a splash of olive oil and vinegar, or paired with a crisp lettuce and celery salad. Tuna salad (see recipe on page 64) is a nutritionally optimal combination of good protein, good fat, and vegetables, and is a great meal in or out of a sandwich. Canned tuna also expands your healthy dinner options greatly: you can use it in chowder, frittatas, fish cakes, noodle or rice casseroles, and so on. (See a few favorite tuna recipes beginning on page 143.) Tuna has also been found to be less environmentally toxic in an office lunchroom than sardines.

… but Give Sardines a Chance

Reputation-wise, sardines are a bit like liver; some people may think they actually exist only in the world of humor. A pity, because they're such nutrient-dense brain food, as well as rich in omega-3 oils, nucleic acid, and protein.

If you are new to sardines I suggest starting out with something like King Oscar Extra-Small Sardines "taken from the icy waters of Norway's purest fjords" (as the label puts it) and packed in olive oil in little cans with rip-off lids. If the sight of a small tail hanging off your fork might bother you, mash the sardines before you use them. Try them mashed on a thin slice of fresh whole wheat bread spread with butter or mayonnaise and sprinkled with salt and pepper. (See *Sardine Paté* on page 65.)

Try kippered snacks if you don't like sardines. These are usually next to sardines on the grocery shelf and are tasty little smoked herring fillets that are ready to eat with a fork right out of the can. (Drain them first.) King Oscar makes a great kippered snack. By the way, read labels carefully to make sure you don't accidentally end up with something packed in cottonseed oil, or some kind of sauce you may not like.)

Avoid Eating Out Regularly

(See *Eat Out Less* on page 25.)
For those of us working out of the home all week it is easy to find ourselves eating out on a regular basis. To get away with this without gaining weight or losing our hard-won high density lipoproteins takes will, discipline, and imagination.

Don't compromise. Choose places that can offer some nutritious options. Thai restaurants can serve up wonderful plates of vegetables, and Greek restaurants usually offer sides like hummus and tzatziki, sometimes served with tomato, cucumber and olives. Mexican restaurants can be sources of some decent alternatives, like sides of black beans and pico de gallo, and fajitas with extra sauteed onions and bell peppers requested.

If eating out is necessary, do some research. When you're eating out for breakfast, ask the waitress if they use real butter. If they only have margarine, that's a bad sign. Even after choosing sensibly from a menu, however, we can neutralize our choice by indulging in the extras that are hard to resist. As with most of life's issues, the bottom line is simple self-discipline.

Restaurant Tips

- When you're choosing a salad, pick one with the most colorful greens. When it comes to lettuce, the darker green, the better. If you're at a salad bar, avoid trimmings like bacon bits, croutons, and roasted salted sunflower seeds.

- Avoid unnecessary trans fats by steering clear of breaded or battered food. The coating is bad, the deep-frying is worse.

- Request extra vegetables to replace sides like French fries and white rice.

- Check the menu for options like sides of sauteed spinach or polenta. The restaurant may even create a side of their vegetables-of-the-day for you.

- Say *no* to soft drinks and fruit juice.

Menu *for* One Week

This section has always been a problem for me. I can understand the general demand for detailed menus, especially for those who are dealing with significant change in their eating habits, but it's an intimidating project. Suggesting a week's worth of dinners was easy. The problem was figuring out breakfast, lunch, and snacks: just *whose* breakfast, lunch, and snacks were we talking about? And are these consumers working in an office building or at home? Alone or not? With children?

I did it, but the next edition of this book will probably offer an improved version, with better integration of leftovers.

These suggestions mostly fit the context of a busy schedule that doesn't allow much time for fussing over food. The purpose is purely to offer ideas on how one might put into practice the principles of eating we have been talking about.

Make Time for Breakfast

… and make your breakfast count. Include a serving of whole grains of some kind. Some of us can eat the same thing every morning for years at a time, but for those of you who like variety there are lots of options. (See *Breakfast Tips*, pages 38 – 43.) It should be added that people who eat breakfast are less susceptible to the tender trap of a mid-morning snack.

Calories? We're Not Counting

The goal is to get as much good food in the form of whole grains, vegetables, fruit, and beans on your plate as possible. Don't fall for the low fat myth. *Good* fat is the goal. If you have a weight problem, first look at your intake of refined carbohydrates, not the healthy fats found in the whole foods you are eating. ***Cut back on serving sizes*** and reduce calories from desserts, breads, pasta, potatoes, corn, sweet drinks, and juices. Keep alcohol to a maximum of one serving daily. And ***exercise daily***, if only for a few minutes.

Cook With Leftovers in Mind

It's a good idea to aim to build your next meal on the last. This means (generally speaking) that a good lunch is always possible with no extra work, and dinner on the following night is much easier.

For example, you may serve *Easy, Cheesy Polenta* (page 138) with *Quick Little Black Bean Chili* (page 121) one night, and serve the leftover chili with freshly cooked rice on another night. You can turn the leftover rice into *Nutty Brown Rice* (page 126) or *Green Eggs & Rice* (page 127) on other nights that week. You should only have to cook from scratch every other day or less.

There Are No Dessert Suggestions

… but fresh fruit is always an option. If our goal is optimum health and a sensible weight, there really is no place for the conventional notion of dessert, like cookies, pie, or ice cream. (Except for special occasions and holidays, of course.)

If you stop having desserts, you will eventually stop missing desserts. On the other hand, if you stop having desserts except when you feel stressed, or depressed, or the need to reward yourself for something, you are making it harder for yourself. None of us can afford to assume we can be anything but very serious about our health.

❧ Day 1 ❧

Breakfast
- ❑ Orange or grapefruit
- ❑ Egg fried with sliced tomato
- ❑ Whole-wheat toast

Mid morning snack
- ❑ ¼ cup mixed raw almonds and raisins

Lunch
- ❑ Whole-wheat pita pocket with tuna salad
- ❑ an apple or fruit in season

Afternoon snack
- ❑ 1 cup plain yogurt with banana

Evening meal

- ❑ *Quick Little Black Bean Chili*
- ❑ *Easy Cheesy Polenta*
- ❑ *Pico de Gallo*

Chili and polenta are natural partners. *Easy Cheesy Polenta* tastes good by itself, and makes a filling and balanced meal with the chili. (Hot brown rice topped with grated cheese is a standard alternative to the polenta in our house.) This combination is a quick and easy dinner to make an hour before you eat. *Pico de Gallo* would go well with this meal, but the simple cucumber and cilantro mixture is less work. (If you use an English cucumber you won't need to remove the skin, and the dark green contrast will be useful if you haven't any cilantro.)

Both polenta and chili make wonderful leftovers. You can store chili in the refrigerator for days and reheat it for lunch or dinner served over brown rice or baked potatoes. Leftover polenta can be reheated and served with any sauce or stew, or sliced and fried in olive oil.

❧ Day 2 ❧

Breakfast
- ❑ Banana or fruit in season
- ❑ Oatmeal: hot (Scottish or steel cut) *or* cold (rolled oats or muesli)

Mid morning snack
- ❑ Celery or carrot sticks with *sharp* cheddar cheese

Lunch
- ❑ Whole-wheat pita pocket with hummus and sliced cucumber and tomato
- ❑ orange.

Afternoon snack
- ❑ ¼ cup *Seductive Soy Beans or* ½ cup cooked soybeans in the pod

Evening meal

- ❑ *Tuna Tetrazzini*
- ❑ *Green Beans in Vinaigrette*

A creamy, brightly-flavored tuna noodle casserole is a dependably popular comfort food liked by most kids and grown ups, but also a natural vehicle for omega-3 rich tuna, vegetables, and whole grain pasta. It can be made a day in advance and chilled, then brought to room temperature before baking. (You could substitute leftover chicken or turkey instead of tuna, and cooked brown rice with or instead of pasta.)

Warm green beans in vinaigrette contrasts nicely with the rich casserole. If you're forced to throw yourself on the mercy of your freezer, you could try the skinny little *haricot verts* available in the frozen vegetable section of some stores. The flavor and texture is naturally never as good as fresh, but slim crisp green beans are rarely available. My solution is to toss the beans in vinaigrette. Fresh steamed broccoli is a good alternative.

❧ Day 3 ❧

Breakfast
- ❑ Fruit smoothie
- ❑ *Serious Muffin*

Mid morning snack
- ❑ Hard boiled egg, halved and sprinkled with salt and pepper *or* deviled egg
- ❑ orange

Lunch
- ❑ Cheese and tomato sandwich on whole-wheat bread, grilled or plain
- ❑ apple or fruit in season

Afternoon snack
- ❑ handful of raw almonds
- ❑ banana

Evening meal

- ❑ *Roasted Chicken Thighs*
- ❑ *Quick Brown Rice Pilaf*
- ❑ *Butternut Squash Purée*
- ❑ *Spinach & Mushroom Salad*

A minimum-effort-maximum-effect type dinner that is pretty safe with any audience: hot roasted chicken thighs sitting on a bed of rich couscous, a delicious scoop of bright butternut purée, and a vivid green salad. Thighs are my favorite chicken body part both to eat and to prepare, and cooking it with skin and bone intact is best for the meat. Roasting a whole chicken is an option if you want the mix of white and brown meat or just need the wishbone.

An alternative to the pilaf would be *Nutty Brown Rice*. *Marinated Carrot Matchsticks* is a good substitute for the squash. (The marinated carrots could then double as salad.)

❧ Day 4 ❧

Breakfast
- ❑ Orange
- ❑ Hot whole grain cereal (oatmeal, cracked rye polenta, buckwheat, millet)

Mid morning snack
- ❑ 1 cup plain yogurt with honey or chopped banana

Lunch
- ❑ Leftover chicken or chicken salad
- ❑ Slice of buttered whole-wheat bread

Afternoon snack
- ❑ Apple

Evening meal

- ❑ *Green Eggs & Rice*
- ❑ *Marinated Carrot Matchsticks*

This is a meatless main dish that begs for all kinds of variations and substitutions. You can stir the ingredients together in the morning or at the last. You can make it unctuous with extra cheese and rich milk or you can add extra vegetables like chopped cooked broccoli.

I like to pair *Green Eggs & Rice* with a marinated vegetable or substantial salad to make sure people get enough to eat. An alternative to the marinated carrots would be *A Greek Salad* or even something like *Warm Lentil Salad*. You're free to work on a salad or vegetable once you put *Green Eggs and Rice* in the oven.

(Other brown rice main dishes are *Kedgeree* and *Mexican Brown Rice & Black Beans*.)

❧ Day 5 ☙

Breakfast
- ❑ Grapefruit
- ❑ Egg scrambled with cheese and tomato
- ❑ Whole-wheat toast

Mid morning snack
- ❑ Celery sticks with *hummus* or *faux ranch dressing* or *The Definitive Dip*

Lunch
- ❑ *Tuna Salad* in pita pocket
- ❑ Pear or peach

Afternoon snack
- ❑ 2 brown rice cakes with almond butter

Evening meal

- ❑ *Black Bean Polenta*
- ❑ *Napa Cabbage Salad with Cilantro*

This is an easy vegetarian meal featuring a layered polenta, cheese, and black bean dish with a bright salsa accent that can be prepared an hour ahead or a day or more ahead. Once Black Bean Polenta is put together, it technically only requires heating. So whether you bake it as a casserole or take a serving to work to heat for lunch, it works just as well.

Pico de Gallo is a particularly good accompaniment: the flavors are harmonious but the crunch is a refreshing contrast to the richness of the polenta.

(Another vegetarian option would be *Spinach & Cheese Crepes with Tomato Sauce*. I would serve the crepes with asparagus in season, or steamed broccoli and cauliflower florets.)

❧ Day 6 ☙

Breakfast
- ❑ *Oat and Wheat Pancakes* with butter and pure maple syrup
- ❑ Plain yogurt with fresh fruit

Mid morning snack
- ❑ Carrot sticks with *sharp* cheddar cheese **or** leftover *Pico de gallo* with ½ cup cottage cheese

Lunch
- ❑ *Tabbouleh* with chickpeas **or** leftover *Black Bean Polenta*
- ❑ Apple or cluster of grapes

Afternoon snack
- ❑ Popcorn (popped with olive oil)

Evening meal

- ❑ *Tuna & Broccoli Pasta*
- ❑ *Fresh Tomato Salad*

This is a fast feast. When a dish is this simple, though, it can be easy to ruin by being casual about the details. Every ingredient matters. The only real work is slicing the florets off the broccoli stalks, and that could easily be done in advance. For the pasta I would suggest a spiral-type shape; something with plenty of surface to catch the sauce. (Avoid penne — it's too substantial for this dish.). Bite-sized cooked chicken is a fine substitute for the tuna. This is wonderful eaten cold the next day with a bit of added vinaigrette.

Fresh Tomato Salad is an easy partner but even easier would be just sliced fresh tomatoes salted and peppered and drizzled with olive oil.

❧ Day 7 ❧

Breakfast
- ❑ Orange
- ❑ *Fast Frittata with Tomato & Onion*
- ❑ Whole-wheat toast

Mid morning snack
- ❑ 1 banana

Lunch
- ❑ 2 *Brown Rice Power Patties* **or** leftover *Tuna & Broccoli Pasta*

Afternoon snack
- ❑ ¼ cup raw sunflower seeds and raisins

Evening meal

- ❑ *Crowded Chowder*
- ❑ *Little Whole Wheat Honey Loaf*
- ❑ *Broccoli, Celery & Apple Salad*

Main dish soups like this chowder (which can be fish or clam or vegetarian) are options that work especially well for the times when I think I can smell smoke from my brain, but I'm committed to producing dinner (or lunch). When everything goes in one pot, there is much less to go wrong, and one is less likely to run into timing issues with side dishes. Make sure the bread you serve is truly 100 percent whole grain.

A great alternative to chowder is my version of *Tom Kah Gai*, which is a shockingly loose translation of the Thai chicken soup by the same name. Believe it or not, *Tom Kah Gai* is also one of the fastest and easiest emergency meals I know. *Napa Cabbage Salad with Cilantro* or *Carrot Slaw* would be alternative salads.

Favorite
3   Bits *and* Pieces

Dressings
Dips
Spreads
Sauces
Bits and Pieces

Vinaigrette

Vinaigrette is one of the most useful items you can have on hand. An instant source of flavor, a best friend of vegetables, easy to tweak in any ethnic direction, and always waiting on the other side of the refrigerator door. You can create it at the last minute directly in your mixing bowl and just add your salad or vegetables, or you can make a couple of cups at a time and use it for weeks. It's a simple process using basic ingredients.

- Vinaigrette is a great all-round dressing for tossed green salads as well as pasta, rice, bean, and potato salads, and is an easy way to dress up canned beans that have to make an unscheduled appearance at the table. Vinaigrette will also pinch hit as a marinade for meat.

- One of vinaigrette's most valuable contributions is in the area of vegetable consumption. Some children (and grownups) who may have a hard time getting excited about eating cooked vegetables will veritably *gobble* steamed or roasted broccoli, cauliflower, carrot, asparagus, and green beans if they are served dressed in vinaigrette. Even Brussels sprouts, beets, rutabagas, and turnips can be appetizing (well, in small pieces) with some help from vinaigrette.

- Once vegetables have been tossed with vinaigrette they can be served at any temperature, which removes a lot of pressure from mealtimes. If temperature isn't an issue, you can blanch, steam, boil, or roast vegetables whenever time allows; apply the vinaigrette; then move on to any part of the menu that may not be so flexible. They even taste good the next day. (Note that broccoli and green beans tend to turn a brownish-yellow by that time, however.)

- Some of the sturdier vegetables are improved after a night in vinaigrette, especially the less popular root vegetables like beets, which are more popular marinated or pickled, anyway.

- Toss whole mushrooms in vinaigrette and you will have a succulent and delicious antipasto dish within a half-hour. (They turn dark and pickled by the next day, but they still taste good.)

- You can make a simple vinaigrette just by combining vinegar, oil, salt, and pepper, and shaking or whisking the mixture before you use it. Or you can mix vinaigrette directly into a mixing bowl; maybe ¼ cup of vinegar, ¼ cup of olive oil, ½ teaspoon of salt, ½ teaspoon freshly ground pepper, and a clove or three of crushed garlic. Then you add a few cups of hot beans or cooked grains or vegetables or pasta and toss.

- If you make vinaigrette using a regular or hand held emulsion blender or food processor, you will end up with a more stable emulsion – rather like a thin mayonnaise. A mini-processor works well for vinaigrette: process everything but the oil for 10 seconds, and then add the oil and process for another 10 – 15 seconds. Depending on the processor, you may not need to bother crushing the garlic first. This is definitely more convenient than the shake-before-using version, especially for last-minute use. You can just scoop the amount you need from the jar. It will soften and liquefy by itself or you can stir it with a spoon to hurry it up.

Garlic and Mustard Vinaigrette

This is my all-purpose vinaigrette with ingredients I always have on hand. There is something about this combination that works, and I think it is both the simplicity of the mixture and the intensity of the flavor. It can turn a tossed green salad into an event, with the help of some freshly grated Parmigiano-Reggiano.

(Makes about 1 cup)

¼ cup apple cider vinegar
1 tablespoon freshly crushed garlic
1 tablespoon whole grain mustard
1 tablespoon honey
1 teaspoon salt
1 teaspoon freshly ground pepper

¾ cup extra-virgin olive oil

- Combine all ingredients except olive oil in a 2-cup measuring jug and whisk thoroughly.

- Slowly add olive oil in a thin stream, whisking steadily. With a blender or food processor you can create a creamy, more stable emulsion that resembles a sauce. It will separate fairly quickly if blended by hand.

- Transfer to a glass jar *(or several containers — see **Note**)* and store in your refrigerator. You can refrigerate the vinaigrette for weeks to use as needed.

Note:
➢ If vinaigrette is solid, just scoop out what you need and put the rest back in the refrigerator. It will return to a liquid quickly at room temperature. However, if the mixture has separated the oil will solidify on top, which means you have to bring the whole batch to room temperature to recombine it. You will find it more user friendly (especially for last-minute needs) to divide the recipe into ¼-cup portions immediately after blending it. Recycled glass spice jars work well, or the little Rubbermaid ½-cup containers.

➢ With my pepper grinder, about 60 grinds gives me a teaspoon of ground pepper. I never bother to measure.

Lemon and Cilantro Vinaigrette

This is ideal for the times when you want a Tex-Mex or Middle Eastern accent. It's also mighty good with a can of black beans. Even if you don't have lemon and cilantro, the presence of cumin, chili, and Tabasco will handle the situation.

(Makes about 2/3 cup)

¼ cup lemon or lime juice
1½ teaspoons freshly crushed garlic
1 teaspoon honey
1 teaspoon chili powder
1 teaspoon ground cumin
1 teaspoon salt
½ teaspoon freshly ground pepper
¼ - ½ teaspoon Tabasco sauce

¼ cup olive oil
¼ cup chopped fresh cilantro

- Combine juice, garlic, honey, and seasoning, then whisk in oil. Stir in cilantro. Mix an hour or more before using, if possible.

Mayonnaise

Mayonnaise is one of the world's most useful foods. It is actually a noble sauce in its own right, but it can also be the main ingredient in salad dressings and dips, and mixtures like tuna, chicken, and egg salad. It adapts instantly to flavors like curry, mustard, chutney, pickles, horseradish, anchovies, herbs, and even fruit. Best of all, it adapts to fresh garlic, as in *aioli*. (See *Rich Yogurt Aioli* on page 58.)

Good Fat

Mayonnaise is also in the category of good fat if it's made with good oil. I suggest using a combination of the mild tasting canola oil and extra virgin olive oil. The proportion of each depends on personal preference.

The versatility of mayonnaise is partly dependent upon its ability to blend in, and some of us find that the aggressive taste of olive oil is not preferable here. Just one part of olive oil to three or four parts of canola oil is subtle enough, however.

Mayonnaise is also one of the easiest foods to make, and virtually foolproof. You could certainly make it by hand with mortar and pestle or in a bowl with a whisk, but I prefer the simplicity of a food processor. (I also always keep a backup of *Best Foods* real mayonnaise in the cupboard for emergencies.)

For a very thick version, I use egg yolks instead of whole eggs, as described in the following recipe. (The only time I have ever had a failure is when I experimented with a one-yolk batch in my KitchenAid mini-work bowl and found that there wasn't egg to form an emulsion. For the same reason, using the wide based VitaMix blender is not an alternative.)

Mayonnaise

The following recipe is easiest made in a small food processor. Made in a blender, the mayonnaise becomes too stiff well before all the oil is blended in.

(Makes about 1¾ cups)

> 2 egg yolks (see note)
> 2 tablespoons apple cider vinegar
> 1½ teaspoons dry mustard powder
> 1½ teaspoons salt
> ½ cup extra virgin olive oil
> 1 cup canola oil

- In a food processor combine everything except the oils, and process for about 10 seconds. Then, with the machine running, add the combined oil in a thin, steady stream. That's it. The finished mayonnaise should be stiff enough to mound on a spoon.

- Scrape the mayonnaise into a clean glass jar and store it in the refrigerator. It can be stored for several weeks if kept cold and tightly sealed.

Note:

➤ You can use whole eggs, or a whole egg and a yolk, but the mayonnaise will turn out more like a thick and creamy sauce than the more traditional stiff texture.

➤ If you are making this for someone who *only* likes *Best Foods* mayonnaise, reduce the vinegar to 1 tablespoon and skip the olive oil.

➤ Store egg whites in the refrigerator until you can make a batch of *Coconut Macaroons*. (See page 186.)

Yogurt

Yogurt is best known for its friendly bacteria that improve immunity, reduce gastrointestinal inflammation, and protect against infection. Yogurt is an important addition to the diet for anyone taking antibiotics, and also has high available calcium content. Even people with lactose intolerance can usually eat yogurt because the bacteria that turn milk into yogurt gobble up a lot of the lactose in the process. Kefir has similar properties.

Which Yogurt?

All yogurts were not created equal, so buy a yogurt in which the only ingredients are milk and acidophilus and other live cultures. Natural yogurts with live cultures will cost more than the common supermarket brands, but if you consider yogurt a nutritional supplement, which it is, it's worth buying the best. My favorite is *Nancy's*, made in Springfield, Oregon.

- *Avoid* mass-market brands. Most include ingredients like gelatin and cornstarch, which keep yogurt from naturally separating and create a smooth texture.
- *Avoid* pre-sweetened and fruited yogurt. The sugar appears to reduce the live cultures over time. As for frozen yogurt, it is both junk food *and* fake food.

How Fat?

Yogurt made with whole milk has richer flavor, better texture, and is less tart—advantages to consider if introducing someone to yogurt for the first time. You may even find unhomogenized whole milk yogurt with a layer of cream on top. Low fat yogurt is sold everywhere, though, and is a better choice than non-fat.

Draining Yogurt

Draining the whey from the yogurt gives it a thick, smooth texture that makes it much more versatile. You can use it as a substitute for sour cream, or even cream cheese, if you leave it long enough. (It is sometimes called "yogurt cheese".) If you sweeten the thick, drained yogurt with honey and soften it with a small bit of thick cream, it is spectacular with fresh fruit or fruit desserts.

Some folks use drained yogurt as a replacement for mayonnaise, spreading it on bread and adding it to tuna salad. I usually blend the yogurt with small amounts of mayonnaise for dips and sauces.

To Drain Yogurt

(For more detail see recipes on page 57-58.)

Drain yogurt in a 2 – 3-cup strainer lined with a disposable basket-style coffee filter. (A paper towel or piece of linen tea towel or some layers of cheesecloth also work perfectly well.) Aim to drain the yogurt for *at least* 1½ hours, but for the ideal thick and creamy texture drain the yogurt in the refrigerator overnight.

If you start with 2 cups of undrained yogurt, you will end up with a scant cup of yogurt cheese in 12 hours. Remember that additives like gelatin and cornstarch will inhibit draining. Read ingredient labels.

I never "discard liquid", as most recipes direct. If it's good enough to eat when it's an integral part of the yogurt, it's good enough to drink after it is extracted. It's cold and refreshing. If you don't want to drink it, add it to soup or a smoothie.

Rich Yogurt *Aioli* (Goop)

This has always been known as *Goop* among family and friends. The name has neither dignity nor appetizing connotations, but it is what has become my culinary signature. Goop is a cousin to *aioli*, (*eye-OH-lee*) the garlic-infused mayonnaise of Provence. The French would be appalled by the presumption, but in any case it is used as an *aioli* substitute in our house.

It is thick and creamy, and usually tongue-biting if I can lay my hands on enough good, fresh garlic. Good garlic is the key to good goop. I generally use more than my recipe calls for because I like to err on the side of *yowza!* Furthermore, you just never know who might need to have their sagging immune system boosted.

It should be added that there is nothing wrong with classic all-mayonnaise *aioli*. Mayonnaise made with good oil is good food. (See recipe on page 56.) We much prefer the taste of the yogurt version, however, and we consider yogurt an important food in its own right. (See *Yogurt* on preceding page.) Even though I call for 2½ cups of yogurt, the final volume is closer to 1 cup after it is drained overnight. Some folks (including me) enjoy goop made from yogurt that has only drained for a few hours; it is more refreshingly potent when its texture is not too thick.

Goop is especially good with roasted vegetables, steamed vegetables, raw vegetables, and salad vegetables — and goop can single-handedly justify the existence of the baked potato. We also serve it as a sauce for fish (or any seafood, for that matter) as well as meat loaf or roast beef or chicken, or any rich meat dishes.

Goop Recipe

(Makes about 2 cups)

> 2½ cups *Nancy's* low fat yogurt
> ½ cup mayonnaise
> 1 tablespoon freshly crushed garlic
> ½ teaspoon of salt
> ½ teaspoon freshly ground pepper

- Drain yogurt for at least 3 hours in a strainer lined with a basket-style coffee filter. (See *Draining Yogurt* page 57.) You will probably end up with a bit more than 1 cup of drained yogurt.

- Stir remaining ingredients into drained yogurt and mix well. Store in the refrigerator. It keeps well for over a week but the garlic loses some intensity. It's best when eaten within a few days.

Note:

➤ The proportion of yogurt to mayonnaise may vary in either direction but there must be enough garlic to raise eyebrows, and enough salt and pepper to round out the flavor. *The freshly ground pepper is critical*; about 30 grinds should give you close enough to a half-teaspoon.

➤ The longer you have allowed the yogurt to drain the thicker the goop. If you want the texture of thick ranch dressing, allow yogurt to drain just a couple of hours. For a very sturdy goop you will need to drain the yogurt about 12 hours.

Faux Ranch Dressing
With Yogurt and Garlic

This mixture serves two purposes for me: it makes food taste better and it gets more yogurt into the diet. Variations of this sauce can be used as dressing for salads or a sauce for any cooked vegetables, especially baked potatoes. This is very basic, which suits me, but it takes well to variations. However, don't be stingy with the garlic, salt, and pepper. If it isn't punchy, it just won't work.

(Makes about 2½ cups)

> 2 cups of plain yogurt
> ¼ - ½ cup mayonnaise
> 2–3 teaspoons freshly crushed garlic
> ½ teaspoon of salt, or to taste
> ½ teaspoon freshly ground pepper

- Stir all ingredients together. *(Don't use the blender or food processor — they break down the yogurt and make it watery.)*

Note:
➤ Use the larger quantity of mayonnaise (homemade or equal quality) if the sauce tastes too stringent to you. A little richness helps balance the garlic, as well.

➤ You can also adjust this dressing with additions like a tablespoon or so of vinegar, finely minced green onion, a half-teaspoon of something like celery seeds, and so forth. You might even find that a teaspoon of honey or sugar rounds out the flavor in a way that makes this a more useful dressing. (Honey is better but it isn't easy to stir in.)

Tzatziki (tzort of)
Yogurt Sauce with Cucumber and Garlic

I like this best served with fresh or grilled pita bread and the hummus (on page 62). You can also use it as a refreshing sauce or salad with rich meat dishes (see note about *raita* below). As a dip it should have a noticeable garlic presence. I suggest draining both yogurt and cucumber for the best results, but it's certainly optional or adjustable, depending on schedule or taste.

(Makes about 2½ cups)

> 2 cups plain yogurt (full fat or 2%)
> 1 medium to large cucumber
> 1 teaspoon salt
> (¼ teaspoon for salting cucumber)
> 1 tablespoon extra virgin olive oil
> 1–2 teaspoons freshly crushed garlic

- Drain the yogurt for an hour in a strainer lined with a basket-style coffee filter. You will probably end up with about 1½ cups yogurt and almost ½ cup of liquid. *(If you would like a thicker consistency, drain yogurt overnight.)*

- Peel, seed and grate cucumber. Place in a colander and sprinkle with ¼ teaspoon salt. Set aside for about 30 minutes and then press out excess liquid.

- Mix together olive oil, garlic, salt, and yogurt, and blend with cucumber.

Note:
➤ If you would like a sort of *raita*, the Indian salad, add ¼ teaspoon ground cumin to the olive oil mixture, and about 1 cup fresh diced tomatoes and ½ cup diced mild onion or green onions.

The Definitive Dip

This is a sprightly but rich-tasting dip with the freshness of parsley, the punch of garlic, and the satisfying note of cheddar. It is remarkable how many garlic-wary people have enjoyed this dip without commenting on the garlic. The reason may be that there are so many flavors jostling for attention that the garlic just falls back into the crowd. Or maybe it is countered by the intense parsley presence. Whatever the reason, it seems to work.

(Makes about 2½ cups)

> 1 bunch minced fresh parsley
> 2 cups plain yogurt, drained
> ½ cup mayonnaise
> 2 cups grated extra-*sharp* cheddar
> 1 tablespoon freshly crushed garlic
> 1 tablespoon lemon juice
> 1 teaspoon salt
> ½ teaspoon Tabasco sauce
> ¼ teaspoon curry powder

- Drain yogurt overnight, if possible. *(See page 57 for more detail.)*

- Wash parsley well, spin or blot dry, and discard stems. Process in food processor for about 15 seconds or until finely minced. (Leave parsley in processor. You should have at least 1 cup.)

- Add drained yogurt and the remaining ingredients to the minced parsley and process until smooth. *If you mix this dip by hand, make sure the cheese is grated finely enough to blend in smoothly.* This dip is best eaten the same day, before it is chilled. (It will thicken when chilled.)

Guacamole

We probably can't do much to reduce America's consumption of tortilla chips, but a good guacamole can help offset the damage, while still tasting decadent enough to fool the consumer. What actually constitutes a good guacamole is a matter of opinion, and *this* opinion favors a simple combination of ingredients with strong notes of lime juice and garlic.

(Makes about 2 – 3 cups)

> 2 – 3 ripe avocados
> 2 – 3 tablespoons lime/lemon juice
> 1 teaspoon Tabasco sauce, or to taste
> ½ – 1 teaspoon freshly crushed garlic
> ½ teaspoon salt

Optional:
> ¼ cup minced mild onion
> ¼ cup chopped fresh cilantro

- Slice avocados in half lengthwise. Remove peel and seed. Dice and then mash roughly in a bowl. *(Try to avoid baby food consistency. Some texture in the finished dip is nice, so I start by dicing the avocado first: by the time the other ingredients have been mixed in, the guacamole is pretty smooth, yet with some recognizable bits of avocado.)*

- Make a separate mixture of lime or lemon juice, Tabasco sauce, garlic, and salt. Blend gently but thoroughly with avocado. Set on table with very good tortilla or pita chips and stand back.

Note: An alternative to guacamole, just as tasty but more versatile, is the *Avocado Salsa* on page 90.

Tofu Paté
(or Faux Egg Salad)

For this recipe use extra firm tofu, which can be found in 5- and 10-ounce packets. Prepared this way, tofu paté makes a convincing stand-in for egg salad. You could also use extra firm tofu to extend egg salad if you don't have enough eggs.
(Tofu is soy bean curd: for more about soy beans and tofu see pages 112 – 114.)

(Makes about 1½ cups)

> 5 ounces extra firm tofu
> ⅓ cup mayonnaise
> ½ cup finely minced celery
> ¼ cup finely minced onion
> ½ teaspoon salt
> ½ teaspoon prepared mustard
> ¼ teaspoon freshly ground pepper
> ⅛ teaspoon curry powder

- Pat tofu dry with a paper towel. Mince tofu finely; or grate on the medium holes of a box grater; or dice and pulse in food processor until it looks finely minced.

- Mix with mayonnaise, celery, onion, and seasoning, and mash together thoroughly. Serve as a dip for crackers or pita crisps, or as a filling for pita bread, or as a sandwich spread.

Note:
➢ It is shocking but true that vacuum-packed extra firm tofu can be perfectly fine after several months in your refrigerator, unopened. I have found tofu to still smell and taste fresh even after 10 months beyond use-by date, so test before you toss.

A Brisk Black Bean Thing

Whether you mash the beans or leave them whole, this is a great little side dish to serve when you find yourself with a ragged smorgasbord of leftovers, even if you don't have fresh cilantro. A good companion for guacamole and salsa, whether you serve it in the form of a dip or as a simple little bean relish to eat with a fork.

(Makes about 2 cups)

> 1 can (15 ounce) black beans
> ¼ - ½ cup finely minced mild onion
> 2 tablespoons lemon or lime juice
> 2 – 3 tablespoons olive oil
> ½ teaspoon freshly crushed garlic
> ½ teaspoon chili powder
> ½ teaspoon ground cumin
> ½ teaspoon salt
> ¼ - ½ teaspoon Tabasco sauce
> ¼ cup chopped fresh cilantro

- Drain and rinse beans and set aside. Mince onion (use smaller amount if onion is not mild) and place in a mixing bowl, and add lemon or lime juice, oil, garlic, and seasonings. Add beans and cilantro (if you have it) and toss thoroughly.

Note:
➢ For a dip-able or spreadable texture, mash the beans or the whole mixture with a fork until you're happy with it. I like to mash roughly enough so that the beans are still recognizable and the onions are still crunchy.

➢ If you want something more salad-y, add finely diced celery and red or green bell peppers.

Hasty, Tasty Hummus
(Chickpea Dip)

Don't say you dislike hummus until you've tried this recipe. It is best eaten right after it's made — creamy, rich, and almost warm. Hummus is delicious as a dip for raw vegetables like carrot and celery, or pita bread, or as a spread in a vegetarian sandwich.

There are countless ways to make hummus and perhaps as many ways to spell it. You can even buy powdered hummus but I've never wanted to get close enough to read the actual ingredients or instructions. Few recipes call for a respectable amount of garlic, but *this one does!*

(Makes about 2½ cups)

> 1 can (15 ounces) chickpeas
> ¼ cup lemon juice
> ¼ cup tahini (raw or roasted)
> ¼ cup extra virgin olive oil
> 1 tablespoon freshly crushed garlic
> ½ teaspoon salt
> ⅛ teaspoon ground cumin
> ¼ cup boiling water

- Drain chickpeas thoroughly. (No need to rinse.) Combine drained chickpeas and all the ingredients except the water in a food processor and blend until smooth.

- With the processor running, pour in the boiling water. The texture should be thick but creamy and pourable. (It will thicken more in the refrigerator.) Taste and adjust the flavor to suit yourself . . . but make sure it's *spunky*. If it's too beany it's boring. Hummus keeps well for at least a week.

Note:
➢ Tahini is sesame seed paste, and you can usually find it in supermarkets as well as natural food stores. I try to find a jar with the thinnest layer of oil on top. (The longer the tahini has been sitting, the more oil will rise to the surface, and the harder the paste will be.) Store in the refrigerator.

Roasted Chickpeas

For another tasty treatment of chickpeas — with *no garlic* — try this simple idea. Nice appetizer to serve with olives. This is a small recipe – I would double it.

(Makes about 1¼ cups)

1 can (15 ounces) chickpeas
1 tablespoon extra virgin olive oil
¼ teaspoon ground cumin or curry powder
¼ teaspoon freshly ground pepper
¼ teaspoon salt

- ***Preheat oven to 450 degrees***. Rinse and thoroughly drain chickpeas.

- In a small mixing bowl, combine olive oil with cumin or curry powder, freshly ground pepper, and salt. Add chickpeas and toss.

- Spread in a single layer in a shallow foil-lined baking pan and roast for about 20 – 30 minutes or until toasty. Shake pan now and them.

Note:
➢ If your oven isn't available, sauté chickpeas in one layer in a sturdy skillet over medium-high heat. Cook until chickpeas begin to brown, shaking pan now and then; about 20 – 30 minutes.

Pita Crisps

Pita crisps stand in nicely for commercially made chips and crisps and are certainly worth the ridiculously small effort they demand. You can make a more exotic version with herbs or spices or sprinkles of Parmesan and so forth, but I rarely do. This recipe is simple and has few ingredients because I'm usually making them when I'm too busy to feel ambitious.

Sometime it's hard to find whole-wheat pita pockets, but even if you use pitas made with white flour it will *still* be a better snack than most commercial crackers.

(Makes about 80 crisps)

>   1 package whole wheat pita bread
>   (about 5 pitas – see *Note*)
>   ½ cup olive oil
>   salt
>   freshly ground pepper
>
>   (*Optional*: ¼ teaspoon dried thyme)

Preheat oven to 300 degrees. Lay out baking sheet.

- Split each pita into 2 disks and lay them out, insides facing up. (*See first note.*)

- Brush each round lightly with oil, and sprinkle with salt and a swift swish of freshly ground pepper over each one. *(Whatever you decide to spread or sprinkle on the crisps, don't forget how thin they are. A little flavor goes a long way. And be sparing with the fat or you'll find the baking sheet awash with it. You can brush more olive oil on the thicker rounds.)*

- *(… and if you decide to use dried thyme, start with about ¼ teaspoon of thyme in your palm, grind it between thumb and forefinger, and then take pinches of the thyme and sprinkle sparingly over the pitas.)*

- Slice each pita round into 8 wedges and place on *ungreased* baking sheets. (You'll probably need two.)

- Bake in the middle of the 300-degree oven for about 20- 30 minutes, or until the wedges turn golden brown.

- Serve pita crisps as you would potato crisps, as an appetizer or accompaniment to dips. They will keep beautifully for at least a week, stored in a cool spot (but not in the refrigerator) in a plastic bag or covered container.

Note:

➢ This is an inspired use for commercial pita bread. Look for a brand that is whole-wheat, and thinner rather than thicker. **If you can't find thin pita pockets, I wouldn't try this recipe –** thicker pita can be hard on the teeth when toasted like this. *(I generally never use homemade pita pockets for this purpose because they always get gobbled up when they're fresh.)*

➢ Some brands of pita pockets have a thin top and thicker bottom, in which case I separate them and cook them on two different baking sheets. The thinner disks turn brown sooner.

Tuna Salad
(As a sandwich filling or pita bread stuffing or salad topping)

*(See **Canned Tuna** on page 142.)*

We make this tuna salad most Saturdays for lunch. It is crunchy and exuberantly flavored, and very different from the traditional version. Because of the deliberate emphasis on crunch this mixture is not cohesive enough to behave properly in a sandwich. We serve it with a fork on the side, or stuffed in pita pockets.

Often those who think they don't like tuna salad find that they like this one. Please don't cut back on the seasoning when you try this recipe for the first time. You can halve this recipe easily but keep in mind that 2½ nephews can easily eat it all in one sitting.

(Makes about 4 – 5 cups)

12 ounces solid white tuna in water
1½ cups finely diced sweet onion
1½ cups finely diced celery
½ cup mayonnaise
1 tablespoon whole grain mustard
¾ teaspoon Tabasco sauce
½ teaspoon salt
¼ teaspoon fresh ground pepper

- Open tuna can and drain tun thoroughly. ***On draining tuna:** This is an important step in the construction of a reputable tuna salad, especially if you expect to have leftovers. The simplest method is to wring out as much of the liquid as you can by pressing the lid firmly down against the tuna and holding the can upside down. Solid tuna is easier to drain than chunk, which tends to squeeze out from under the lid. However, even solid tuna has a proportion of mushy bits as well. For best results squeeze the liquid from the tuna literally by hand or in a small sieve.*

- You will have a scant 2 cups of drained tuna. Scrape into mixing bowl and break up clumps with a fork.

- Add onion and celery, mayonnaise (see page 56), mustard, Tabasco, salt, and pepper. Mix thoroughly.

Notes:

➤ For tuna salad some prefer the solid white tuna for its mild flavor and distinct texture, but chunk light tuna is possibly higher in omega-3 fatty acids, potentially lower in mercury content, and cheaper. The water-packed is best in recipes using drained tuna because with oil-packed tuna the good omega-3 fatty acids are leached out of the tuna and into the oil.

➤ As with any other recipes calling for raw onion, I use the sweet variety (Walla Walla, Mayan, Vidalia, etc.). If you only have regular yellow onions on hand, use less. (How much less depends on who is eating it.)

➤ For a more cohesive and sandwich-friendly mixture, reduce the onion and celery to about 1 cup each.

➤ Tuna salad is best eaten on the same day it's made, but it can be stored in the refrigerator for several days; just mix before using to recombine liquid that will collect, or drain off the liquid, if you prefer. Less liquid will collect if you squeeze it out thoroughly to begin with.

Sardine Paté

Now, I generally like sardines but I much prefer the dainty ones — the smoky, rich, extra-small brisling sardines. However, there are many kinds of sardine lovers out there, which probably accounts for the fact that lots of sardines are not dainty. Some are the sardine version of linebackers. If you happen to peel back the lid of a sardine tin and find yourself looking down at a row of oversized sardine torsos instead of the more delicate fish, it may be a good time to try this little recipe for sardine paté.

I believe this stuff is delicious — assuming you don't have an anti-sardine bias — and I would not hesitate to serve it to a visiting head of state, preferably a state that maintains friendly relations with sardines, like Spain or Greece. I would serve it in teaspoon-sized scoops on crispy, thin little squares of buttered whole-wheat toast.

> 1 tablespoon extra virgin olive oil
> 1 tablespoon lemon juice
> 1 teaspoon lemon zest
> 1 tablespoon whole grain mustard
> ¼ cup minced onion
> ¼ teaspoon salt
> ¼ teaspoon freshly ground pepper

- Combine oil, lemon, mustard, onion, salt, and pepper in a small mixing bowl.

- Drain a tin of sardines (3½ - 4 ounces) packed in water. Chop roughly or mash, depending on your taste. Add to onion mixture and blend thoroughly.

Chicken or Egg Salad

Here are general directions for chicken or egg salad that can be eaten alone with perhaps a stalk of celery as a spoon, or used as a sandwich filling or in pita pockets. If you use pita pockets you can get away with a crunchier version.

> ½ cup finely diced celery
> ½ cup finely diced onion
> ¼ cup mayonnaise
> 1 – 2 teaspoons grainy mustard
> ¼ teaspoon salt
> ¼ teaspoon curry powder
> ¼ teaspoon freshly ground pepper
> (¼ teaspoon Tabasco sauce)
>
> 1 cup chopped cooked chicken
> *or* 4 peeled chopped boiled eggs

- Dice celery and onion and combine in small mixing bowl with mayonnaise, mustard, salt, and pepper.

- Add chopped chicken or eggs and blend thoroughly.

- Stuff these mixtures into pita bread pockets, or make into sandwiches, or combine with salads.

Note:
➢ A 6-ounce can of solid white tuna packed in water, drained and flaked, is an alternative to the chicken and boiled eggs. See *Tuna Salad* recipe for details.

➢ See more on hard-boiled eggs on the following page.

Hard-boiled Eggs

Hard-boiled eggs are efficient, clean, and no-nonsense. You can boil a bunch at once and eat them all week. A hard-boiled egg cut in half and salted and peppered can be eaten on your way through the kitchen or even on your way to your car. Or it can be packed intact and peeled as needed.

There is a lot written about the best ways to boil eggs. There at least is agreement on the importance of keeping the water at no more than a simmer while the eggs are cooking. For those of us easily distracted cooks I would recommend the following method for hard-boiling eggs.

- Put the eggs from the fridge into a small saucepan. (The size of the pan would depend on the number of eggs: 6 eggs fit nicely in a 1-quart saucepan.) Cover with a couple of inches of cold water.

- Bring the water to a brisk, rolling boil, then **immediately remove the pan from the heat,** cover, and set aside for 10 minutes. (See note below.)

- Pour off the hot water and submerge the eggs in ice water for 10 minutes. *(This is supposed to shock the eggs into contracting slightly, which should make them easier to peel. HAH!)*

Note:
➢ If you want soft boiled eggs, check one after about 5 – 7 minutes, depending on how soft you want them to be.

Deviled Eggs

These are remarkably popular. They are a handy item for a hot night if you have some hard-boiled eggs waiting in your refrigerator. These directions call for 3 boiled eggs but I would usually make double this amount. I estimate about 1 teaspoon of mayonnaise per yolk but some prefer more.

> 4 boiled eggs, halved lengthwise
> 1 tablespoon mayonnaise
> 1 teaspoon prepared mustard
> ⅛ teaspoon curry powder
> ¼ teaspoon salt
> ¼ teaspoon freshly ground pepper
> (2 teaspoons sweet pickle relish)

- Carefully peel and rinse eggs. Crunchy bits of shell can ruin a good deviled egg. *(If your eggs emerge as misshapen little lumps with only about half the egg whites still desperately clinging to their yolks, consider a nice egg salad. See previous page.)*

- Cut hard-boiled eggs in half and carefully extract the yolks. Mash the yolks with the mayonnaise, mustard, curry, salt and pepper. Fill each egg white. *(Some people love a bit of sweet pickle relish.)*

Note:
➢ For a packed lunch stick the egg halves back together and wrap in a bit of plastic wrap, gathering the plastic at one end of the egg and twisting snugly, like you were wrapping a rum truffle. Yum.

Hot Stuff

This is hot. It has to be hot. If it isn't hot enough to make you exclaim when you taste it, hot it up some more. Horseradish is a noble decongestant, as is mustard, and a sensible diet supplement for anyone with chronic congestion and a handy box of Kleenex. Try this sauce with meat loaf (page 156) or aggressive vegetables like Brussels sprouts. (You may even forget you never liked Brussels sprouts.)

(Makes about 1½ cups)

>   2 tablespoons Coleman's dry
>   mustard
>   2 tablespoons apple cider vinegar
>   2 tablespoons extra-hot horseradish
>   ½ cup mayonnaise (see page 56)
>   ½ cup sour cream *(see note)*
>   1 teaspoon salt
>   1 teaspoon sugar

- Mix together the mustard and vinegar, then blend with the remaining ingredients until smooth. This will hold nicely in the refrigerator for weeks.

Note:

➤ Instead of sour cream, which I generally never have in the refrigerator, I prefer whole milk yogurt that has been drained at least overnight.

➤ It is worth going to some trouble to track down an honest, vicious horseradish with fumes that make your eyes water when you take off the lid. I've found that the product called creamed horseradish can be hotter than the pure grated stuff, although I don't know why.

Whole-wheat Scones
(Biscuits)

I use this recipe for scones or shortcake (with an extra tablespoon of sugar added) or as the top crust for chicken potpie *(see page 69)*. If you don't keep a back-up supply of butter in the freezer, I suggest you put a stick of butter into the freezer when you plan to make this recipe. It is easier to grate butter if it is at least half-frozen.

(For about 12 scones)

>   2 cups whole-wheat pastry flour
>   2 teaspoons baking powder
>   ½ teaspoon baking soda
>   ½ teaspoon salt
>   2 tablespoons white sugar
>   1 stick (¼-lb or 8 tablespoons) butter
>   ¾ – 1 cup full fat milk or buttermilk

Preheat oven to 425 degrees.
- Combine flour, salt, baking powder, and sugar, and blend thoroughly. (I use a wire whisk.) Grate stick of butter into flour mixture and toss together until well mixed.

- Pour ¾-cup milk over the flour mixture and blend briskly with a fork. Add only as much of the remaining milk as you need to incorporate any floury residue, and knead briefly in bowl to blend in the dry bits. Try not to handle dough any more than necessary.

- On a floured countertop, roll out dough to about ½-inch thick. Using a biscuit cutter or a knife, cut into circles or wedges and arrange on an ungreased baking sheet. Bake for 15 – 20 minutes or until golden brown and puffy.

Mirepoix
(Sautéed Vegetable Base)

Mirepoix (pronounced *meer-PWAH*) is a simple sauté of diced vegetables and aromatics, but is one of the most useful cooking basics you can know. The classic French version is about two parts onion to one part each celery and carrot, and can provide the critical underpinning for soups (like the *minestrone* on this page), chowders (see page 148), pot pies (see next page), stews, and sauces. In Italy it is called *soffrito,* a more fitting name for my olive oil version, anyway. Whatever the name, it can be adjusted to suit your purpose or supplies. Mine sometimes has bell pepper instead of carrots and/or celery (see *Chili* on page 122 or *Tuna Tetrazzini* on page 145), but it is usually the one below.

(Makes about 2½ cups)

> ¼ cup olive oil
> 3 cups diced onion
> 1½ cups diced carrot
> 1½ cups diced celery
> 1 tablespoon freshly crushed garlic
> (¼ cup of minced fresh parsley)

- Heat oil in a heavy wide-bottomed pot or large skillet over medium-high heat. When oil is hot, add vegetables (they should sizzle when they hit the oil) and sauté for about 12 minutes or until vegetables are barely tender. *(After about 10 minutes begin to stir vegetables more diligently. They brown quickly once they have begun to soften.)*

- Add garlic (and parsley, if you have it) and sauté for another minute, stirring constantly. Remove from heat.

Basic Chicken Soup

(Serves 4 – 6)

Mirepoix (this page)
6 cups chicken stock
1½ teaspoons salt
1 teaspoon freshly ground pepper
4 cups shredded cooked chicken

- Combine mirepoix, broth, salt, and pepper in a 5-quart pot and bring to a simmer.

- Add cooked chicken pieces and bring back to a simmer. The soup is ready when you are. Mmmm.

A Minestrone

(Serves 4 – 6)

Mirepoix (this page*)*
6 cups of chicken broth or water
4 cups of bite sized cauliflower florets
3 cups diced zucchini
1 can (28 ounces) diced tomatoes
1 can (15 ounces) chickpeas
1 teaspoon of salt
1 teaspoon of freshly ground pepper

- Combine mirepoix and broth in a 5-quart pot and bring to a simmer.

- Add cauliflower and simmer for 10 minutes before adding zucchini, tomatoes with their juice, chickpeas, salt, and pepper. The minestrone is ready when the vegetables are tender.

Béchamel Sauce
With Parmesan and Lemon

Béchamel (*bay-sha-MEL),* also called white sauce, is a useful recipe that serves as a basis for dishes like pot pies, soufflés, lasagna, macaroni-and-cheese, casseroles, and simple creamed vegetables like onion or spinach. It can take on all kinds of accents just with additions like herbs, cheese, and spices (or lemon and Parmesan, as in this variation). It is based on a *roux* (pronounced as in *kangaroux*), a mixture of butter and flour which is also useful for enriching and thickening soups. Roux smells delicious, too — like shortbread cookies baking. (If you replace the milk in this recipe with meat stock, you have – *voila!* – *veloute* sauce.)

(Makes about 2½ cups)

> ½ stick butter (4 tablespoons)
> ⅓ cup white flour (5 tablespoons)
> 2 cups whole milk
> ½ teaspoon salt
> ½ teaspoon freshly ground pepper
> ½ cup freshly grated Parmesan
> 2 tablespoons fresh lemon juice
> (zest from 1 lemon)

- **The roux:** Heat butter over medium low heat, preferably in a sturdy 1½-quart pot. When butter is melted sprinkle the flour over the butter and blend thoroughly. Stir over a medium-low heat until the mixture bubbles. Cook for another 2 minutes, stirring. Don't let it brown — it will gain flavor but lose thickening power.

- **The sauce:** Slide pot off heat and whisk ½ cup milk into the roux. When mixture is smooth add another ½ cup and whisk vigorously until smooth before blending in the remaining milk. Return to the heat, whisk in the seasoning, and bring sauce to a simmer. Simmer gently about 15 minutes, whisking often. It should be nicely thick. Stir in Parmesan and lemon juice (and zest, if the lemon has it to spare).

Chicken Pot Pie

(Serves about 4)

Béchamel Sauce (this page)
Mirepoix (page 68)
4 cups cooked chicken in bite-sized pieces
½ teaspoon dried thyme
½ teaspoon salt
½ teaspoon freshly ground pepper.

Whole-wheat biscuit topping (page 67)

Preheat oven to 400 degrees.
- Combine béchamel with mirepoix and cooked chicken. Scrape into 8 x 8-inch baking dish and top with squares of biscuit dough rolled out to ¼ - ½ inch. *(You won't need the whole recipe. Too much biscuit topping overwhelms the filling.)* Bake in a 400-degree oven for 30 minutes, or until crust is golden.

Note:
➢ If you are starting with raw chicken, I suggest poaching about 2 lbs chicken according to the recipe on page 153. I prefer shredding into delicate pieces rather than chopping.

➢ A cup of frozen peas can be stirred directly into the mixture, and you can substitute 2 – 3 cups of any cooked chopped vegetables for the mirepoix.

Tomato Sauce

This recipe is simple – pay no attention to the number of ingredients. It is also quick – I only simmer it for 20 minutes or so. Nobody needs to be told the many uses for tomato sauce: you can serve it over pasta, polenta, crepes, fish, pizza, meatloaf, and so forth. However, if you decide to make this and actually *can't* think of a use for it, you can always turn it into cream of tomato soup (see note following), or add it to a pot of chili or minestrone.

(Makes about 4 cups)

> ¼ cup olive oil
> 2 – 3 cups finely diced onion
> 1 tablespoon freshly crushed garlic
> 1 can (28 ounces) crushed tomatoes
> 1 tablespoon honey
> 1 teaspoon salt, or to taste
> 1 teaspoon freshly ground pepper
> 1 teaspoon dried oregano
> ½ teaspoon dried thyme

- Heat oil in 2½-quart saucepan over medium heat. Add onions and sauté until very soft, about 10 – 15 minutes.

- Add garlic and cook for another 2 minutes. Stir in remaining ingredients, bring to a simmer, and simmer gently for about 20 minutes, uncovered. If making in advance, cool thoroughly before covering and refrigerating.

(If you use regular diced tomatoes, purée slightly cooled sauce in a food processor. You can use the pulse button to retain texture rather than purée the sauce to smithereens.)

Note:

➤ For more texture, I like to use S&W "petite-cut" diced tomatoes instead of crushed.

➤ For a Bolognese-style sauce, just add a pound of ground meat after you add the garlic, and sauté until the meat is mostly brown before adding the tomatoes.

➤ For a Puttanesca-type sauce, add a half-cup of pitted and chopped olives (your choice), a few minced anchovies, and a couple of tablespoons of capers.

➤ Leftover tomato sauce is a beautiful thing. Use it to top a meatloaf (page 156) or crepes (page 158), or add to chili (page 121-122), or add it to the *Smoooth Butternut Bisque* (page 98) before you puree it. For that matter, make yourself a little batch of cream of tomato soup. For example, to about 2 cups of tomato sauce you can add a cup of chicken stock or water, and a cup of half-and-half or evaporated whole milk. (A 5-ounce can of evaporated milk is ¾ cup; just add milk to make a cup.) *(See page 97 for a recipe for a Thai style cream of tomato soup.)*

Cooking tomatoes with olive oil improves the availability of the lycopene contained in the tomatoes. Lycopene and similar nutrients are strongly associated with reduced age-related eye diseases, cancers, and heart disease. The addition of the onions and herbs strengthens the nutritional punch with lots of micronutrients that are anti-inflammatory and reduce cancer and heart disease risk.

4   Vegetables

Fresh Vegetables
Frozen Vegetables
Vegetables to Keep Handy
Roasted Vegetables
Simple Salads
Vegetable Soups and Sides

Fresh Vegetables

Vegetables are protective against just about everything you want to be protected from, so it makes sense to take care of them. Don't buy vegetables that you won't realistically use before their prime passes. Freckled cauliflower, limp broccoli, shriveled bell peppers, blotchy zucchini, spinach beginning to dissolve around the edges — it would certainly discourage anyone trying to learn to love vegetables. How popular would bread be if it were served stale half the time?

Clean and Trim Them Early

Wash vegetables like celery and greens as soon after you buy them as possible so they will be available for instant use. A salad spinner (the Zyliss brand is my favorite) is a good investment: it's important to spin greens almost dry before storing or dressing them. Seal them in clean plastic bags lined with paper towel to help absorb excess water to keep them crisp.

Keep the more perishable vegetables like bell peppers and cucumbers toward the front of your refrigerator so they won't sneak off behind the leftovers and emerge a week later looking wrinkled and dissolute. Try to use them while they are at their best, even if you just slice them up and serve them as finger salad.

Take a few minutes to slice broccoli florets from their stems: it's easy and relatively quick to do, and you'll be so glad when you suddenly need a vegetable to serve. Store the broccoli stalks separately, ready to use for salad or soup. The stalks will keep better if you peel them the same day you use them.

Keep It Simple

For a busy cook it makes sense to lean heavily on vegetables that are always available, and that wait patiently until you need them. It helps if they are versatile enough to be useful raw *or* cooked, and if they are equally comfortable playing a leading or supporting role.

Some vegetables that fulfill all four qualifications are onions, celery, carrot, and napa cabbage, and potatoes. (It's true that potatoes are hardly useful raw — although you should try a slice of raw salted potato, if you haven't already.) For more on these, see *Vegetables to Keep Handy* on page 77.

Butternut squash and sweet potatoes deserve at least honorable mention. Both keep well in a cool, dry, place, are easy to peel, and have bright orange and creamy-textured flesh. Both work well as solo vegetables, whether baked, puréed, or roasted. (Sweet potatoes are not related to potatoes or yams, by the way.) Both are especially rich in carotenoids (like beta-carotene).

The Salad Vegetables

Then there are the salad vegetables, like cucumber, bell peppers, and tomatoes. Simple sliced cucumbers and peppers make instant salads, if you slice them and serve them crispy and cold with a side of dip, like *Hasty Tasty Hummus* or *Rich Yogurt Aioli*. It's a nice change from chopped or tossed salads and so much less work for the cook.

English (hothouse) cucumbers are seedless, thin-skinned, and ready-wrapped: a wonderfully convenient alternative when regular cucumbers are not exciting. They are generally more expensive and usually worth it, but examine them very carefully for soft spots or tips. Tomatoes sliced into wedges and sprinkled with salt and freshly ground pepper make a delicious salad.

... and Greens

Romaine lettuce, as long as it's fat and fresh, is my choice of the lettuces. It has a crunchy stem and substantial leaf and is the easiest of the greens to clean.

However, if you want something as easy to use as iceberg lettuce, try napa cabbage. (See page 81 for more about this wonderful vegetable.) Iceberg lettuce does not count as a serving of vegetables, by the way; in the world of lettuce, the deeper green, the better.

For tight schedules, it's hard to beat a bag of ready-to-use mixed greens, those colorful mixtures of lettuces, bitter greens, fresh herbs, and spinach. As for those handy bags of baby spinach, what a boon to the overextended cook! A case can no doubt be made for those fresh-picked muddy little bunches of spinach, but the cleaning and preparation are not acceptable uses of time, in my opinion. When I want fresh spinach for salads I would rather pay for the triple-washed bags of baby spinach available in most supermarkets. (Always triple-check use-by dates, by the way.)

I'm puzzled by people who wouldn't dream of spending extra money on pre-washed greens, yet think nothing of throwing out bags of vegetables that die of exposure and hypothermia before anyone finds time or energy to clean and trim them.

In Season?

Vegetables are at their best in season. In the case of spring vegetables like asparagus and summer vegetables like corn on the cob, I'm perfectly happy to serve them every day while they're locally picked and at their best, and then pretty much ignore them the rest of the year. Cucumbers in season can be sweet and succulent with innocuous seeds, but most of the year they are just — ordinary. Variety is not more important than quality: it makes perfectly good sense to focus on the vegetables or fruit in season.

Certain vegetables like zucchini are not as distinctly seasonal, but in summer you can find skinny little zucchini with tender velvety skin and crisp, creamy flesh; these are delicious sliced raw and served with dip. I wish they were easier to find.

Although acceptable supermarket zucchini are generally available year round, they are *not* on my list of staples for a few reasons. They don't store very well, have a fleeting prime, and threaten to cook down into a translucent mush if you're not careful. But sliced thinly or shredded and then cooked fast and hot in olive oil, garlic, and salt, even so-so zucchini can be memorable. (For more zucchini ideas see about roasting them on page 87 or *Zucchini Frittata* on page 157.)

The Organic Question

The question often comes up concerning whether or not to insist on organically grown vegetables. However, so far there is not enough data to make a strong case for an organic-only position. At this point the evidence for benefit is still lacking despite decades of research, but there is nothing vague about the evidence for eating at least 5 servings of vegetables and fruit each day. Whether or not they are from organically grown produce is secondary.

Unfortunately, we can't always trust the accuracy of the claim or the definition of organic in each case. However, I often find reasons to buy organic produce: for example, when I need green onions and the regular ones are limp and broken, it may be that the organic versions are exuberantly fresh. I'm happy to pay more for a superior product.

Frozen Vegetables

Frozen vegetables are considered to be nutritionally superior to canned, but they are more perishable. It usually doesn't pay to stock up on more than you will use in a month or so. (You don't know how long they have languished in the supermarket freezer, either.) Taste them before you use them.

I use a narrow spectrum of frozen vegetables because the fresh versions taste so much better and are convenient enough, for the most part. (See *Vegetables to Keep Handy* on page 77.) However, I would not like to do without a few frozen vegetables like corn, beans, peas, and chopped spinach. (For frozen baby lima beans and green soybeans (edamame), see the chapter on *Beans* starting on page 107.)

Frozen Corn

This is a convenient vegetable to have available when you need an extra side dish and a good source of cholesterol-lowering insoluble fiber. It doesn't need to be cooked and stands up well to vinaigrette so is adaptable to salads (see *Succotash Salad* and *Black Bean, Corn and Jicama Salad*) as well as hot dishes (see *Scalloped Corn*).

I always buy petite yellow corn. White corn is delicious but it can be disconcertingly sweet. (Good for snacking straight from the freezer, however. I like eating frozen corn a few kernels at a time like candy. Once the kernels thaw, the thrill is gone.)

Draining the corn well before using in salads is critical; one method that works well as a final step is to toss the drained corn in a sieve with a paper towel, replacing the paper towel until it stops getting wet. Sometimes I've shaken it in a hot skillet to cook off any residual water or roasted it briefly in the oven, but it's not necessary.

Emergency Corn Sauté

As a last minute cooked vegetable, frozen corn is almost instant. (For a premeditated frozen corn dish see page 102.)

(Serves 4 – 6)

>   2 tablespoons extra virgin olive oil
>   ⅛ teaspoon red chili flakes
>   1 bag (16 ounces) frozen petite corn
>   ½ teaspoon salt
>   ½ teaspoon freshly ground pepper

- Heat olive oil in a skillet over medium heat and add chili flakes. When oil is hot add frozen corn and sauté until the kernels are hot, about 10 minutes. Add salt and pepper, and your corn is ready to serve.

Note:

➢ If you have the time, sauté 1 cup minced onion and an extra ¼ teaspoon of salt before adding the corn. *(Remember that a cup of diced onion cooks down to only ½ cup: that's none too much onion.)*

➢ If you don't have time but want some interest, add a drained 4-ounce can of diced green chilies with the corn.

➢ The flavor begs to be taken to another level, too. A pinch of dried basil rubbed between the fingers and added at the beginning of the cooking added an unpretentious little flourish. Or for something more outspoken, ⅛ teaspoon each of curry powder and ground cumin added with the chilies.

➢ Leftovers are a great addition to polenta. (See page 138.)

Frozen Green Beans

Frozen baby green beans are convenient when fresh are hard to find. This is actually most of the year, in my experience. The flavor and texture of frozen beans is never as good, though: they can be a bit tough and watery.

A solution is to toss the hot, just-cooked green beans either in vinaigrette (see page 55) or in olive oil with garlic, grated Parmigiano-Reggiano, salt, and pepper. The added flavors will distract nicely from any freezer taste or texture.

There are the skinny little green beans (*haricot verts*) imported from France, petite green beans, or cut green beans. The best choice is whatever sells the fastest, so buy carefully and use quickly.

Frozen Peas

Frozen peas are not as dependable as frozen corn. They tend to shrivel and lose the plump sweetness that makes young, fresh-picked peas so incomparably delicious. As with all frozen vegetables, try not to let them linger long in your freezer.

The simplest way to prepare them as a side dish is to quickly sauté them with olive oil or butter, salt, and pepper. Cook them just before you serve: they cool quickly and overcook just as fast. Sauté only until hot.

Plump green frozen peas need only to be thawed (under hot running water works) to be recipe-ready. If added to something like a stovetop rice pilaf, they only need to be heated through.

Last-Minute Green Beans

16 ounces frozen slim green beans
(1 cup water and 1 teaspoon salt)
3 tablespoons extra virgin olive oil
1 tablespoon apple cider vinegar
½ teaspoon freshly crushed garlic
½ teaspoon salt
¼ teaspoon freshly ground pepper
¼ cup freshly grated Parmesan

- Bring 1 cup water to a boil in 3-quart saucepan, and add 1 teaspoon salt.

- Place frozen beans in saucepan. Cover and boil approximately 6 minutes, or until beans are barely tender but not soft. Drain thoroughly.

- Meanwhile combine olive oil, vinegar, garlic, salt, pepper, and Parmesan (optional) in serving bowl. Add drained hot cooked beans to bowl and toss thoroughly. Serve hot, warm, or room temperature.

Quick Green Pea Soup

3 cups water or stock or both
1 large onion, chopped (3 – 4 cups)
1 small potato, peeled, sliced thinly
1 teaspoon salt
½ teaspoon curry powder
1 bag (16 ounces) frozen petite peas
½ teaspoon freshly ground pepper
5-ounce can evaporated whole milk

- Bring water to a boil in a 3-quart soup pot. Add onion, potato, salt, and curry powder, and simmer 20 minutes or until vegetables are very soft.

- Add peas and pepper and cook gently for another 10 minutes. Turn off heat and allow mixture to cool for half an hour.

- Puree in food processor or blender in one or two batches. Return to pot and bring back to a simmer. Add milk. Taste for flavor. Makes about 6 cups.

Frozen Spinach

I only use frozen spinach as an ingredient, never as a cooked vegetable in its own right — unless you count the following recipe or the occasional speedy spinach soup, which I make just like the preceding *Quick Green Pea Soup.*

I occasionally can find a 16-ounce bag of frozen chopped spinach, but the most commonly available form of frozen spinach is the 10-ounce solid block, which amounts to less than 1 cup of thawed, drained spinach. (If you accidentally buy frozen *UN*-chopped spinach, which in my experience is stringy with spinach stems, you can chop it yourself after it's thawed or cooked.)

Preparing Frozen Spinach

The easiest way to thaw frozen spinach is to leave it in the refrigerator overnight (in a dish to catch the draining liquid).

For stovetop method, place the frozen spinach into a skillet or pot with a lid. Place over a low heat, covered, and cook very gently for about 20 – 30 minutes or until spinach is fully thawed and hot through. Check after 10 minutes and break up icy center if needed. Press out excess liquid in a sieve: you should easily collect ¼ — ½ cup, depending on whether you are working with 10- or 16-ounce packages. (The texture of cooked spinach makes it harder to squeeze out than barely thawed spinach.) The extent to which you drain the spinach depends on the recipe. You don't need to be fussy for the following *Spinach Timbale*.

If you must microwave frozen spinach, place in a Pyrex dish and microwave uncovered for about 6 minutes. ***(Use this method for emergencies only because there may be evidence that microwaving vegetables reduces the antioxidant levels.)***

Spinach Timbale (Custard)

This is a side dish that allows you to serve spinach where no spinach has dared to go before. Even those hostile to the very suggestion of spinach can probably enjoy this timbale (*TIM-bul*). It is simply constructed and seasoned, with nothing to distract from the spinachness, yet with the spinachy edges softened by some creaminess.

(Serves about 4 – 6)

> 10 ounces frozen chopped spinach
> 3 eggs
> 5-ounce can evaporated whole milk
> *or* ¾ cup half-and-half
> ½ - 1 teaspoon salt
> ½ teaspoon freshly ground pepper

Preheat oven to 300 degrees

- Place ¼ cup of water and frozen spinach into a pot with a lid. Bring water to a boil over medium-high heat, then reduce heat to low, cover, and cook for about 15 minutes. Check spinach in 10 minutes and break up icy center if needed. Drain off excess liquid in a sieve; you should be able to easily extract ¼ cup.

- Meanwhile, whisk together eggs, milk, and seasoning. Add spinach and mix well. *(This may be mixed the day before and chilled. Remove from the refrigerator an hour before cooking, and stir again before the next step.)*

- Scrape into a buttered 1½ -quart casserole dish and bake in a 300-degree oven for 45 minutes, or until no longer wet in center.

Vegetables *to* Keep Handy

There are certain vegetables I *always* try to have on hand; these are onions, carrots, celery, potatoes, cabbage, and garlic. (Butternut squash is also on the short list, but is *often* rather than *always* on hand.) They have year-round availability, durability, and versatility.

Last minute or unexpected meals aren't so much of a problem when you know your basic ingredients are waiting for you. It works best to have a core group of recipes that use all these vegetables so you don't need to be inventive unless you feel like it. Depending on the way you cut them, cook them, and combine them, most of these vegetables can be a main feature or just as easily play in a supporting role. (See *Roasted Vegetables* on page 83 and the vegetable recipes in this chapter.)

Onions

As this cook's best friend, the onion ranks right up there with fire and ice. If you can't decide what to fix for dinner, you are never wasting time if you peel an onion. You can serve them roasted, sautéed, pickled, marinated, and raw, alone or otherwise. The hottest onion is mild and almost sweet when cooked. At *least* one onion can disappear into any soup, stew, sauce, sauté, casserole, pilaf, stir-fry, potato dish, and even salad. Onions wait patiently, are modestly priced, and available everywhere all the time.

Choose onions that are hard and fairly smooth-skinned, and store loose in a dark, cool place. Sweet onions like Walla Walla, Vidalia, or Mayans have a shorter shelf life than the regular yellow onions (sometimes called "storage onions"). I store

them like yellow onions but make a point of using them quickly.

A fine strategy is to keep a peeled and ready-to-dice-or-slice sweet onion in the refrigerator — it lasts much longer than an onion in its skin, for some reason, and is so convenient when you just want some for sandwiches or salads.

There are *lots* of onions in my recipes, both because I love them and because the onion is a phenomenally healthy vegetable whether raw or cooked. I buy sweet onions almost exclusively. Their milder flavor allows me to use more of them, especially in recipes where I use them raw. I ignore any recipe's demands for red or white onions or shallots.

The sweet varieties are the nicest to work with but are not always available or affordable out of season — which is most of the year. The imported Mayans are generally available year round and are often competitively priced.

Everyday yellow onions are all-purpose and can be mild, but they are generally aggressive. Sweet onions almost never make me cry when I cut them, but remember that even the hottest onions become mild and almost sweet when cooked.

Using Onions

When chopping vicious onions, one defense is to wear swimming goggles, according to *Cooks Illustrated* magazine. Another technique is to chill the onion before slicing it, which apparently slows the chemical reaction that causes the tears. You can also burn a couple of candles right next to the chopping board; it's a tip that I believe has worked for me, and candlelight is certainly more flattering than goggles.

Recipes that call for only half an onion are generally improved by a whole onion. In my world a medium onion equals about 2 cups diced, and a large onion equals

3 – 4 cups diced. (I don't know much about small onions.) Generally, "diced" means chopped into roughly ¼ inch squares and "minced" means finely diced into pieces smaller than ¼ inch. Cooked diced onions are reduced by about half when cooked.

Sautéed Onions

- For about 2 – 3 cups of diced onions, heat a 10-inch skillet or pot over a medium-hot burner and add 2 – 4 tablespoons extra virgin olive oil.

- When the oil is hot (but not smoking) add diced onion. If the oil is hot enough, the onions should sizzle when they hit the pan. Toss the onions to coat with oil and then sauté until onion is tender, shaking the pan and giving the onions a toss regularly to keep them cooking evenly.

- Depending on the amount of onion, the level of heat, and the surface area of the skillet this can take 10 – 15 minutes. The smaller the amount of onions, the faster they will cook.

Fresh Garlic

Garlic gets plenty of credit for its benefits to the immune system and its role as a natural antibiotic, but it is rare for garlic to be any more than a token presence in actual recipes.

Even in recipes that traditionally headline garlic, like *hummus* and *aioli,* one might see instructions to add *one clove*! In fact, I have found a recipe for hummus in which the chef-author calls for "¼ garlic clove, finely minced". Whether or not my interpretations happen to exceed even the most relaxed cultural limits, it still should be hard to defend the use of only ¼ clove of garlic in *anything*.

I do tend to use garlic in therapeutic quantities. The effect of fresh crushed garlic in certain dishes (the two mentioned above, for example) is critical to their success.

Something as pungent and aggressive as garlic, however, is going to stir up some strong feelings, especially when there are no warning labels. Even so, it is surprising how the most often requested recipes are the ones with the most lethal levels of fresh crushed garlic.

(I do agree that garlic should be consensual. The risks of secondhand garlic fumes are very real, especially in a short car on a long trip. The chances of a tragic conclusion of some kind are high.)

Still, most people I meet who *think* they hate garlic have not been exposed to fresh garlic that has been treated with respect. Dehydrated garlic is *not* interchangeable with fresh garlic. Even the broad-minded *Joy of Cooking* says "Always use fresh garlic. Powdered and salt forms tend to have rancid overtones." (Bottles of peeled or pre-crushed garlic are as close as some people ever come to fresh garlic, but there is simply no comparison.)

Good garlic can be hard to find, even in the best supermarkets. Produce departments with otherwise high standards can occasionally offer a heap of aged and rickety garlic. It may *look* fine, but always be alert.

Hold any suspect garlic in your hand and rub it with your thumb; if it feels dented or soft, or if you can see any hint of mold or tips of green sprouts, don't buy it. A head of garlic should feel heavy for its size, and the cloves should feel hard and smooth.

(If you find yourself alone in your kitchen with some veteran garlic, see if you can salvage any of it. Throw out any shriveled cloves. Split the others open with a small knife and remove the bitter-tasting green sprout, then use as usual. It won't be juicy, but it will at least have garlic flavor.)

Store garlic as you do onions, in a cool, dark, well-ventilated place — never the refrigerator! And if you feel tempted to keep a bottle of store-bought minced garlic at the back of your refrigerator in case of an emergency, be assured that there will never be an emergency serious enough.

Using Garlic

It rarely makes sense to go to the work of mincing garlic. Garlic is sticky, potent, and often comes in cloves too small to control easily. Crushing is simpler and cleaner if you halve *but don't peel* the clove and if you have a good tool for the job.

That is one of the reasons it's worth paying for a well-designed garlic crusher like the Zyliss brand. I've had other brands backfire. The best and freshest garlic has no sprout and is juicy when you crush it — and it hurts *horribly* if it squirts in your eye.

Crushing Garlic:

- Cut *unpeeled* clove through its equator and place in the garlic press, cut side down and skin side up. No need to cut small cloves – just crush them whole.
- Squeeze garlic press tightly, and then scrape (an oyster knife works well) off the pure garlic pulp extruded from the press.
- Remove the little mat of garlic stuff remaining inside the press. (Another good use for the oyster knife rather than the more delicate point of your paring knife.) Sometimes it lifts out cleanly and other times you have to scrape out bits that cling in and around the holes.
- **This method does not work on peeled cloves**: it is the presence of the husk that helps drive the flesh of the garlic so efficiently through the holes of the press, as well as leave behind the often-neatly-removed garlic remains.

Peeling Garlic:

Whack each clove with a paperweight, or some solid object with a flat bottom. **Use only enough force to crack the clove**, not smash it. You should find it easy to peel. You can also peel a clove of garlic by placing the flat side of a chef's knife over it and then leaning on the blade until you hear the clove crack. On older cloves I usually trim the root end and remove any green sprouts.

Garlic Oil

If you want the convenience of bottled garlic, make your own garlic oil. This is a good way to use small cloves that are a nuisance to crush in the press (see peeling suggestion preceding) or for those times when you want to take advantage of a good supply of fresh juicy garlic. For most purposes you can use it as you would fresh garlic. It's a wonderful back up when you find yourself out of fresh garlic or don't want to take the time to crush it.

> ½ - 1 cup peeled whole garlic cloves
> ½ - 1 cup extra virgin olive oil

- Combine garlic and oil in your blender or mini food processor and blend until smooth. Scrape into a bottle with a tightly sealing lid and refrigerate. It will become firm as the oil chills.

Note:

Keep garlic oil chilled, taking it out of the refrigerator just long enough to scoop out what you want. Use within a month. Use in place of fresh garlic, according to taste.

Celery

When buying celery, check the cut ends for freshness (you don't want brown withered tips) and wiggle a stalk to make sure the celery is not tired or cracked. Celery lasts wonderfully sealed properly in a plastic bag; *not* stored in the ventilated open bag it often wears in the supermarket, and in which the celery turns limp within 2 or 3 days. (If you leave the celery in the ventilated bag, at least seal the top of the bag.)

Juicy, crunchy celery sticks are crucial to dips, tuna salad, potato, rice or bean salads, and, well, family life as we know it today. The coarse outer leaves and strongish-tasting outer stalks can be minced and used in soup or broken up and added to stock. The tender inside leaves should be chopped and added to salads or tuna or whatever. (I use celery leaves a bit like parsley, which I rarely have on hand.)

Celery is so useful that it pays to clean and trim it all at once, as soon after you buy it as possible. It is especially useful stuffed with something like tuna salad or peanut butter and handed to a child who is certain of imminent starvation when dinner is still an hour away.

Carrots

These are dependable vegetables to have in your refrigerator and easy to prepare. Peeled and sliced on the diagonal in thin discs, they make the perfect raw dipping vegetable.

Then, if you cut those slices into matchsticks, steam them for about 7 minutes (or until barely tender), and toss them with vinaigrette, you have a great side dish that's good warm, cold — or the next day. Add some minced fresh basil or cilantro and you have a company dish. Chopped fine and sautéed in oil or butter with celery and onion they make a base for soups or sauces or stews. (See *Mirepoix on page 68.*)

Grated carrot salad is an easy fresh addition to a last-minute dinner, tossed with vinaigrette and a handful of raisins, and a couple of grated raw carrots can be tossed through cabbage or green salads. Carrots are definitely more popular raw than cooked, texture and flavor-wise, but they can be hard to chew raw for the very young and old.

One way to make cooked carrots popular is to make them explode with bold flavors like curry, cumin, fresh cilantro, and lemon juice or vinegar. (See *Marinated Carrot Matchsticks* on page 103.) You could also transform their texture in a bright purée, allowing them to blend quietly into soups, or mashing them in equal amounts with potatoes. Carrots are too useful and nutritious to give up on easily.

Potatoes

Nobody has to be told that potatoes are marvelously versatile and popular. I always have Yukon Gold or red skinned potatoes on hand for steaming, roasting, soups, or potato salad, and some russets for baking or mashing.

The potato is especially valuable to the cook in a hurry because it can be cooked and mashed within 20 minutes and provide a filling and satisfying base for a quick and easy sauce made with a bit of leftover meat. Potatoes can make it easy to be a hero.

As for versatility, they're a favorite appetizer (crisp-roasted potato slices or wedges), side dish (roasted, baked, scalloped, mashed, steamed), or main course (baked and topped with some delicious mixture like chili and grated cheese, with a crunchy topping of diced onion and tomato).

You can turn potatoes into a warm or cold salad, use them in just about any soup, or combine them comfortably with just about any other vegetables. For instance, mashed and blended with a tender sauté of onion and cabbage, which is an interpretation of the Irish classic, *colcannan*. (See page 100.)

Stored loose in a cool, dark, and ventilated place, (*never* in a plastic bag), potatoes usually last easily for several weeks. In fact, store potatoes as you would onions, but not mixed *with* onions; apparently they shorten each other's shelf life.

A potato that is beginning to soften is fine to use but peel away any green patches. (As an aside, I have to say that there are few things that smell *worse* than a rotten potato, so don't store them where they may have any opportunity to roll out of sight.)

It is important to note that potatoes are mostly easily digested starch and should be considered a carbohydrate like white bread or white rice, rather than a vegetable.[1]

Napa (or Chinese) Cabbage

In some ways this could be called the iceberg lettuce of cabbage – crispy, juicy, and mild – but with more flavor, more dignity, and more food value because of its cruciferous nature. (It is also the basis for *kimchee*, the very hot and crunchy Korean condiment.)

Napa cabbage has enough character to stand on its own, yet is too mild to offend anyone who hates cabbage. In fact, it's so mild that it benefits from the association with bold flavors, like green onion and cilantro. Like others in the cabbage family, it waits cheerfully in the refrigerator until you need it, and seems amazingly unaffected by age.

Napa cabbage is tender and crispy, and ideal for stir-frying because it barely needs cooking. It's also marvelous as a quick, easy last-minute salad, alone or added to other greens. Just remove any bruised or

---

[1] Walter C. Willett, M.D. *Eat, Drink, and Be Healthy* (2001) 19-20, 115

broken outer leaves, and then slice off whatever you need. The top half is fluffy and the bottom half is crunchy and juicy.

I usually leave it undressed until shortly before serving it; napa cabbage wilts and weeps quickly. It is better dressed with vinaigrette — a mayonnaise-based dressing should be saved for the sturdier types of cabbage.

One of my favorite beat-the-clock company salads is the top half of a large specimen chopped into bite-sized pieces and tossed with an 8-ounce package of sliced mushrooms, a small bag of ready-to-use baby spinach, and some vinaigrette.

(Actually, I toss the mushrooms separately first with a couple of tablespoons of vinaigrette to give them a head start.) Another favorite is shredded napa cabbage dressed with a lemon, garlic, and cumin vinaigrette with a few sliced green onions and cilantro. (See *Some Simple Salads*.)

For an instant home-alone meal of soul-satisfying dimensions, try a bed of napa cabbage (about 2 cups sliced), a chopped tomato, some leftover brown rice (about ½-cup), some *Faux Ranch Dressing*, and a scoop of leftover tuna salad. Mmm-mm.

Green Cabbage

I prefer the taste and texture of the crinkly-leafed Savoy cabbage over regular cabbage. In any case, green and red (purple, really) cabbage is available year round and lasts an astounding length of time in the refrigerator.

In fact, its sturdiness and good sportsmanship is why we see so much cabbage, red and green, represented on the fast food front, mainly in the form of coleslaw. Cabbage is a member of the *brassica* family of vegetables, which means it is a fiber-rich nutritional powerhouse.

Cabbage is one of my favorite cooked vegetables, although one of the most bitterly joked about, usually in the context of boarding schools or grandmother's house. If you cook cabbage quickly you can avoid the smell and texture that has made cooked cabbage so famous.

("*Even today, well-brought-up English girls are taught by their mothers to boil all veggies for at least a month and a half, just in case one of the dinner guests turns up without his teeth.*" This quote is from Calvin Trillin, who may have been thinking of cabbage.)

The easiest way to serve cooked cabbage is to include it in a minestrone-style soup. My favorite way, though, is thinly sliced and sautéed in butter until tender, and either eaten as is with lemon juice, salt, and pepper or stirred through mashed potatoes. Cabbage and potatoes are very happy together. (See *Colcannon* on page 100.)

Butternut Squash

This is virtually always available, all-purpose, and bursting with beta-carotene. Even its name is delicious. It is easy to prepare for purées, soups, or curries, or to roast in bite-sized chunks as a scrumptious accompaniment to roasted meat.

People who think they don't like squash have discovered they love it roasted with olive oil and salt. (See *Squash* in roasted vegetable section.) I've even eaten raw grated butternut squash in salads! (It was similar to raw grated carrot.)

It will hang around happily for weeks, if necessary, but it will gradually dry out and develop a whitish layer under the skin and a spongy texture. Look for a smooth, hard butternut squash that feels heavy for its size with no sign of wrinkles. Try to pick one with the longest, fattest neck for the maximum amount of solid flesh.

A simple but good side for any meat dish is puréed squash. (See page 99.) A creamy squash soup is a bit of a cliché, but a great one.

Squashes are no fun to peel raw, but butternut squash is easier than most. When I'm in a hurry I don't bother with the bulb end where the seeds are. I just use the neck, peeling it as I would a carrot while using the bulb end as a grip. (The surface of peeled squash leaves a funny coating on the hands.)

I set aside the bulb end in a cool place and use it within a week, when there's time to also roast the seeds. (See following directions.) There are plenty of ways to use a small amount of such an agreeable vegetable: simply roast it or steam it and either serve it hot with whatever else you're eating or store it in the refrigerator for another time.

If you don't need to cut it while it's raw, however, simply halve and bake on a foil-lined roasting pan until the flesh is soft when you poke it with a knife or a skewer. Then you just scoop the flesh out of the skin.

As for the squash seeds, scoop them out, roughly separating them from the fibrous stuff they're attached to. Rub the seeds lightly with olive oil, spread them on an oiled square of tin foil on a baking sheet, salt lightly, and roast in a 325 degree oven for about 15 minutes or until they're golden-brown and crunchy. Don't let them get too brown or they'll be bitter. Then eat them just as they are, shells and all.

Roasted Vegetables

Even people (children as well as adults) who think they don't like vegetables generally like roasted vegetables. The explanation is pretty simple; when you apply fat, salt, and high heat, you are simulating the fast food effect without the downside. Instead of a bath in hot partially hydrogenated fat, the real food method calls for a coating of olive oil and a very hot oven. The roasting method intensifies the flavor of the vegetable, caramelizes the sugars, softens the inside, and crisps the outside. Following are some vegetable roasting steps and tips.

- The equipment and method is generally the same regardless of the vegetable: use the largest roasting pan that will fit into your oven and line it with heavy-duty foil. (The foil makes cleaning up simple but I find that regular foil is a waste of time because it rips too easily when you do any scraping.) You may or may not choose to mist the foil with non-stick spray: vegetables with less moisture, like potatoes, tend to stick.

- Toss vegetable pieces with olive oil and spread in one layer: if you add more vegetables than will fit in one layer, they will steam where they are stacked, and you will end up with semi-stewed vegetables. Sprinkle with salt and (usually) freshly ground pepper.

- Place uncovered in the top third of a preheated 450-degree oven for 10 – 45 minutes, depending on the vegetable and the size of the pieces. At this temperature the liquid will tend to evaporate from the vegetable instead of collecting in the pan, and you will probably notice the steam steadily escaping from the closed oven door toward the end of the roasting process. *Be careful opening the oven!* Make sure and turn your eyes away from the initial burst of steam.

- There's generally no reason to interrupt a vegetable while it's roasting. Once you are comfortable with the process, and know how long to leave the vegetables in the oven, just set the timer and get busy doing something else. When you test for doneness, poke the bigger pieces. It's better for the smaller pieces to be overcooked than to serve any undercooked vegetables. In fact, people who wouldn't care – or maybe even notice – if they never saw another vegetable in their life may fight over the blackened and caramelized crispy bits.

- At times when you would normally sauté or steam vegetables, you can usually roast them instead. It's certainly easier than sautéing and allows you to do other things while the vegetables are cooking. It also gives you a flavorful and ready-to-serve vegetable. However, as delicious as roasted vegetables are, it should be noted that they are generally best eaten on the same day — they are cooked pretty enthusiastically.

- It should also be noted that the vegetables at our table are always accompanied with a side of an all-purpose sauce we call Goop, formally called *Rich Yogurt Aioli*. This is a mixture of drained yogurt, homemade mayonnaise, salt, pepper, and enough freshly crushed garlic to cause an involuntary gasp. (See recipe for *Rich Yogurt Aioli* on page 58.)

Asparagus

This is the *only* way we have prepared asparagus ever since we first discovered the roasting method. Break off tough ends by holding both the top of the spear (below the head) and the stem end and bending it until it snaps. There is no need to use a peeler.

Clean thoroughly in a bath of cold water. If you are not going to use them the same day, store them in the refrigerator with their stem ends in about ¼ inch of water and the spears upright, like a bouquet of flowers, loosely covered with plastic or a damp paper towel. (A Pyrex measuring jug works well.)

Drain and pat dry, and coat with olive oil: my method is to heap them up, pour two or three tablespoons of oil on top, then gently toss them with my hands. Spread in a roasting pan (crowding is fine, but one layer only), sprinkle with salt and freshly ground pepper, and roast at the top of the oven for about 10 minutes for slim asparagus and 12-15 minutes for fatter spears. The timing obviously depends on whether you prefer your asparagus tender-crisp or soft. A slight browning of the spears and crisping of the tips adds a flavorsome touch.

A plate of hot roasted asparagus can be served as an appetizer, or as a salad course tossed in vinaigrette. It is also fine on the dinner table even though the spears cool quickly.

Beets

The beet is not a fiercely popular vegetable, but please linger briefly while I put in a word for a side dish of slim, gleaming deep-red beet wedges tossed in vinaigrette. You'll feel gratified when a guest notices them and cries "Beets? Are those *beets?* I *love* beets, but I haven't had any since my grandmother died!"

To prepare for this moment, place the rinsed beets exactly as you bought them (tails intact but greens chopped to an inch in length) on a large enough piece of foil to allow you to enclose beets completely. Seal beets inside the foil and place in any old baking pan that fits. Roast in the middle of the oven for about 1½ hours.

(Beets can take an amazing amount of time to cook, and you don't want to have to bother unwrapping them until you're sure they're done. If you must interrupt earlier because you're in a hurry or the beets are small, test for doneness by poking with a skewer.)

When beets are cool enough to handle, poke a fork in the greens end and peel with a paring knife. Skins should slip off easily. Slice peeled beets into slim wedges (or cubes or straws) and toss while still warm in vinaigrette. Make sure to check your fingernails for beet stains.

Brussels Sprouts

You thought beets were bad! Well, Brussels sprouts also have a relatively small but passionate following, and you never know when someone is going to ask you to cook some up as a special birthday treat. So, pull off loose outer leaves and trim the stem so it is almost flush with the sprout. Cut a tiny but deep **x** in the stem with the tip of your paring knife.

Add Brussels sprouts to a pot of boiling salted water, boil for about 5 minutes, and drain very well. Leave whole or cut in half, depending mainly on their size. Then, lay the Brussels sprouts in a foil-lined roasting pan, drizzle with olive oil, and shake pan gently to make sure all the sprouts roll around in the oil. (A rubber spatula helps.) Sprinkle with salt and roast, shaking pan once or twice, for about 20-30 minutes or until browned and luscious.

(If the oven isn't available for roasting, you could just continue boiling the Brussels sprouts for another 5 minutes, or until just tender; drain well, then cut in half and roll around in garlicky vinaigrette.

Good whether hot, warm, or at room temperature. Irresistible with a side of the *Rich Yogurt Aioli* on page 58.)

Cauliflower

Roasted cauliflower is a delicacy to be shared between two or three who can be trusted to eat no more than their share. Cauliflower can vary quite a bit in size but two people can easily dispose of an average sized head if it's roasted as described below. (I have also served it as an appetizer straight from the oven to surprised friends.)

Separate cauliflower into clumps and carve or split clumps into smaller florets with a paring knife. Toss gently in at least ¼ cup olive oil and place in one layer in a foil-lined roasting pan or baking sheet. Sprinkle with salt, and roast for about 15 – 25 minutes, or until cauliflower is browning. We like an almost toasted effect, blackened bits and all. Eat right away, if possible.

Eggplant

A note about buying eggplants: only settle for one that is firm, glossy, and smooth-skinned, with a perky-looking green cap, and try to use it the same day. The most dependable for mild flavor and tender skins are the Japanese eggplants. A good fresh eggplant requires no salting and draining to remove bitterness. There is generally no need to peel an eggplant unless you suspect the skin is tough or waxed.

So, trim off the stem end, and cube the eggplant in ¾ inch chunks. Toss with a few tablespoons of olive oil (which is absorbed as fast as you add it, so be aware) and spread in a foil-lined roasting pan. Salt and roast until soft and beginning to brown, which will be about 25 minutes.

For eggplant lovers, the simplest preparation is to slice into ½ inch rounds. Line a baking sheet with foil, then brush both sides of the eggplant rounds with olive oil and crowd them on the sheet like cookies (except they don't spread). Sprinkle with salt, and roast for about 25-30 minutes or until eggplant is buttery soft to the touch.

Garlic

You'll have to read about roasting garlic somewhere else. I don't roast garlic. Fresh garlic, however, is about the best friend a roasted vegetable can have. (See recipe for *Rich Yogurt Aioli*.)

Green Beans

Roast these as you would asparagus. A plate of roasted and salted green beans makes a great appetizer. However, I've had mixed success; they can be tough and dryish, possibly because they weren't as fresh as they seemed. Still delicious, though.

Onions

The sweeter varieties with their thicker layers are the best choice for roasted onions. Trim and peel onions, then cut the onions into wedges or quarters, and toss with about 1 – 2 tablespoons of olive oil per onion.

Or cut them into ¾-inch slices, lay them on the oiled foil, brushed with oil and salted. Some people like to roast them whole, in or out of the skin, with a chunk of butter stuck into a plug cut out of the center. Anything is fine as long as there is at least an onion for each person planning to eat. (Onions reduce by about half when they're cooked, as well as becoming mild and sweet.)

Spread onions in an oiled foil-lined roasting pan, and sprinkle with salt and a bit of freshly ground pepper. Roast them high in your oven until the onion flesh is almost melting and the edges are blackened, about 30 minutes.

(…or you may prefer your onions less radically roasted. You can also use this method as an alternative to sautéing diced onion to add to other dishes.)

Parsnips

How can you bring up the subject of parsnips with a straight face? But how can you possibly *ignore* them with a name like that? Now that we have mentioned them, though, choose slim and smallish ones, peel and cut them in half-inch chunks, roast them to within an inch of their lives, and don't be stingy with the oil and salt.

Peppers

If there is one roasted vegetable that evokes the Mediterranean best for me, it is the sweet red (or yellow or orange) bell pepper. Especially when the peppers are broiled and marinated, a surprisingly easy operation, except for the fact that it always sets off our smoke alarm with invisible smoke.

So, remove the stem, core, seeds, and white pithy bits, and quarter lengthwise. Lay skin-side up on a shallow foil-lined baking pan. (There's no need to oil anything, but use enough foil to allow you to enclose the peppers later.)

Place under the broiler and keep an eye on them. The skin should blacken within 20 minutes. You may choose to move them around to broil more evenly or use an egg turner to flatten any that are curving up too high. Basically the peppers are ready when most of the skin area is charred.

Pull pan out of the oven and bring the edges of the foil over and snugly wrap the peppers up for about 10 minutes. The skin will scrape off easily. (*Please* don't skin the poor peppers under running water like some instructions say. It's appalling to think of mixing water with the fragrant pepper juice just for the sake of a few bits of blackened skin or whatever.)

Roll the delicious and still warm pepper sections in a few tablespoons of vinaigrette or a quick mixture of a couple of tablespoons of extra virgin olive oil, a tablespoon of vinegar, a half-teaspoon of crushed garlic, and some salt and pepper.

Potatoes

This is a roasted vegetable that virtually everyone loves. There are lots of options here, both in variety (white, red, Yukon gold, russet, and so on) and method.

My favorite is baby red potatoes boiled in a big pot of water for 15 minutes and then rolled in olive oil, salted and peppered, and roasted for about 30 minutes or until soft inside. (You can roast them without parboiling them first, but the texture inside and the crunch outside may not be as good.) Depending on their size, you can quarter them, halve them, or leave them whole to roast them.

For roasting potato wedges I prefer Yukon gold. Aim for slimmer rather than fat specimens, scrubbed but not peeled, sliced lengthwise in at least eighths, tossed in olive oil, and crowded in the foil-lined pan curved skin side down. (I actually take the time to set each wedge on its back, because it is least likely to stick to the foil that way. I don't disturb them while they're cooking, naturally.)

Sprinkle with salt and pepper, and roast until they are golden-brown, blistered, and crunchy on the outside, and molten soft on the inside. Allow about 45 – 60 minutes, depending on the size of the pieces, and serve straight from the oven with a side of *Rich Yogurt Aioli.* (See page 51.)

To substitute for baked potatoes, cut potatoes in half lengthwise, rub with olive oil, sprinkle with salt and pepper, and roast about 45 minutes, or until tender inside and crisp outside.

For the quickest-cooking version and a great appetizer, make potato crisps: slice potatoes lengthwise into thin slices, brush with olive oil and a bit of salt, crowd on a foil-lined baking sheet, and roast until browned — about 10-15 minutes.

Squash

To me, squash automatically means butternut squash. As well as having the most appetizing name, this variety is easy to prepare with its smooth shape, thin skin, and sensible seed arrangement. When you buy, look for one with a long neck and an abbreviated bulb end – the neck is easiest to chop into regular pieces. (Use a sharp chef's knife and be careful when cutting this vegetable; it is hard and dense, and its shape makes it tricky to handle.)

Trim the stem end, and peel with a vegetable peeler. (Handling the peeled squash leaves a funny coating on the palms of your hands: I try to hold onto the unpeeled section as long as I can.) Slice the neck into about 1-inch wheels, and then cut slices into sixths or eighths, depending on the size of the squash.

Toss with a few tablespoons of olive oil, and then lay in the foil-lined roasting pan curved side down where possible. Sprinkle with salt and pepper, then roast 30 – 45 minutes, or until blackened on the points of the wedges and very soft. If you are roasting the squash for purée or soup, see recipe for *Butternut Squash Purée* or *Smoooth Butternut Bisque*.

Sweet Potatoes (Yams)

I mean the orange-fleshed sweet potatoes, often called "garnet yams" and among the richest sources of beta-carotene in the vegetable world. It is completely unrelated to yams or potatoes. The jewel or garnet sweet potatoes have generally smooth reddish-brown skins that peel easily, and are actually delicious sliced and eaten raw – crisp, mild, and slightly sweet.

They can also be baked like potatoes in their skins (but on a piece of foil because the sugar can escape and burn late in the cooking) at 400 degrees for about an hour or until tender. Split and mash with a bit of butter, salt, and pepper. It tastes almost illicit. (For a bit more on the subject of so-called yams, see *Two Potato Soup* on page 58.)

To roast sweet potatoes for a vegetable side dish, peel and slice into ¾ - inch chunks and roast them just as you would butternut squash, allowing the edges to blacken slightly.

For roasted sweet potato cookies, slice peeled raw sweet potatoes into ¼ -inch slices, brush with olive oil, sprinkle with salt and pepper, and roast in the top third of a 450-degree oven for about 30 minutes or until starting to brown.

Zucchini

If you can't find small-to-moderate, slim, hard zucchinis, I don't recommend buying them at all. The bigger they are, the tougher the skin and the more spongy and seedy the centers.

So, clean and trim them, but don't peel them, of course. (Only the large zucchinis have tough skin.) Slice them down the middle lengthwise, and then cut them into 2-inch chunks. Toss in olive oil and lay them skin side down in the foil-lined roasting pan. Sprinkle with salt and freshly ground pepper, and roast high in a hot, hot oven for about 20 minutes, or until the zucchini is tender and beginning to brown. (Some like zucchini very soft, but I prefer it with some texture intact.)

A good side dish is roasted zucchini and onion: slice zucchini in quarters lengthwise and then in 1-inch chunks. Chop 2 onions in 1-inch dice. Add to chopped zucchini and toss vegetables in olive oil. Spread in one layer in a foil-lined shallow roasting pan, sprinkle with salt and freshly ground pepper, then roast on the top shelf of a 450 – 500 degree oven for about 20 minutes, or until onions begin to blacken on the edges and the zucchini begins to brown. Beware! It shrinks quite a bit, so make sure there's enough to go around.

Simple Salads

- The very simplest salad is sticks or slices of raw vegetables like celery, carrot, cucumber, tomato, bell peppers, broccoli or cauliflower, baby zucchini, Jicama (see page 119), turnip, radish, and so forth, served with a little bowl of some sort of dip or thick dressing. (See *Dressings and Dips*.)

- Almost as simple is just about any combination of the same vegetables grated, thinly sliced, diced, or julienne (sliced into matchsticks) and dressed with vinaigrette, salt, and freshly ground pepper.

- The sturdy and versatile vegetables like carrots, celery, and cabbage are easy to recruit for salad duty just about any time. You can't be as spontaneous with the more delicate and perishable greens, but the variety is nice.

- Don't forget the option of steamed or roasted vegetables tossed with vinaigrette — salads don't have to be raw. In fact, there are many people who would ignore a conventional salad but enjoy a lightly cooked and marinated vegetable like asparagus, carrots, or green beans.

Fresh Tomato Salad

This is one of the most useful and certainly easiest salads in existence. Good color accent on the table *and* the plate, easy to eat, and generally acceptable to most audiences. A plain tomato salad is simple to jazz up with green or white onions, diced avocado, olives, fresh herbs, and so on. The option I use most is sweet white onions. (You can usually find sweet onions year round, imported or otherwise.)

- Just dice or slice fresh tomatoes — ½ - 1 per person — into chunks, wedges, or slices and serve them sprinkled with salt and freshly ground pepper. You may prefer a bit of vinaigrette, but you will find that the salt draws out the juices of the tomatoes, which combines with the pepper to make its own dressing. It is best done within a half-hour of serving.

- *Onion Option*: Peel onion and halve lengthwise. Lay one half cut side down on cutting board and slice slim wedges (no more than ¼ inch at widest point) from the rounded edge. You will need about ½ - 1 cup of onion slices (depending on quantity of tomatoes and mildness of onions). Combine with 2 tablespoons vinaigrette and set aside to marinate for 15 minutes, if possible. Mix gently with chopped tomatoes.

Apple, Broccoli, and Celery Salad

This is my favorite way to use broccoli stems. (Check for solid, fresh looking stems when you buy broccoli.) Some chopped broccoli florets can help give a deeper green accent.

(Serves 4 – 6)

> 1 – 2 crisp apples, peeled or not, in ½ x ¼ inch dice (about 1½ - 2 cups)
> 1 – 2 cups sliced peeled broccoli stems
> 2 cups sliced celery, ¼ -inch or less
>
> 3 tablespoons mayonnaise
> 1 tablespoon apple cider vinegar or lemon juice
> ½ teaspoon salt
> ½ teaspoon freshly ground pepper
>
> ½ cup broken fresh or toasted walnuts or pecans
> 2 tablespoons dried currants or raisins

- Strip thick skin from broccoli stems using a small knife, starting with the base of stem and peeling upwards. Halve lengthwise and slice in ⅛ – ¼ inch slices.

- Mix together vinegar, mayonnaise, salt, and pepper and thoroughly blend with broccoli, celery, apple, nuts, and currants.

Spinach, Napa, and Mushroom Salad

The contrast of the deep green spinach with the pale inside leaves of the napa cabbage is striking enough to make this salad get away with this simplicity.

(Serves 4 – 6)

> 8 ounces sliced mushrooms
> ¼ cup vinaigrette (*Vinaigrette with Mustard and Garlic*)
> 4 cups sliced napa cabbage (about ½ head)
> 6 ounces pre-washed baby spinach
> ¼ - ½ cup freshly grated Parmesan

- Place mushrooms in salad bowl and toss with 2 tablespoons vinaigrette.

- Add sliced cabbage and spinach with remaining 2 tablespoons vinaigrette and toss thoroughly. Add Parmesan, toss again, and serve as soon as possible.

Pico de Gallo (with Cabbage Variation)

Naturally you can fool around with the proportions and ingredients here, but this is a version I like to serve with rich dishes like chili and salmon.

(Serves 4 – 6)

> 2 tablespoons lime or lemon juice
> 2 tablespoons extra virgin olive oil
> 1 teaspoon freshly crushed garlic
> 1 teaspoon salt
> 1 – 2 tablespoons minced jalapeno chili
> ¼ - ½ cup chopped fresh cilantro, if available
> 1 cup diced (¼ -inch) mild onion, like Mayan or any sweet variety
>
> 2 – 4 tomatoes (about 2 cups) seeded and in ¼-inch dice
> 2 cups cucumber, peeled and seeded if necessary, in ¼-inch dice
> *or* 2 cups green cabbage in ¼ inch dice

- In a small mixing bowl combine lemon juice, olive oil, garlic, salt, jalapenos, and fresh cilantro. Add diced onion and set aside.

- Core and quarter tomatoes, and scoop out seeds. (Don't discard! Eat them or save them for soup.) Dice tomatoes and cucumber or cabbage. (English cucumbers need no peeling or seeding.)

- Add tomatoes and diced cabbage and toss thoroughly.

Avocado Salsa

This is *so* good and *so* simple. It even looks and tastes fresh the next day.

(Makes about 2 cups)

> 2 large or 3 small avocados, ripe but firm
> 1 cup diced sweet onion
> 2 – 3 tablespoons fresh lemon or lime juice
> 1 tablespoon extra virgin olive oil
> ½ teaspoon freshly crushed garlic.
> ¼ teaspoon salt
> ¼ teaspoon Tabasco sauce

- Dice avocados in ¼ - ½ inch cubes, and the onion in ¼-inch dice. Combine in bowl and gently toss with juice, olive oil, salt, and Tabasco. Taste for flavor. Try to leave some for others.

Tossed Green Salad with Vinaigrette and Parmesan

The makeup of the greens can vary according to whatever you happen to have on hand: if you can plan ahead you can have bags of mixed greens and baby spinach to combine. The crispier and meatier romaine lettuce provides a nice contrast to the more delicate specialty greens. A handful of shredded red cabbage provides some nice color. Any salad greens work, but they should be clean, dry, and fresh. You can have the greens waiting in their serving bowl an hour or so ahead as long as you cover them with a damp paper towel and store them in the refrigerator. Dress the greens just before serving because they wilt quickly.

(Serves about 4, but easily adjusted for any number)

> 8 – 10 cups of bite sized greens
> ¼ cup *Vinaigrette with Mustard and Garlic*
> ½ cup grated *Parmigiano-Reggiano*

- Toss the greens with the vinaigrette. Add Parmesan and toss again. Serve right away while greens are still perky.

Napa Cabbage Salad with Cilantro

If making this salad a day in advance, I would suggest leaving it undressed until shortly before you plan to serve it; napa cabbage is not as sturdy as regular cabbage, and so tends to wilt as its liquid drains from its leaves into the bottom of the bowl. But wilted or not, it makes a refreshing snack the next day.

(Serves 4 – 6)

> About 6 cups thinly sliced napa cabbage
> About 3 green onions, sliced thinly on the diagonal
> ¼ - ½ cup chopped cilantro
>
> **Lemon & Cumin Vinaigrette:** *(makes about ⅓ cup)*
> 2 tablespoons lemon juice
> ½ teaspoon ground cumin
> ½ teaspoon salt
> 1 teaspoon honey or sugar
> 1 teaspoon freshly crushed garlic
> 2 tablespoons extra virgin olive oil

- Combine cabbage and cilantro in mixing bowl.

- Whisk together vinaigrette ingredients. Add to cabbage mixture and toss.

Carrot Slaw

This is bright looking and punchy tasting with a sweet twist. (You could use a pre-shredded cabbage mixture instead of preparing them yourself, and dress the salad with ¼-cup of vinaigrette from page 55.)

(Serves 4)

> 2 cups grated carrot (about 2 – 3 medium)
> 2 cups thinly-sliced green cabbage (like Savoy or Napa)
> ¼ cup raw sunflower seeds
> ¼ cup currants *or* finely minced or sliced candied ginger
>
> 1 tablespoon cider vinegar
> 1 tablespoon honey
> 2 tablespoon extra virgin olive oil
> ½ teaspoon freshly crushed garlic
> ½ teaspoon salt
> ½ teaspoon freshly ground pepper

- Combine carrots, cabbage, sunflower seeds, and ginger/currants. *(The dainty little currants or dark raisins give a vivid accent to this salad.)*

- Mix together vinegar, honey, olive oil, salt, pepper, and garlic. Add to vegetable mixture and toss thoroughly.

Mediterranean Salad

Any variation on the theme here works. If you happen to have a few crisp radishes to slice, or a particularly nice little zucchini to dice, add or substitute. Use whatever you like or happen to have available, adjusting amounts of each to your taste.

> 1 cucumber peeled and quartered lengthwise
> 2 medium tomatoes
> 1 cup diced sweet onions
> 1 sweet bell pepper, gold if possible for color
> ¼ cup *Garlic and Mustard Vinaigrette,* or *Lemon and Cumin Vinaigrette*

- Seed cucumber if necessary and cut into ¼- ½-inch dice. Dice tomatoes, onion, and bell pepper into ¼- ½-inch dice.

- Combine vegetables with vinaigrette and toss. Add more salt and freshly ground pepper to taste.

Greek Salad

A mild onion is important in this salad — one of the sweet varieties like the seasonal Walla Walla, or the Mayan onion which is widely available year-round. If you have only hot onion, make a different salad. If you're not a feta cheese user already, try a mild domestic brand made from cow's milk, like *Athenos*. Don't be intimidated by the use-by date; it lasts an amazingly long time in the refrigerator in its original package. Its rich, salty bite mingles with the dressing and is not at all intrusive, even for those who think they don't like feta. This is one of those recipes where every ingredient is critical.

(Serves 2 – 4)

> 2 tablespoons apple cider vinegar
> 2 tablespoons extra virgin olive oil
> ½ teaspoon salt
> ½ teaspoon freshly ground pepper
> 2 cups sweet onion sliced
> 1 cucumber or about 2 cups chopped
> 4 – 6 Roma tomatoes or at least 2 cups chopped
> ½ cup Kalamata olives, pitted and halved or quartered
> 4 ounces mild feta cheese, thinly sliced and crumbled

- Place vinegar, oil, salt, and pepper in mixing bowl. Peel onion and halve lengthwise. Lay one half cut side down on cutting board and slice slim strips, no more than ¼ inch at widest point, from the rounded edge. *(Cut strips in half if onion is big.)* You will need about 1 – 2 cups of onion slices, depending on mildness of onion. Add onion to dressing in bowl and toss. Set aside while you prepare rest of salad.

- Peel and quarter cucumber lengthwise, and scoop out seeds. Cut in ¼-inch slices. (If you are using a thin-skinned English cucumber you don't need to peel or seed it.) Quarter tomatoes lengthwise and remove bits of core, then cut crosswise into ½-inch slices. *(You should have at least 2 cups of each.)* Add to onion mixture.

- Prepare Kalamata olives (see ***Note***) and feta. I prefer to slice the feta thinly so it crumbles and blends into the salad. Add to salad and toss. Mmmm.

.Note:

➢ One way to pit Kalamata olives is to score each into quarters while intact, then massage the olive gently, with a finger and thumb on the pointy ends, until the pit disengages from the neatly quartered flesh. Be careful not to lose any pits in the salad — they look dangerously like olive quarters.

Gazpacho
(Cold Mediterranean Soup)

Salad in a blender! Summer in a glass! Cold and zesty, and a pleasant way to perk up wilted limbs and drooping taste buds. This traditional Spanish soup has countless versions, but this is mine and it may be one of the simplest. You can make and chill the vegetable base days ahead (except for the tomato juice, which makes more sense to chill in its can), and transport it to a picnic or potluck in a bottle surrounded with ice.

(Makes about 8 cups)

> about 2 pounds ripe tomatoes (about 6 – 8 medium)
> 1 large cucumber
> 1 cup chopped onion
> 2 – 4 cloves garlic
> ¼ cup apple cider vinegar
> ¼ cup extra virgin olive oil
> ½ teaspoon salt
> ½ teaspoon Tabasco sauce
>
> 2½ cups tomato juice, or to taste
> ¼ - ½ cup fresh chopped cilantro (for garnish)

- **To prepare tomatoes:** Place a couple at a time in a pot of boiling water for about 10 seconds, then peel. (I stick a fork in the core end and strip the skin off with a paring knife.) Slice into quarters, core, and scoop seeds into a sieve. *(You can strain about ¾ cup of juice from the seeds to add to the gazpacho ingredients.)*

- Peel cucumber, quarter lengthwise, remove seeds, and chop roughly. Peel and chop onion and peel garlic.

- Combine tomatoes, cucumber, onion, garlic, vinegar, oil, salt, and Tabasco in food processor in two batches and process for about 30 seconds, or until smooth. If made in advance, transfer to a bottle and chill at least overnight. You should have about 5½ cups of gazpacho base; add tomato juice to taste.

Note:
➢ Traditional garnishes are croutons and finely diced green peppers and cucumbers. I prefer the gentle bite of some diced avocado perched on a dollop of drained yogurt that has been mixed with just enough heavy cream to make it smooth. Cooked, chilled shrimp would be spectacular additions.

Vegetable Soups and Sides

By keeping ingredients and methods simple, we are more likely to include an extra serving or two of vegetables in our meals. These are very basic recipes that I can generally put together without planning ahead: most of the ingredients are my pantry standards. With a handful of these easy recipes standing by, you can add a vegetable without much trouble.

Two Potato Soup

This is a simple and luscious soup. Not complex, but comforting and easy to make. Because I always have the ingredients on hand, and because the soup takes only an hour from start to finish, this is a favorite last-minute meal, especially with red lentils added (see note) and whole grain bread and butter on the side.

(Serves about 4)

> 3 cups water
> 1 large onion in ¼-inch dice (3 – 4 cups)
> 1 medium – large sweet potato/garnet yam, grated (3 – 4 cups)
> 1 large baking potato, grated (3 – 4 cups)
> 2 teaspoons salt
> 2 teaspoons freshly crushed garlic
> ½ teaspoon freshly ground pepper
> ¼ teaspoon Tabasco sauce
> 1 can (14 ounces) coconut milk (not *lite* or low fat)

- Bring water to the boil in a 5-quart soup pot over medium high heat. Add diced onion and grated vegetables as you prepare them. Add salt and bring back to the boil, then reduce heat and simmer gently for about 30 – 45 minutes, stirring or whisking at least every 10 minutes to keep it from sticking. (Don't worry if it seems too thick.) Add garlic and simmer 10 minutes longer.

- Add pepper, Tabasco, and coconut milk. Whisk vigorously, both to blend ingredients and to smooth the texture of the soup. For a creamy version use an immersion blender or food processor. Bring back to a simmer and serve.

Cauliflower Butter Broth

The cauliflower is one of the most sensible vegetables a busy person could have in the refrigerator, as long as you take a moment in the produce department to make sure its snowy complexion is natural and not the result of cosmetic surgery. (Few vegetables age gracefully.) They're quick to clean and easy to prepare, with almost no waste. The cauliflower is mild mannered enough to be generally liked but with enough of the crucifer family spunk to be interesting. This is a simple, satisfying, single-note soup that uses the whole cauliflower, and makes a good first course while giving you one or two servings of vegetables. Cauliflower Soup #2 that follows is simpler, faster, and uses cream instead of butter.

(Serves about 4 as a first course)

>   4 tablespoons butter (½ stick), or olive oil, or mixture of both
>   1 medium-large onion, diced (about 3 cups)
>   1 tablespoon freshly crushed garlic
>   2 tablespoons all purpose flour
>   4 cups water
>   1½ teaspoons salt
>   1 teaspoon freshly-ground black pepper
>   1 cauliflower, chopped (about 6 cups)

- Heat a heavy 5-quart pot over medium-high heat. Add butter (and/or oil). When bubbling, add onions. Sauté 12 minutes or until onion is tender.

- Reduce heat to low, add garlic, and sauté another minute. Sprinkle the flour over the top and blend in thoroughly. Add 1 cup of water and blend until smooth. Scrape the corners of the pot to make sure that no pockets of floury onion escape notice. Add remaining water, salt, and pepper.

- Meanwhile, rinse and trim cauliflower of leaves and stem. Separate into clumps and carve or split clumps into smaller florets with a paring knife. Dice the core and the remaining bits and pieces. You should have at least 6 cups total. Scrape it all into the soup. The cauliflower will probably poke above the surface, but that's fine. Bring soup to a simmer and cook for about 35 minutes or until cauliflower is very tender.

For a creamy alternative, try this simple variation with curry and cream: Bring water to a boil and add diced onions. Quarter cauliflower lengthwise and slice into ¼ - ½-inch slices, including core. Add to pot, bring back to a boil, and then reduce heat and simmer 35 minutes. Add garlic, salt, and pepper, and *½ teaspoon curry powder*, and simmer another 10 minutes. Add *½ cup cream or evaporated whole milk* and purée until smooth.

Creamy Thai Tomato Soup

The Thai reference is actually culinary license on my part but this is a great soup: rich and vivid, yet with the comforting quality of creamy tomato soups. This can be made from scratch quickly and uses ingredients I always have on hand.

(Serves 6)

¼ cup olive oil
½ teaspoon crushed chilies
1 medium – large sweet onion, diced (about 3 cups)
1 tablespoon freshly crushed garlic
1 can (28 ounces) crushed tomatoes
1 can (11.5 ounces) Campbell's tomato juice (1½ cups)
1 teaspoon salt
1 teaspoon minced fresh ginger
2 teaspoons fish sauce
1½ tablespoons honey
1 can (14 ounces) coconut milk (not *lite*)
2 tablespoons fresh basil leaves, thinly sliced

- Heat the oil over medium-high heat in a heavy 5-quart soup pot. Add chilies and onion. Sauté 15 minutes, or until onions are very soft. Add garlic and sauté another minute.

- Add crushed tomatoes, tomato juice, salt, ginger, fish sauce, and honey. Bring to a simmer, then reduce heat and simmer for about 20 – 30 minutes, stirring now and then. Remove from heat, add coconut milk, and blend thoroughly with whisk or purée. (See note below.) Add fresh basil just before serving.

Note:

➢ I like the smooth-textured version of this soup. If you have an immersion blender, purée soup directly in pot. If you use a food processor, purée cooled soup in 2 batches. Return soup to pot and bring to a simmer again. The fresh basil is a grand addition, but the soup is bright enough in color and flavor to stand alone.

Smoooth Butternut Bisque

This can be made from scratch very quickly, and takes kindly to experiments in the field of flavors, especially the spices. The heat of this soup is important, I think, and depending on the audience you could add more chilies or add Tabasco sauce at the end. You could use all kinds of squash for this soup, leftover or fresh-cooked, roasted or steamed. Butternut squash happens to have the smoothest texture. The tomato juice counters the sweetness of the squash and onions nicely.

(Makes about 8 – 10 cups)

2 – 3-pound butternut squash, or about 3 – 4 cups cooked

¼ cup olive oil
1 medium-large onion, chopped (3 – 4 cups)
1 teaspoon curry powder
1½ teaspoon salt
1 tablespoon freshly crushed garlic
(1 tablespoon finely minced fresh ginger, if available)
2 cups water
¼ – ½ teaspoon Tabasco sauce
3 cups tomato juice
1 can (12 ounces) evaporated milk

- ***To roast squash:*** *Preheat oven to 450 degrees and place the rack in top third of oven.* Halve squash lengthwise and scoop out seeds. Line a baking sheet or shallow pan with foil. Mist with non-stick spray or rub cut side of squash with olive oil. Place squash cut side down on foil. *(The foil simply makes the clean up easy.)* Roast for about an hour, or until squash is very tender. When cool, scrape squash from skin and chop roughly.

  To steam squash: Peel squash and slice off each end. Separate neck from bulb end. Stand squash neck up and halve vertically, then cut into 1 – 2-inch chunks. Halve bulb end and scrape out seeds. *(For directions on roasting seeds see page 82.)* Chop bulb end and add to the rest of the squash chunks. Steam in a 4-quart saucepan for about 30 minutes or until tender.

- Meanwhile, heat the oil in a heavy 5-quart soup pot over medium-high heat and add onions, curry, and salt. Sauté 10 – 15 minutes or until onion is soft. *(I would always use the larger quantity of onion. You don't need to be fussy about chopping when you're going to purée the soup anyway, but make sure the onion is sautéed until soft.)* Add garlic and sauté another 2 minutes.

- Stir in ginger (if you have it), Tabasco, water, and cooked squash pieces. Bring to a boil, and simmer 15 minutes.

- Remove from heat. Add tomato juice and evaporated milk.

- Purée soup in 2 or 3 batches in food processor or blender. *(At this point you could store soup in the refrigerator for several days.)* Return soup to pot. Bring to a simmer and serve.

Butternut Squash Purée

This is fun to serve to people who don't trust squash under any circumstances. I have seen some touching scenes of reconciliation. The preparation is simple and each ingredient important. Butternut squash is dependably smooth and creamy, and has easy-to-peel thin skin. Also, puréed squash is a tastier leftover than the roasted squash described on page 87, which is best eaten freshly roasted.

(Serves about 4 – 6)

> Butternut squash (about 3 lbs or approximately 4 cups cooked)
> 2 tablespoons butter
> ½ teaspoon salt
> ½ teaspoon freshly ground pepper

- Peel squash and chop into roughly evenly sized chunks. (For squash-chopping suggestions see directions for *Smoooth Butternut Bisque* on preceding page.) Place squash chunks in a steam in a 4-quart saucepan for about 30 minutes or until tender.

- Purée in a food processor or in a bowl with an electric mixer, with butter, salt, and pepper. *(This re-heats well if you want to prepare it in advance.)*

Note:
➢ The simplest steaming method is with a collapsible steamer basket. The hot metal baskets of steamed vegetables are not easy to extract from the pot but they're available in 2 sizes just about everywhere including supermarkets.

➢ You could purée carrots or small parsnips the same way, using the steaming method to cook them. Carrots tend to make a more watery purée, so I usually add a small peeled and chopped potato to steam with the carrots.

Colcannon
(Mashed Potatoes with Cabbage)

Colcannon is a traditional Irish mashed potato and cabbage dish that lends itself to all kinds of variations. (One suspects that the garlic and olive oil would *not* be an Irish variation. Call it poetic license.) This is a clever way to serve green cabbage, cooked to a buttery tenderness and stirred through the mashed potatoes with or without the onion suggested here. *(See Note for other options.)*

(Serves about 4 – 6)

> 3 – 4 medium potatoes (russets or Yukon gold)
> (1 medium onion or about 2 cups in ¼-inch dice - optional)
> ¼ cup extra virgin olive oil
> 1 teaspoon freshly crushed garlic
> ¼ - ½ green cabbage, or about 4 – 8 cups shredded
> 1 cup milk
> 1½ teaspoons salt
> 1 teaspoon freshly ground pepper

- Peel and cut potatoes into quarters or eighths. Steam or boil until tender, about 30 – 40 minutes. *(I prefer steaming to boiling; boiled potatoes tend to break down and dissolve into the water if left too long.)*

- ***Optional but strongly recommended:*** Meanwhile, peel and dice onion. Heat olive oil in skillet over medium heat, add onions, and sauté for about 10 minutes or until very tender. Stir in the garlic, turn off heat, and set aside.

- Combine cabbage and milk in a skillet over medium heat. Bring to a simmer and cover; reduce heat to low, then cook gently for 20 minutes or until very soft. *(If you don't include the sautéed onion, stir the garlic and olive oil into the cabbage in the last few minutes of cooking.)* Add salt and pepper.

- Mash cooked potatoes, and then combine with onion and cabbage mixtures. Blend well.

Note:
➤ The creamy blandness of the mashed potato is a natural vehicle for other vegetables to be slid into the meal almost undetected. Two or three small turnips cooked and mashed with the potatoes are generally safe for any audience, and rutabagas, too, although the yellow tint is not as subtle. But you can *always* get away with a cup or two of tender sautéed diced onions with the mashed potatoes. (Two cups of raw diced onions cook down one cup.)

Cauliflower Custard

Using custard as a vehicle is a great way to serve cauliflower, and lots of other vegetables, for that matter. This dish is bliss for cauliflower lovers and pretty good for the rest of you. It is a bit pallid without the chopped parsley, and the fresh green bite provides a contrast in flavor that is even more important than the color.

(Serves 4 – 6)

> 1 cauliflower
> 3 eggs
> 1½ cups 2%, whole, or evaporated milk
> 4 ounces *sharp* cheddar cheese, grated (about 1 cup)
> 1 teaspoon salt
> ½ teaspoon freshly ground pepper
> ¼ cup minced fresh parsley, if possible

Preheat oven to 325 degrees. Mist a 1½-quart casserole with non-stick spray.

- Clean and trim cauliflower of leaves, and trim stem. *(I prefer to remove stem and most of the core up inside the cauliflower and save for Cauliflower Butter Broth on page 96. However, if it's a small cauliflower I use the whole thing.)* Place cauliflower in steamer basket, stem side down. Steam until tender, about 15 – 25 minutes, depending on the size of the cauliflower. Set aside until cool enough to handle.

- Meanwhile whisk eggs in a mixing bowl (an 8-cup Pyrex jug works well) and add milk, cheese, and seasoning.

- Chop steamed cauliflower into bite-sized pieces. You will probably have between 4 – 6 cups. Add to egg mixture and mix gently.

- Scrape cauliflower mixture into oiled casserole dish. Don't worry if there are bits of cauliflower sticking up. Bake in the middle of the oven for about 50 – 60 minutes or until custard is golden on the edges and no longer wet in the center. *(I suggest reducing the heat to 300 degrees after 30 minutes.)*

Note:
➢ An all-onion version is real soul food for us onion lovers, especially during Walla Walla season. I use 1-inch chunks of roasted or sauteed sweet onions. It takes about 3 large ones, or about 9 cups of chopped fresh onion.

Scalloped Corn

This is a variation on a traditional American recipe, sometimes called corn pudding, and is solidly in the category of comfort food. Those who like vegetables to arrive at the table subdued and creamed especially appreciate it. You can use canned or fresh corn instead of frozen, of course. More importantly, you can hide at least one onion in this dish without anyone noticing!

(Serves 4 – 6)

>10 ounce or 16 ounce frozen petite yellow corn (2 – 3 cups)
>2 tablespoons olive oil
>1 medium onion in ¼-inch dice (about 2 cups)
>1 red or green bell pepper in ¼-inch dice (at least 1 cup)
>4 eggs
>1 cup 2%, whole, or evaporated milk
>8 ounces *sharp* cheddar cheese, grated (about 1 cup)
>1 teaspoon salt
>¼ - ½ teaspoon Tabasco sauce
>(***Optional:*** 4 ounce can green mild chiles, diced – see note)

Preheat oven to 300 degrees. Mist a 1½-quart casserole with non-stick spray.

- Empty frozen corn into a strainer and run under very hot water for about 10 seconds, then set aside to drain. Drain very well.

- Heat oil in 8 – 10-inch skillet over medium high heat and sauté onion 5 minutes. Add bell pepper and continue sautéing another 5 – 10 minutes or until barely tender. Add drained corn and sauté for another few minutes to cook off any water still hanging onto the kernels. (An optional step.)

- Whisk eggs in a mixing bowl (an 8-cup Pyrex jug works well) and add milk, cheese, seasoning, sautéed vegetable mixture, corn, and chiles.

- Scrape into oiled casserole dish and bake custard in the middle of the oven for about 1¼ hours or until custard is golden on the edges and no longer wet in the center. *(Custards tend to separate if not cooked slowly and evenly.)*

Note:
➢ If you have no bell peppers, the canned green chiles are especially welcome. A more serious chile is another option for some who like their food to pack some heat. As for the canned option, I suggest buying whole chiles and dicing them yourself — diced canned chiles may include bits of tough skin and stem.

Marinated Carrot Matchsticks

Cooked carrots are hard for some of us to enjoy but they are easy to prepare *plus* they provide a splash of bright color. A solution is to slice carrots into thin sticks, steam until barely tender, and toss in vinaigrette. Carrots are dominant enough to handle aggressive flavors like cumin, cilantro, and garlic, and a recipe like this allows one to sneak a few of the more assertive root vegetables onto the table. A turnip sliced into matchsticks can be steamed with the carrots; the peppery flavor and clean white color contrast nicely with the carrots. (See *Note* below.)

(Serves 4 – 6)

> 4 – 5 cups ¼-inch matchstick carrots and turnips
> 2 tablespoons lemon juice or cider vinegar
> 2 teaspoons honey
> 1 teaspoon freshly crushed garlic
> 1 teaspoon salt
> 1 teaspoon ground cumin
> 1 teaspoon freshly ground pepper
> 3 tablespoons extra virgin olive oil

- Trim and peel vegetables. Slice carrots diagonally into ¼-inch slices, and then into ¼-inch matchsticks. Slice turnips in half lengthwise, then into ¼-inch slices. Slice into matchsticks, as with carrots. Combine matchsticks to make about 5 cups, and steam for 7 – 10 minutes, or until tender-crisp. *(If you overcook them they will fall apart when you toss them in the vinaigrette.)*

- Combine dressing ingredients in mixing bowl and whisk together. Add steamed matchsticks and toss gently but thoroughly to mix. Serve hot, warm or room temperature. Makes great leftovers.

Note:

➤ Two other vegetables I like to bring in under cover of vinaigrette are rutabagas and kohlrabi. Their names may make it difficult to take them seriously but the point here is not to bring these vegetables to the table just for the sake of diversity or a concern for their self-esteem. (Although how can we like them if they don't like themselves? There are some deep issues here.) More importantly, the peppery brightness of these root vegetables is a welcome foil for the sweetness of the carrots. (Kohlrabi or rutabagas are best when quite small, about the size of plump lemons.)

➤ You can buy julienne carrots in some stores, if you need to. You can also make matchsticks with a food processor attachment or a tool like a mandolin. There is even a peeler look-alike that is actually a julienne slicer made by Oxo, which can create linguini-type matchsticks.

Ratatouille
A (Roasted) Mediterranean Medley

Ratatouille (Rah-tah-TOO-ee) was born in the Provence region of France, and could define the term "Mediterranean" both by its ingredients and simplicity. *Ratatouille* pops up commonly in cookbooks and menus in this country and it is probably safe to say that rarely is justice done to it. *Ratatouille* is juicy, flavorful, rich, and particularly good served over the polenta (on pages 137-138), potatoes, pasta, or as a pizza topping, omelet filling, or in a *frittata*. It can be served at any temperature, from hot to room temperature, and is especially delicious the day after it's made. And the day after that. And so on.

(Serves 6 – 8)

> 1 eggplant (about 1 pound), firm and dark purple, unpeeled
> 3 sweet red, orange, green, and/or gold bell peppers
> ⅔ cup extra-virgin olive oil, divided
> 2 medium – large onions, preferably sweet
> 1 can (28 ounces) peeled diced tomatoes, drained
> ¼ cup finely chopped garlic *or* 2 tablespoons freshly crushed
> ¼ cup fresh chopped basil or 1 teaspoon dried basil
> 1½ teaspoons salt, or to taste
> 1 teaspoon freshly-ground black pepper

Preheat oven to 450 degrees.

- Line a large shallow roasting pan, about 11x16 inches or the largest that will fit into your oven, with heavy duty foil coated with non-stick spray. Trim eggplant (I prefer to leave the glossy purple skin intact) and cut into 1 x ½-inch chunks. Core and seed peppers, and chop into 1-inch chunks. Toss eggplant and peppers together in a large bowl with 1/3-cup olive oil. Spread in the pan, sprinkle with about half the salt and pepper, and roast in the top third of the oven for 20 minutes, or until just barely tender.

- Peel onions and chop into 1 x ½-inch chunks. *(Onion plays the part of a vegetable here, not just a flavoring. Sweet onions tend to have thicker, juicier layers.)* Heat ¼ cup of the oil in a sturdy pot (4 – 5-quart) and sauté onions briskly for 10 minutes or until tender. Add garlic and sauté another 2 minutes. *(You could roast the onions like the eggplant and peppers if you prefer.)*

- Empty diced tomatoes into small strainer to drain. You do not want "petite diced" tomatoes here, by the way. Larger chunks are better. As for fresh tomatoes, they don't have enough flavor for this dish. *(Save the juice, which should amount to about 1 cup or more, for something like Creamy Thai Tomato Soup or Smoooth Butternut Bisque on pages 97 – 98.)*

- Add eggplant and pepper mixture, drained tomatoes, basil and remaining salt, and pepper. Mix gently to avoid mushing soft vegetables. *(The name ratatouille translates literally as "stirred dish", but this recipe tries to avoid any unnecessary stirring. This dish is so much prettier and more appetizing when it's not mushy.)*

- Reduce oven temperature to 350 degrees and bake *ratatouille*, uncovered, for about ½ hour to meld the flavors. *(If you have chosen to roast and sauté more vigorously, as I tend to do, the ratatouille obviously needs no cooking, but the tomatoes need some time to get acquainted.)*

- Serve at any temperature. Liquid will collect, so serve the ratatouille with plenty of good dipping bread.

- *Ratatouille* will keep for several days in the refrigerator, but make sure it has completely cooled before covering and chilling.

Notes:

➤ I never bother with the salting-rinsing-drying business with the eggplant. However, always buy eggplants that are smooth, shiny, and tight in their skin or don't bother buying them at all.

➤ The extra virgin olive oil is an ingredient in its own right, not just a sautéing medium. If you have to substitute with another kind of oil for some unthinkable reason, there's nothing I can do about it: just don't call the dish *ratatouille*. Fresh garlic also has no substitute, but if you choose to use less than this recipe calls for, the dish will still be perfectly legal.

➤ It's important not to roast the vegetables beyond the just-tender stage. The eggplant will melt into indistinguishable blobs and the skin will lift off the peppers. It's best if the vegetables maintain their shape while you combine everything, and they will cook a bit more during the brief baking.

➤ Many *ratatouille* recipes call for zucchini. If you decide to include zucchini, choose slim, smallish ones, if possible. Trim both ends, quarter lengthwise, and slice into 1-inch lengths. Toss with 2 tablespoons extra virgin olive oil, spread in a foil-lined pan, sprinkle with salt and pepper, and roast in the top third of a 450-degree oven for about 15 – 20 minutes.

➤ … but I like zucchini served just about anywhere but in a stew. Texture is not a quality for which zucchinis are admired, and I love them sliced or diced and cooked quickly and uncovered in olive oil, salt, and pepper.

Caponata
(A Sicilian Antipasto)

For every one of us who loves eggplant, there may be three who don't. There is a lot of passion on both sides. A good caponata is so lively and rich, however, that it has a good chance of slipping under the most highly sensitive eggplant radar.

Caponata is related to ratatouille, but is a sort of sweet-and-sour relish than stew. It can be served as a sauce for pasta or rice, or cooked fish, or as a topping for pizza, or with hot or cold meat as a relish, or on bruschetta, and so on and so forth.

(Makes about 6 cups)

> 1 small firm eggplant, unblemished
> 2 – 3 stalks celery
> 1 medium onion
> 1 red bell pepper
> ½ cup olive oil (divided)
> ¼ teaspoon crushed chilies
> 1 fat teaspoon freshly crushed garlic
> 15-ounce can *petite* diced tomatoes
> ½-cup pitted chopped green olives
> 2 tablespoons apple cider vinegar
> 2 tablespoons honey
> 1 teaspoon salt, or to taste
> 1 teaspoon freshly ground pepper
> 1 tablespoon capers
> ¼ cup currants
> ½ cup minced fresh parsley

- Preheat oven to 450 degrees. Line a large baking pan with foil and mist with non-stick spray. Trim ends of eggplant and cut into ½-inch cubes. Toss with ¼ cup olive oil and spread evenly in one layer in pan. Roast eggplant in oven for 20 minutes or until beginning to soften.

- Meanwhile prepare other vegetables. Slice celery lengthwise into halves or thirds, and slice crosswise into ¼ -inch dice. Peel onion, and core, quarter, and seed pepper. Cut each into ¼-½ inch dice. (You should have about 2 cups of onion and 1½ cups each of celery and peppers.)

- Heat remaining ¼ cup olive oil in a heavy 5-quart pot over medium-high heat. Add dried crushed chilies and celery. Sauté 5 – 7 minutes, and then add onion and bell peppers. Sauté until just tender, about 10 minutes longer, depending on the level of heat and the sturdiness of the slices. Add garlic and cook for another minute.

- Stir in half-roasted eggplant and sauté until eggplant is soft. Add petite diced tomatoes with their juice, olives, vinegar, honey, salt, and pepper. (Add capers, currants, and parsley, if you have them) Bring to a simmer and cook gently for about 10 minutes, uncovered. If making in advance, cool thoroughly before covering and refrigerating.

One of my favorite uses for *caponata* is with fresh halibut, as follows:

Place half of the *caponata* recipe in a shallow 1½-quart casserole dish. Place 1 – 2 pounds of fresh halibut filets on top, and cover fish with the remaining *caponata*. Bake uncovered for 30 – 45 minutes in a 350-degree oven until fish can be flaked gently with a fork at its thickest point. This dish pairs nicely with roasted asparagus. The presentation is stunning, and leftover fish and sauce makes can be made into a tasty and colorful chowder.

5

Beans

Beans

Why eat beans? Besides being rich in protein, iron, and B vitamins, beans are a superb source of soluble fiber, and one of this world's best defenses against diabetes, heart disease, cancer, obesity, and osteoporosis. Beans are perhaps the cheapest and safest lipid lowering drugs on the market, *and* they come in pretty colors. In fact, the colored varieties are more antioxidant rich.

Beans also happen to be cheap, available everywhere, simple to cook, and easy to store. You don't even have to *cook* them yourself: you can find a bean for any occasion canned and ready to drain and use in soup, chili, salad, dip, or whatever.

Canned beans

- Home-cooked beans are easy but for spontaneous bean eating there are canned beans. These should be absolute standards in any pantry. They easily stand in for home-cooked beans, and have all the health benefits *plus* a great shelf life, huge variety, and wide availability. (A standard 15 ounce can is about 1¾ cups of beans.) At any time there are about 6 cans each of black beans (I use them the most) and chickpeas in my cupboard.

- For me the most useful canned beans are black beans. They contrast nicely with rice and polenta, and they are small. (Bean size can be important when you are feeding anti-bean folks.) Larger beans like red or white kidney beans are not as easy for non-bean-lovers to eat, and have a firmer texture.

- Chickpeas (garbanzo beans) are among the richest sources of the anticancer

compounds called *protease inhibitors*[1], as well as soluble and insoluble fiber, folate, and iron. They are probably best known for their role in the Middle Eastern dip called *hummus*. (See page 62.) Red kidney beans are also usually represented partly because they're so pretty, but mainly because they feature nicely in bean marinades and some chilies.

Frozen beans

- You should also be able to find fresh frozen beans, like baby lima beans, speckled butter beans (delicious name!), black-eyed peas, and fresh soybeans (*edamame*) in the frozen vegetable section of your supermarket. These cook quickly straight from the freezer, and are delightful hot and buttered with salt and pepper, or tossed with olive oil, freshly crushed garlic, salt, and pepper, or dressed with vinaigrette and served at any temperature.

To prepare dried beans

- Check beans for sick, shriveled or broken beans, or any non-bean material like rocks or little lumps of dried mud, both of which can look bean-like if you're not alert. (Sometimes other types of beans will turn up, like a glossy red kidney bean in a batch of chalk-white Great Northern beans, which is fun. You can always include visitors.)

- Rinse in a strainer and place in a large heavy-bottomed pot or saucepan (at least 3-quart size) and add enough cold water to cover beans by about 3 – 4 inches. Remember that beans can swell to almost 3 times their original volume. Remove any floaters.

---

[1] *The Food Pharmacy Guide to Good Eating*, Jean Carper©1991

- If you opt to soak the beans, set them aside for 4 – 12 hours. For a pound of beans, which is about 2 cups, use about 10 cups of cold water.

To cook beans
- For about 5 – 6 cups cooked beans, start with 2 cups of dried beans. (This is about 1 pound of beans.) Place beans in a 5-quart pot and cover with about 8 cups of cold water. Beans should be covered by about 3 inches of water.

- Place pot over a medium heat and bring to a rolling boil. Reduce the heat to low and let the beans simmer very gently for about 1 – 3 hours, depending on the size and age of the bean, or until tender. (Lentils take only about 30 – 40 minutes to cook, while chickpeas can take 3 hours.) Don't try to rush the cooking — slow and gentle is best for beans. Boiling beans damages their little coats and they tend to disintegrate.

- After about 30 minutes, add a couple of teaspoons of salt. It is said that cooking beans with salt toughens them, but the fact is that beans taste *much* better cooked with salt; adding salt in the second half of the cooking period is a good compromise.

- Cool beans in their cooking broth (if the recipe allows) for better texture and flavor. It's also handy to store the beans in the refrigerator in the cooking liquid: they keep nicely, and the bean broth can be added to soup, with or without beans.

- Never add acidic ingredients like tomatoes or vinegar to beans before they are completely cooked; the acid will inhibit the softening process.

More about soaking
Bean-cooking experts still seem to disagree as to whether or not soaking beans is important. Soaking may improve the texture of the beans and help them cook more evenly, as well as reduce the cooking time a bit. Soaking also reduces the potential for certain digestive problems, if you discard the soaking water. I never discard the soaking water. *(More about the digestion issue further on.)*

If you're in a hurry or gripped by a sudden and impatient craving, skip the soak step or use the quick-soak method: bring beans to a hard boil in lots of cold water, then remove from heat, cover, and let sit for an hour. ***However***, some experts say that if you can't soak the beans for at least 4 hours, just cook them longer, as the quick-soak method is ineffectual. One begins to suspect that soaking beans before cooking is simply not a life-or-death matter.

The digestion issue
It is suggested by other experts, or perhaps even the same experts, that the digestive problems associated with beans are minimized by pouring away the soak water with most of the pesky water-soluble oligosaccharides. But you're also pouring out nutrients and antioxidants leached out by soaking. A better solution is to cook them longer, eventually making the offending carbohydrates more digestible. (Julia Child suggests that anyone concerned about the minimal loss of nutrients that get thrown out with the bean soaking water should just eat a minimal amount *more* of the beans.) Also, cooking the beans with garlic is said to help – although I'm not sure it should be legal to cook beans *without* garlic. One sensible approach would be to eat two or three tablespoons of beans every day until your digestive system learns to appreciate them.

Easy Beans

You could call this a sort of soup. Should you prefer something soupier, add more liquid and mash some of the beans. If you choose to double the recipe, turn leftovers into a type of minestrone by adding broth and the mirepoix recipe on page 68, or use the mini-minestrone recipe on the same page. My favorite beans are Anasazi, but a white bean like cannellini may be more traditional.

> 1½ cups dried beans
> 6 cups water
> 1 large onion in ½-inch dice
> 1 tablespoon chopped fresh garlic
> 1½ teaspoons salt
> ¼ teaspoon dried thyme
> ¼ teaspoon dried oregano
> ¼ - ½ teaspoon crushed red chilies
> ¼ cup extra virgin olive oil

- (See *Beans* on the preceding pages for more preparation information.) Combine beans and cold water in a 3-quart pot and bring to the boil. Reduce heat to low and cook uncovered at a slow simmer for about 1 hour.

- Add diced onion, garlic, salt, herbs, crushed chilies, and olive oil, and stir into the beans. Continue simmering gently until beans are very tender. (If the water level drops to the bean level, add another cup or so of water.) Cooked beans should mash easily with a fork.

- Serve the beans in bowls with their broth, like soup. A side of freshly grated Parmesan is a good idea, and a buttered slice of whole-wheat honey bread.

Lazy Lentils

I love lentils for their peppery nuttiness and simplicity of preparation. Whether or not *you* love them, they are useful beans to know because they cook so quickly. This is a favorite last-minute dinner, but lentils work equally well as salad, soup, or main dish. There are red, yellow, brown, black, and little French green lentils, but the brown are the biggest and most versatile.

> 1½ cups brown lentils
> 6 cups of water
> 1½ teaspoons of salt
> ¼ cup extra virgin olive oil
> 1 large onion, diced (3 – 4 cups)
> ½ teaspoon crushed chilies
> 1 teaspoon ground cumin
> 1 tablespoon freshly crushed garlic
> ½ teaspoon fresh ground pepper
> (¼ cup chopped fresh cilantro)

- Combine lentils and cold water in a 3-quart pot and bring to the boil. Reduce heat to low. Add salt and cook partly covered at a slow simmer for 40 minutes or until tender.

- Meanwhile, dice onion (about 3 cups). Heat the oil in a non-stick 10-inch skillet and add the onion, chilies, and cumin. Sauté about 10 minutes or until onion is tender. Add garlic and sauté another 2 minutes.

- Add onion mixture to pot of cooked lentils. Add pepper and simmer for another 5 minutes. Stir in fresh cilantro, if you have it, and serve in soup bowls with a side of hot brown rice.

Sprouting Lentils

There are just a few steps to sprouting anything; pick over, rinse, soak, drain, and then rinse and drain about two times each day until sprouts are to your liking. Lentil sprouts are my personal favorites among sprouts; they're plump and crunchy and delicious tossed through a salad. Plus, they're easy to do.

- First, find ½ cup of brown lentils. Check them as usual for rocks or other foreign bodies, then place into a wide-mouthed jar, and rinse by filling the jar with water, stirring vigorously to settle the floating lentils, and pouring off most of the water and any floating things. Repeat, then half-fill the jar with water and set aside for about 6 hours or overnight.

- Tip soaked lentils into a wire meshed sieve, rinse well, and cover with a couple of layers of wet paper towel. Place in a bowl or something to drain. (I use a 6-inch sieve that fits perfectly inside a 1½-quart bowl.) *If you are using a jar with a screened sprouting lid, which you can generally find at natural food stores, simply drain the lentils, then fill jar with fresh water and drain again immediately.*

- Set drained lentils aside in a cool spot out of direct light. Now, all you have to do is to remember to rinse and drain the lentils twice a day. **Drain thoroughly.** That's all there is to it. The lentils will have sprouted enough to be eaten in just a couple of days.

- Keep refrigerated.

Note:
➤ You can apply the sprouting instructions above to many other grains, seeds, or beans. Some seeds or beans require a longer soaking time than wheat, and most require a longer sprouting time, but one sprouting rule never varies: sprouts will spoil if allowed to stay too wet or too warm. (Bad bacteria flourish under these conditions.) The idea is to maintain a moist, cool environment.

Other Sprout Options

- **Wheat** sprouts are a delicious addition to cold cereal like rolled oats or muesli. Wheat sprouts taste best if the sprouts are about ¼-inch. This takes just a couple of days.

- **Sunflower seeds** are *fast*: they sprout in about one day, and become delicately crunchy. Eat them when their sprouts are only barely showing. I only soak them for two hours or so before draining and setting aside to sprout. They don't store well after they've sprouted (they develop black speckles) so eat them or toss them into salads within a day or two. They taste so good that it is hard *not* to eat them quickly.

- **Mung bean** sprouts are good, but you need to shake the sprouted beans a handful at a time in a metal pie pan to check for the rock-like unsprouted beans. You can find them by the distinctive rattle they make in the pan. Home-sprouted mung beans are nothing like the long, juicy bean sprouts you find in Asian markets and some produce sections of supermarkets, but are still tasty stir-fried briefly in butter with lemon juice.

Fresh Frozen Beans

Most common are baby green lima beans, green soybeans, speckled butter beans (delicious name) and black-eye peas. Check for freezer burn: if the beans look shriveled when you open the bag or box, the situation is possibly hopeless. They will probably taste freezer-burnt and won't soften much as they cook. Try to buy beans that break up fairly easily when you handle them. If the beans are in a solid icy clump it's a bad sign. If you want to try anyway, cover with water and simmer until tender. Fresh frozen beans, whether leftover or straight from the freezer, are a good addition to minestrone-type soups.

Green soybeans cook in about 5 minutes, baby limas in about 10 minutes, speckled butter beans in about 15 minutes and black-eye peas in about 30 minutes.

Fresh Soybeans
The Japanese call them *edamame* (*ed-uh-MAH-may*). They have a nutty, sweet quality and firm texture that some may prefer to the more beany texture of the similar looking baby green lima beans. The availability of fresh soybeans in supermarket freezer departments is amazingly widespread, probably because they are arguably the most delicious soy product on the market. You can even find them fresh in the pod (Asian markets are your best bet) as well as cooked and ready-to-eat.

Fresh green soybeans are a particularly sensible source of soy because they are unprocessed. I usually serve them on their own, whether in or out of the pod (see recipes on following page), because they are such a pretty shade of green and taste so good. They make a fine replacement for lima beans in my *Succotash Salad* (page 116) or anywhere else.

Tofu

There are those who consider tofu to be a sort of practical joke played on the gullible Americans (the same ones who eat shark cartilage) by a fun-loving Japan. And it may be true, but it's nice when something as practical as tofu can be fixed up to taste so good.

The two tofu recipes in this book use extra firm tofu — *Tofu (in soy ginger marinade)* on page 114 and *Tofu Pâté* on page 61. The marinated tofu doesn't last long in our house: if I marinate tofu for the purposes of a stir-fry, I have to make extra for snacking. Tofu Pâté is a wonderful egg salad substitute.

What is it?
Tofu is pressed soy milk curds made from soybeans. Tofu's very blandness and ability to absorb flavors makes it a perfect candidate for marinating, and then either being served as an appetizer or tossed through a stir-fry. It comes in a wide range of textures, from "silken", which is soft enough to disappear into dips and smoothies, to "extra firm", which you can buy in a ready-to-prepare form that requires no draining or pressing to remove excess liquid.

Draining Tofu
If you buy tofu packed in water in a plastic tub, you should press out the excess water. Wrap tofu in a clean kitchen towel and place on a plate. Place another plate over the wrapped tofu, and put something heavy on top, like a telephone book. Set aside for about ½ hour or so. (If you're hungry, 15 minutes works fine, too.) Tofu absorbs flavors more effectively after this step.

Seductive Soybeans
Edamame

This is a very simple treatment and a lovely side dish all by itself.

(Makes about 3 cups)

> 16-ounce bag frozen green
>   soybeans (*edamame*)
> 1 cup water
> 1 teaspoon salt
>
> 2 tablespoons extra virgin olive oil
> 1 tablespoons apple cider vinegar
> 1 teaspoon freshly crushed garlic
> ½ teaspoon salt
> ¼ teaspoon freshly ground pepper

- Bring water to a boil in a 2-quart saucepan and add salt and soybeans. Bring back to a boil, gently shaking the pan to break up any clumps of beans. Reduce heat to low, cover, and simmer for about 5 minutes.

- Meanwhile combine olive oil, vinegar, garlic, salt and pepper in a mixing bowl.

- When soybeans are cooked, drain and add to the oil and vinegar mixture. Toss to thoroughly coat beans. Let sit for 10 minutes, tossing a few times. Serve at any temperature. (Freshly cooked or room temperature is best, I think.)

Soybeans in the pod

These are generally in the freezer next to the regular green soybeans. They make great finger food; some Japanese restaurants serve a little bowl of them on the table as a sort of pre-appetizer.

> 16 ounce bag frozen soy bean pods
> 1 tablespoon of salt

- Bring 2 – 3 quarts of water to a boil. Add a heaping tablespoon of salt. Empty frozen pods into the boiling water. Bring back to the boil, and cook for about 3 – 5 minutes. (Alternatively, steam the pods for 5 – 7 minutes.)

- Drain and sprinkle with salt, and then serve anywhere, anytime. Just squeeze the soybeans from their pods straight into your mouth. (Lay out a bowl to hold the empty pods.)

Note:
➤ These are good hot, cold, or anywhere between. You can snack on them for days: just store them in a bag or covered dish and pull them out of the refrigerator whenever you feel like nibbling. These are also great company on car trips.

Tofu
in Soy Ginger Marinade

These tasty tofu sticks have been gobbled happily by people who have assured me they *hate* tofu. And it's so easy with extra-firm tofu vacuum-packed in minimal water; all you have to do is pat it dry with a paper towel.

10 ounces extra-firm tofu

Soy Ginger Marinade
⅓ cup soy sauce
2 tablespoons toasted sesame oil
1 tablespoon apple cider vinegar
1 tablespoon honey
1 tablespoon freshly crushed garlic
1 tablespoon finely minced fresh ginger
½ teaspoon crushed red pepper, or to taste

- Drain tofu, pat dry, and slice into sticks about ½-inch x ¼-inch. For that matter, make any sized sticks you want: if you want tofu to marinate quickly, make the sticks thinner, but if you plan to store the marinated tofu in the refrigerator to snack from during the week, chunkier slices are easier to handle.

- Combine marinade ingredients in a shallow storage dish and whisk to blend. (A container wide enough to hold the tofu sticks in one or two layers is ideal.)

- Add tofu, making sure all surfaces are covered with marinade. Set aside for at least 10 minutes, and then tilt dish back and forth to allow marinade to flow around tofu before setting aside for another 10 minutes or so. Taste. It should be ready to eat. It will keep happily in your refrigerator for several days although the tofu will darken to the color of the soy sauce. *(I recycle the marinade in a stir-fry, with or without the tofu.)*

Note:

➢ It's easy to keep fresh ginger on hand; just buy a firm, smoothish knob of ginger, cut into walnut sized chunks, and store them submerged in sherry in a glass jar in the refrigerator. Peeling the ginger is optional, but it's easy to remove the thin skin with a vegetable peeler. You can store it for months.

➢ The marinade works equally well for marinating chicken, or for saucing a stir-fry, or for dressing an oriental noodle salad. Your personal tastes can dictate amounts of ginger, garlic, or crushed peppers.

Luscious Lima Beans

The lima bean is a victim of a cultural bean bias. There are otherwise open-minded grown-ups who won't touch lima beans on principle, and who think lima beans aren't even an acceptable subject of conversation. Unlike canned peas, which some consider irredeemable, lima beans don't deserve their reputation. At least green baby lima beans don't.

Innocent children, untainted by the cultural bias and with tastes uncorrupted by their parents' preconceptions, generally love these particular lima beans. I presented this recipe for the first time to my buddy Robbie when he was about 1½ years old, and he thought they were *very* good. (He was a man of few words but he had strong opinions about food, and his judgements were usually accurate.) At the time of this writing Robbie is now a teenager, but he *still* thinks these lima beans are good. Is there a higher recommendation?

(Enough for Robbie and me, and maybe a few close friends.)

> 1 bag (16 ounces) frozen baby lima beans
> 1 cup water
> ½ teaspoon salt
>
> ¼ cup extra virgin olive oil
> 1 – 2 tablespoons apple cider vinegar
> 1 teaspoon freshly crushed garlic
> ½ teaspoon salt
> ¼ - ½ teaspoon freshly ground pepper

- Bring water to boil in a 2-quart saucepan, and add salt. Add frozen lima beans and bring back to a boil, gently breaking up any big clumps of beans. Reduce heat to low, cover, and simmer for about 7 – 15 minutes. Beans should be tender but not mushy. *(Packet directions may say anything from 10 – 20 minutes, but the key words are "until tender". Don't judge doneness by testing beans with wrinkly skins: they take much longer to soften.)*

- Meanwhile, combine the olive oil, vinegar, garlic, salt, and pepper in your mixing bowl. When lima beans are cooked, drain in a colander and add to the oil and vinegar mixture and toss. Let sit for 10 minutes, and then toss again. Yum. Serve hot, warm, or room temperature.

Note:
➢ If lima beans are unable to gain a toehold in your freezer for whatever tragic reasons, you can substitute any fresh frozen beans, like speckled butter beans, green soybeans (edamame), or black-eye peas. Robbie found them all acceptable. Check for freezer burn: if the frozen beans look shriveled they will probably taste freezer-burnt. Yuck. Not a good way to introduce *Luscious Limas* to your family.

Succotash Salad

This is a good dish for a picnic, a potluck, or any kind of hungry gathering. It looks pretty and is sturdy enough for even hot weather. I think it tastes better if it isn't eaten straight from the refrigerator. You can substitute the lima beans in this succotash with green soybeans (*edamame*) or speckled butter beans. (See note following the recipe for *Luscious Limas* on the preceding page.)

(Serves 4 – 6)

>1 box (10 ounces) frozen baby lima beans (about 2 cups)
>1 cup water
>½ teaspoon salt
>
>1 box (10 ounces) thawed petite corn (about 2 cups, very well drained)
>1 cup finely diced sweet onion
>1 sweet red pepper in ¼-inch dice (or about 1 cup)
>¼ cup extra virgin olive oil
>¼ cup vinegar
>1 teaspoon salt
>½ teaspoon freshly ground pepper

- Bring water to boil in a 2-quart saucepan, and add salt. Add frozen lima beans and bring back to a boil, gently breaking up any big clumps of beans. Reduce heat to low, cover, and simmer for about 7 – 15 minutes. Beans should be tender but not mushy.

- Combine diced onion and peppers with oil, vinegar, salt, and pepper in a mixing bowl. Add drained corn and lima beans and toss gently with a large rubber spatula. *(Don't be stingy with the salt and pepper. Beans and corn can overwhelm your average flavoring efforts.)*

Note:
➢ To thaw frozen corn, empty into a colander and run under very hot water for a few seconds, then shake off excess water and toss gently in a colander lined with paper towels. Alternatively, heat a tablespoon of olive oil in a hot skillet, add the thawed corn, and then sauté the corn quickly to cook off any residual water. It's not necessary, but it does make the corn taste better.

➢ For warm winter succotash, add the onion and peppers to 2 tablespoons of olive oil in a hot 8-inch skillet, sauté briskly for about 5 minutes, and then add the corn and sauté for another 5 minutes. Then add to the lima beans and remaining olive oil, vinegar and seasoning.

Tuscan Bean Salad

This is an example of a classic Mediterranean treatment of beans, and a point of departure for your own tastes. You can turn this salad into a Tuscan meal by adding a finely sliced fennel bulb and some very good tuna packed in olive oil. Bean salad variations are endless, and their relaxed attitude toward time and temperature are legendary, but the mix of tang and richness make practical considerations seem irrelevant. It's nice to know a salad you can trust.

(Serves about 6)

> 1½ cups small white beans, uncooked (or about 3½ cups cooked)
> several cloves of garlic, peeled and sliced or smashed (see ***Note***)
> 1 tablespoon salt
>
> ¼ cup lemon juice
> (zest from lemon – see page 36 for more on lemon zest)
> ¼ cup extra-virgin olive oil
> 2 teaspoons freshly crushed garlic
> 1 teaspoon salt
> 1 teaspoon freshly ground black pepper
> 1 cup finely diced red pepper
> 1 cup finely diced sweet onion
> ½ cup minced fresh parsley

- Check and rinse beans, then place in a 3-quart pot or saucepan with the garlic and enough water to cover by 3 inches. Bring to a boil, then reduce heat to low and simmer quietly for about 1 — 1½ hours or until beans are tender. *Add salt after 45 minutes.*

- Scoop out ¼ cup of the bean cooking water and set aside. Pour cooked beans into a strainer, and then tip drained beans into a large mixing bowl. Add the ¼ cup hot cooking water and the remaining ingredients. Toss thoroughly but gently with a big rubber spatula. It may seem wet just after it's made but the beans absorb liquid as time goes by, which is the reason for the dollop of bean water. Bean salads should be luscious.

- Serve any time. This salad is especially good when eaten while still warm, but is also delicious after a night in the refrigerator.

Note:
➢ For the garlic cooked with the beans this is a good time to use those skinny slippery little cloves that tend to cluster at the center of the heads. One firm but restrained tap with the bottom of a glass should barely crush the cloves and conveniently loosen their skins for easy peeling.

Black Bean, Corn, and Jicama Salad
with Lemon & Cilantro Vinaigrette

This salad is crunchy, colorful, flavor-packed, easily made, and good for two or three days of snacking or supplementing a meal. Leftovers are intentional. Sometimes it can be difficult to track down a happy, healthy-looking jicama but it's actually a fine salad without it. The red bell pepper is important for color, however. (For more on jicama, see final *Note*.)

(Serves about 6 – 8)

1 can (15 ounces) black beans
1 box (10 ounces) frozen corn (about 2 cups)
1 medium-sized jicama (1 – 1½ lbs)
1 red bell pepper
1 cup ¼-inch diced sweet onion

Lemon & Cilantro Vinaigrette:
¼ cup lemon or lime juice
2 teaspoons freshly crushed garlic
1 teaspoon chili powder
1 teaspoon ground cumin
1 teaspoon salt
½ teaspoon Tabasco sauce
½ teaspoon freshly ground black pepper
¼ cup olive oil
½ cup chopped fresh cilantro

- Rinse black beans and set aside to drain very well. Place frozen corn in a strainer and thaw by running briefly under hot water while shaking the corn gently. *(Make sure corn is thoroughly drained by tossing in a colander lined with paper towels until the towels stop absorbing water. Use the same method for beans, if necessary.)*

- If jicama has tough brown skin, strip off with paring knife, and then peel once more with regular peeler. Slice into ¼-inch dice. *(You will have 2 – 3 cups.)* Dice onion and red bell pepper.

- Combine all vinaigrette ingredients in a mixing bowl. Add beans, corn, jicama, onion, and bell pepper, and mix thoroughly with a rubber spatula. Cover and chill until ready to serve, mixing again just before serving.

Note:
➢ This salad should be lively: the beans and corn tend to absorb a lot of flavor, so don't skimp on the salt and heat.

> Green bell pepper substitutes nicely for red, but the salad could use a bit of red color. I like to peel the peppers with a regular vegetable peeler. The skins can be a bit tough and they are certainly easier to slice without their skins.

> Jicama (*HEE-kuh-muh*) is a vegetable that looks like a tan oversized turnip, has the crisp texture of a water chestnut, and a flavor that is both slightly sweet and starchy. Choose a jicama with smooth, hard skin.

Three-Bean Thing

Variations of this appear on salad bars everywhere. Something only becomes a cliché when it is used often, and it usually means that it works. You can use any beans you like but these are sturdy and still look fresh a week later. If the onion is mild I would definitely use 2 cups. Diced bell pepper of any color is a good addition (and traditional, too) if you have some.

(Makes about 5 cups)

    1 cup onion, sliced in thin strips, about 1/8-inch x 1 inch
    2 tablespoons extra virgin olive oil
    2 tablespoons apple cider vinegar
    2 – 3 cloves garlic, crushed
    1 teaspoon salt
    ½ teaspoon freshly ground pepper

    1 can (15 ounces) red kidney beans
    1 can (15 ounces) garbanzo beans (chickpeas)
    1 can (15 ounces) cut green beans

- Combine onion with oil, vinegar, salt, pepper, and garlic and set aside. *(This marinates the onions slightly, making them tastier and milder if they are hot.)*

- Drain and rinse kidney beans and chickpeas and set aside in colander to drain thoroughly. (Tossing beans in the colander with a dry paper towel helps.)

- Drain green beans. (S&W cut green & wax beans are pretty if you can find them.) Combine all drained beans with onions in dressing and mix well.

Note:
> This makes quite a bit (I can't find these beans in smaller tins) but you can combine leftovers with cooked pasta spirals, chopped fresh tomatoes, and extra vinaigrette as a quick main dish salad.

Warm Lentil Salad

People who recoil at bean salads can relax. Lentils have a peppery nuttiness and a disarming daintiness that allow them to slip under the radar. Furthermore, this is possibly impossible to dislike. As well as being simple and relatively last minute (lentils cook in about 30 minutes), this recipe is very forgiving. You can use ½ cup of any dressing you happen to like or have already made. You can substitute your own choice of vegetables, like green onions and sweet red bell peppers, or just minced onion. It's an especially good dish to have ready when you're expecting to feed a group that may include vegetarians. Personally, I like to make enough for me to snack on for a week.

(Serves 6)

> 1½ cups brown lentils
> 6 cups water
> 1 tablespoon salt
>
> ¼ cup apple cider vinegar
> ¼ cup olive oil
> 1 teaspoon freshly crushed garlic
> 1 teaspoon salt
> ½ teaspoon freshly ground pepper
> ½ teaspoon ground cumin
> 1 cup minced sweet onion
> 1 cup ¼ -inch diced cucumber
> 1 cup ½ -inch diced tomato
> (½ cup chopped fresh cilantro, if you have it)

- Rinse lentils, and then combine with the water and the tablespoon of salt. Bring to a simmer and simmer until lentils are tender, 30 – 40 minutes. (Check after 30 minutes.) You should have about 4 cups of cooked lentils.

- While lentils are cooking, combine vinegar, olive oil, garlic, seasoning, and onion in a mixing bowl. Set aside until lentils have finished cooking. Drain lentils in a colander. Add hot, drained lentils to dressing and onion mixture and toss thoroughly but gently. Set salad aside for about 15 minutes to marry flavors, tossing once or twice.

- Add cucumber, tomato, and fresh cilantro, if you have it. Toss again. Serve hot, warm, or room temperature.

Note:
➢ Like any type of bean salad, this begs to be part of a buffet. It pairs nicely with something like *Marinated Carrot Matchsticks* on page 103.

Quick Little Black Bean Chili

Serious chili cooks would probably object to the use of the name *chili*, given that there is neither meat nor an honest chile in this dish. It doesn't even use pinto beans! Its attraction is that it is quick, satisfying, and assembled from ingredients I always have on hand. We love it, whatever it is. You can add meat, naturally, although it doesn't need it. This is also easily expanded to serve more people. For more on expansion and additions see *Note*.

(Makes about 4 cups of chili)

> 2 – 4 tablespoons olive oil
> 1 medium – large onion in ¼ inch dice (2 – 3 cups)
> 1 tablespoon chili powder
> 1 teaspoon ground cumin
> 1 – 3 teaspoons freshly crushed garlic
> 1 teaspoon salt
> 1 plump teaspoon honey
> ¼ teaspoon Tabasco sauce, or more to taste
> 1 can (14 ounces) black beans, rinsed and drained (about 1½ cups)
> 1 can (14 ounces) crushed tomatoes in purée
> 1 can (7 ounces) mild whole green chilies, diced

- Heat olive oil in a heavy 3-quart pot over medium-high heat. Sauté diced onion for 10 minutes or until onions are tender.

- Add chili powder, cumin, garlic, and salt. Sauté for another two minutes.

- Add honey, Tabasco sauce, black beans, tomatoes, and diced chilies. Bring to a simmer, and then cook gently for about 10 minutes. Mighty tasty served over *Easy Cheesy Polenta* (page 131). Or melt some grated cheddar cheese over a pile of hot brown rice, then top with chili.

Note:
➢ To make enough for leftovers I use 2 cans of beans, a 28-ounce can of tomatoes, and increase the seasoning by about half. If I have any bell peppers or celery tops that look like they might be feeling neglected I usually dice them finely and sauté with the onions.

➢ Of course, minced fresh hot chiles are an authentic alternative to Tabasco, but fresh chile users don't need me to tell them. For more on chili see the following recipe for *Chili*.

Chili
(*con* beans & maybe *con carne*)

This can be simple or complex, fancy or plain, vegetarian or not. You can use whatever beans you like. (I cook Anasazi beans or use canned pinto beans, and some prefer kidney beans.) You can make it hot, or tame like this version. You also may prefer a soupier chili than this one. Sides of grated cheese, sliced green onions, and sour cream can round out the dish nicely. Chili goes equally well with brown rice (with a layer of grated cheese to be melted by the hot chili), polenta, or baked potatoes, but I like it best served over *Easy Cheesy Polenta* (page 138) with sides of *Pico de Gallo* and *Avocado Salsa* (both on page 90.)

(Serves 4 – 6)

> ¼ cup olive oil
> 2 medium-large onions, diced (at least 4 cups)
> 1 – 2 green bell peppers, diced
> 1 tablespoon freshly crushed garlic
> 2 tablespoon chili powder
> 2 teaspoons ground cumin
> 1 teaspoon oregano
> 1 fat tablespoon honey
> 2 teaspoon salt
> 1 teaspoon freshly ground pepper
> 1 can (28 ounces) petite diced or crushed tomatoes
> 3 – 4 cups cooked beans (15 ounce can is about 1½-cups drained beans)
> (2 – 4 cups diced, minced or shredded cooked meat or leftover meatloaf)
> ½ - 1 cup chopped cilantro, if available

- Heat oil in 4 – 6-quart heavy pot over medium high heat and sauté onions briskly for about 5 minutes, then add peppers and cook for 5 more minutes, or until both are softened. Stir in garlic and seasonings and cook for another few minutes. *(If you would like to add a few cups of cooked and shredded or diced meat, or a pound or so of raw ground beef, this is the time to stir it in.)*

- Drain and rinse canned beans. (To cook them yourself, see *Beans* on page 108 – 109.) Add tomatoes and beans to vegetable mixture. Bring to a simmer and cook very gently, uncovered, for about 30 minutes, stirring from time to time. Avoid letting the chili boil. Keep in mind that the longer you cook it, the drier it gets. Taste for flavor – the chili may need more salt and pepper, or a dose of bottled fire of your choice, depending on the amount of beans and/or meat you ended up using. Add cilantro within an hour of serving, if possible. *(If made in advance, let cool completely, uncovered, before storing in refrigerator.)*

6   Whole Grains

Brown Rice
Other Grains
Polenta
Grain Salads and Sides

Brown Rice

Brown rice has twice as much fiber as white rice because it has not been stripped of its bran. It may be the least likely of all grains and cereals to provoke intestinal gas and is anti-diarrheal as well as a natural laxative. It will not irritate sensitive colons and discourages peptic ulcers. Brown rice contains anti-cancer protease inhibitors, lowers cholesterol, and tends to block the development of kidney stones. However you happen to feel about brown rice, it certainly seems to like you, anyway.

Brown rice is nutrition-dense, fiber-rich, and fluent in just about any language or culture you choose. It can be a side dish, main dish, salad, bread, or dessert. Also, brown rice is equally agreeable with beans, cheese, meat, eggs, nuts, fish, and cooked or raw vegetables. Some of us even enjoy brown rice as a hot or cold breakfast cereal with milk and honey.

This is the most useful of all the grains, in my opinion, which is why most of my whole grain recipes call for brown rice. I suggest making a batch at least once a week and storing it in the refrigerator for snacks or meals any time of day.

Which Variety?
In large stores with bulk grain sections you can find a mind boggling selection of long, short, and medium-grain rice, both domestic and imported, organic and otherwise, and including brown, white, red, black, sticky, sweet, jasmine, and basmati. (Wild rice, by the way, is the seed of a wild grass and not technically part of the rice family.)

The delicate and aromatic brown basmati rice is my preference for most purposes, so I tend to buy it and cook it without giving any thought to other varieties. Short grain brown rice, however, is better for recipes where plumper, moister rice is appropriate, like *Brown Rice Power Patties* (page 128). Also, if you are serving rice as a simple side dish, the stickier short grain rice is easier to pick up with a fork.

For *Mother's Brown Rice Pudding* (page 129) my choice is the short-grain sweet (also called sticky) brown rice. It is very glutinous and clumpy when cooked, and it really is a better texture in rice pudding (or rice patties) than the dryer basmati.

If you cook sticky rice as you do regular brown rice, it will turn into wet, glutinous sludge. Sticky rice should be soaked for 8 – 24 hours, and then steamed for an hour. (I use a sieve that fits snugly in a 3-quart saucepan. The lid happens to fit the rim of the sieve perfectly, but you can use foil to make your own lid.) Make sure the water underneath doesn't touch the rice.

Reheating
The best way to reheat brown rice is by steaming. It will taste freshly made, as well as wait patiently over the steam until you are ready to serve. Don't let the pot boil dry! I set a basket steamer in a saucepan (the size of the basket and saucepan depend on the amount of rice I'm heating) with water added to just below the basket. I then place the cold cooked rice in the basket, bring the water to a boil and cover. Three cups of cold cooked rice takes about 15 minutes to heat through.

Brown rice freezes well. I pack it in 2-cup portions that will fit in my rice steaming pot.

Basic Baked Brown Rice

A lot of people think they don't like brown rice because they have only eaten badly cooked or undercooked brown rice. This is the only way I cook rice; starting it on the stove top, then sticking it in the oven and forgetting about it until the timer rings an hour later.

The most common cooking directions for brown rice involve simmering the rice and water on the stovetop for about 45 minutes. My directions call for baking the rice in the oven for an hour. With the baking method I can forget the rice while it is cooking and am never at the mercy of capricious burners.

There are other cooking options you may prefer — like steaming, pressure-cooking, or using a rice cooker — but the important thing is that final texture of the rice should be tender and moist. In any case it is one of the most intelligent leftovers you could hope to find in your refrigerator.

(Makes about 5-6 cups cooked brown rice)

> 2 cups brown *basmati* rice (see note)
> 4 cups water
> 1 teaspoon salt

Preheat oven to 300 degrees.

- Bring the water to a brisk boil in a heavy 2½-quart pot. Stir in salt and rice and bring back to the boil. Stir again, cover, and transfer to the oven. Bake 1 hour.

- Remove lid, fluff with a fork, and cover with a towel (a paper towel works fine) until cool. Whatever you don't use the same day, store in the refrigerator, covered tightly. *(Make sure rice is completely cool before you cover it.)* Keeps well for a week. See reheating suggestion on previous page.

Note:

➢ If you use *short grain* brown rice, use 3¾ cups of water to 2 cups of rice.

➢ *Basmati* rice has a nutty fragrance and a more delicate texture than regular brown rice and I use it for most purposes.

➢ I never cook less than 2 cups of rice at a time, which makes about 5 – 6 cups of cooked rice. I sleep a lot better if I know there is leftover rice in the refrigerator.

Nutty Brown Rice

This is a great rice dish; simply made, interesting-looking, and decadent tasting. It is a particularly good last-minute dish if you keep pecans and sesame seeds on hand in the refrigerator, as I do. My quick version leaves out the green onions and nuts.

(Serves 4 – 6)

¼ cup olive oil
¼ teaspoon crushed red chili flakes
1 bunch green onions, thinly sliced
3½ - 4 cups *cooked* brown rice
1 scant teaspoon salt
½ cup raw or toasted chopped nuts (walnuts, almonds, or pecans)
¼ cup sesame seeds, toasted

- Heat oil over medium heat in large skillet (preferably a heavy stovetop-to-table sort of pan) and add chili flakes. Cook gently in the oil for a couple of minutes, then add green onions. Sauté for about 30 seconds: onions should be barely softened and still bright green.

- Add rice, salt, nuts, and seeds. Toss until heated through.

Toasting Raw Sesame Seeds:

Tip about ½-cup or so (you might as well toast enough for a couple of batches) into a shallow baking pan and toast in a 325-degree oven for 5 – 10 minutes. Keep an anxious eye on the seeds and shake the pan after a few minutes. They cook quickly and it takes very little time for golden and sweet to become brown and bitter. Remember also that they will continue to cook in the hot pan even after you take them out of the oven.

Quick Brown Rice Pilaf

This is another easy way to present brown rice to an unsympathetic audience. In pilafs the grain is cooked with the liquid (often broth) and vegetables. Here the pilaf concept is an afterthought, but it works well with leftover rice and last minute dinners.

(Serves 4 – 6)

¼ cup extra virgin olive oil
1 medium onion in ¼-inch dice
1 red bell pepper in ¼-inch dice
8 ounces fresh mushrooms, chopped
1 teaspoon freshly crushed garlic

3 cups *cooked* brown rice
1 teaspoon salt
½ teaspoon freshly ground pepper
½ cup of minced parsley

- Heat oil in 10 – 12-inch skillet over medium high heat. Sauté onion (1½ - 2 cups) 5 minutes, then add peppers and/or mushrooms, if you have them. Sauté until tender. Add garlic and sauté another minute.

- Add rice, salt, and pepper (and minced parsley, if you have it) to onion and garlic mixture. Toss to blend thoroughly and reduce heat to low. When mixture is hot, it's ready to serve. Depending on amount of rice and onion used, you may need a little extra salt and pepper.

Note:
➢ Instead of rice you could use cooked pearled barley, bulgur, or *kasha* (see page 132.)

Green Eggs and Rice

This is an easy one-dish whole food meal rich in protein, fiber, healthy fat, and vegetables. It also allows lots of flexibility. You can replace the spinach with other fresh or frozen greens, or something like chopped cooked broccoli or asparagus. You can use sliced green onions instead of regular onions, or a different type of cheese or milk. You can use any leftover rice — but keep in mind that white rice does not have the nutritional caliber you need. For people getting used to brown rice you can reduce the amount of rice *or* replace it with something like cooked quinoa or millet, whole grain pasta, or a combination of any. Leftovers are delicious heated for lunch the next day. Using this recipe as a basic model, and given that you probably always can have eggs, milk, and cheese on hand, you may want to put this on the *Ten Most Useful Recipes* list.

(Serves 4 as a main dish, more as a side dish)

> 1 bag (16 ounces) or 2 boxes (10 ounces each) frozen chopped spinach
> 2 tablespoons olive oil
> 1 medium-large onion in ¼-inch dice (2 – 3 cups)
> 4 eggs
> 1 teaspoon salt
> 1 teaspoon freshly ground black pepper
> 1½ cups milk, fresh or evaporated whole milk
> 6 ounces *sharp* cheddar cheese, grated (about 1½ cups)
> 2 cups cooked brown rice

Preheat oven to 300 degrees. Oil a shallow 1½-quart casserole dish.

- Place frozen spinach into a pot or skillet with a lid. Place over a low heat, covered, for 20 – 30 minutes or until completely thawed and hot through.

- Heat oil in 10-inch skillet over medium-high heat and sauté onion for 10 – 15 minutes or until tender. Remove from heat and set aside.

- Whisk eggs in a mixing bowl or an 8-cup Pyrex jug. Add seasoning, milk, cheese, and rice, and mix well. Blend in spinach and onions. *(You can combine the whole mixture hours or even a day ahead, but bring to room temperature and stir again before you transfer it to the cooking dish.)*

- Scrape into oiled casserole and bake uncovered at 300 degrees for about 60 minutes or until it is no longer wet in the center. *You can cook it at 325 degrees if you want it to finish cooking a little sooner, but a custard-based dish like this will have a better texture cooked at a lower temperature. If you notice mixture bubbling around the edges, reduce heat to 300 degrees.*

Brown Rice Power Patties

These nutty little patties are convenient for lunch at your desk, snacks when you're peckish, meals on the road, or after-school snacks. They're good straight from the refrigerator or at room temperature, which makes them ideal for hiking or camping.

(Makes 12 patties)

> 2 cups *cooked* brown rice
> 6 ounces *sharp* cheddar cheese, grated (about 1½ cups)
> 1½ cups finely-grated carrot (about 1 large)
> ½ cup raw sunflower seeds
> *and/or* ½ cup sesame seeds, raw or toasted)
>
> 3 eggs
> 1 teaspoon dried basil
> 1 teaspoon salt
> ½ teaspoon freshly ground pepper
> 1½ cups toasted slivered almonds or dry roasted peanuts

Preheat oven to 350 degrees. Mist a baking sheet with non-stick spray.

- In a mixing bowl, combine *cooked* rice, grated cheese, carrots, and seeds.

- Combine the eggs and seasonings in the food processor and blend for about 5 seconds. Add nuts and process another 5 seconds. If using dry roasted peanuts you may need to process them an extra 5 seconds. *Don't over-process the nuts; their texture is important.* Add to rice mixture and mix thoroughly.

- Use a ¼-cup measuring cup to scoop mixture onto baking sheet, and form into plump patties about ¾ inch thick. *I pack the measuring cup firmly and rinse it between scoops so that the mixture drops out more or less cleanly formed, ready to be patted out a bit more and shaped the rest of the way.* Bake at 350 degrees for 15 minutes, then turn patties over and bake 10 minutes more. Transfer patties to rack, flipping them so their toastier side shows.

- If you're not eating them the same day, keep in the refrigerator. They will easily last at least a week if kept cold and stored in an airtight container.

To toast slivered almonds, spread them in a shallow baking pan and toast for about 10 minutes in a 325-degree oven. (For sesame seeds, see *Nutty Brown Rice* on page 126.) You want them barely golden, not browned. Cool before using.

Mother's Brown Rice Pudding

This is actually rice custard, but Mother calls it rice pudding. It is best warm from the oven, but straight from the refrigerator at midnight works just fine, too. You can use any kind of leftover rice, any kind of milk, including soy milk or rice milk, and so forth. I think the milk needs to be rich, though, to balance the assertive rice and maple syrup. Mother happens to like raisins in the rice pudding but I prefer a diced ripe banana. This recipe has neither.

(Serves 4)

> 1½ cups ***cooked*** brown rice
> 1 can (12 ounces) evaporated whole milk (1½ cups)
> ½ cup pure maple syrup or honey
> 4 eggs, beaten
> ½ teaspoon salt
> 1 teaspoon lemon zest (see page 36 for more on zest)
> 1 tablespoon lemon juice
> 1 tablespoon butter

Preheat oven to 300 degrees, and set rack in middle of oven.

- If rice is in clumps, break up completely with wet hands or wet wooden spoon, which will keep the rice from sticking. Combine rice, milk, and maple syrup or honey in a 1½-quart pot and set over a low heat. Heat until milk is beginning to steam, and then turn off heat and let it sit.

- Meanwhile whisk eggs in an 8-cup measuring jug, and then add salt and lemon. Add hot rice mixture and whisk thoroughly.

- If butter is soft, spread over bottom and sides of shallow 1½-2 quart casserole. Otherwise, melt butter in casserole (easily done by popping it into the preheating oven for about 5 minutes). Or if you prefer, use non-stick spray.

- Scrape rice mixture into casserole and bake for about 1 hour, or until just barely set in the middle. Check pudding after 30 minutes. If it is bubbling around the edges, reduce heat to 250 degrees. (Custards should be cooked very gently or they will separate.)

Note:
- ➤ One or two finely diced ripe bananas or ½ cup raisins or whatever are additions enjoyed by some. If you use honey, it should be a mild clover honey or it will affect the flavor of the custard. If you have neither mild honey nor maple syrup, use ½ cup brown sugar.

Mexican Brown Rice
with Black Beans

This is a last-minute one-skillet dinner that also offers complete protein in the bean-and-rice partnership. If *Mexican Brown Rice* didn't taste so good, you might suspect some other reason for its existence, like nutritive value or ease of preparation. It is at its best freshly made, but it still makes lovely leftovers. It should be mentioned that if you don't have fresh cilantro on hand when the occasion for this dish presents itself, nobody would probably miss it.

(Serves 3 – 4 as main dish)

> ¼ cup olive oil
> 3 cups diced onion (a medium-large onion)
> 1 tablespoon chili powder (mild)
> 1 teaspoon ground cumin
> 1 teaspoon salt
> 1 green bell pepper, diced
> 1 fat teaspoon freshly crushed garlic
> 2½ cups cooked brown rice
> ¼ cup lemon juice
> ½ teaspoon freshly ground pepper
> 1 can (14 ounces) black beans, rinsed and drained
> 1 can (14 ounces) diced tomatoes, drained
> (½ cup chopped fresh cilantro, if available)

- Heat oil in 10-inch skillet over medium high heat and sauté onion, chili powder, cumin, and salt for about 5 minutes.

- Add diced green pepper and sauté for another 5 minutes. Reduce heat to medium. Add garlic and sauté for another 2 minutes. *(This dish seems to call for a fresh crunchiness, so sauté with an easy hand and a reckless Latin spirit. The green pepper should be tender but still bright green.)*

- Add rice, lemon, pepper, black beans, tomatoes, and cilantro. Toss gently, breaking up any lumps of rice, until the mixture is hot throughout. *(Check to make sure there's enough salt – you may need to add another ¼ teaspoon.)* Serve and eat while steaming hot.

Note:
➢ If you use chopped fresh tomatoes, use plenty – they have a milder flavor than the canned, and their fresh juiciness is a lovely addition. Make sure you add them just before serving, if possible — cooking tends to turn them to mush.

Brown Rice Salad

This salad can be a meal in itself if you toss it with cooked chicken or shrimp. Like any grain salad it's a sensible choice for buffets or picnics: it can be served warm, at room temperature or chilled, and can be made a day before or an hour before it's served. Leftovers can be transformed with additions like chopped olives or fresh tomatoes or marinated beans, or enjoyed for lunch or snacks until the last spoonful is gone.

(Serves about 6, hopefully with leftovers)

> **Lemon Vinaigrette**
> ¼ cup lemon juice
> 1 teaspoon freshly crushed garlic
> 1 tablespoon honey
> 1 teaspoon salt
> 1 teaspoon freshly ground black pepper
> ¼ cup extra-virgin olive oil
> (*Optional*: 1 tablespoon anchovies in olive oil, drained and mashed.)
>
> 3½ cups cooked brown basmati rice, still hot or warm, preferably
> 1 bunch (or at least 1 cup) thinly sliced green onions
> 1 – 2 cups celery in ¼-inch dice
> 1 red bell pepper (the color is important) in ¼-inch dice
> ½ cup raw almonds with skins, chopped in thirds

- Combine lemon juice, garlic, honey, salt, pepper, and oil in a 2-cup measuring jug and whisk thoroughly. Drain anchovies, mince and smash into a smooth paste, and add to dressing. (See **Note**.)

- Pour lemon vinaigrette over rice (freshly cooked, if possible) and toss. Add green onions, celery, bell pepper, and almonds. Set aside for about 30 minutes, tossing a couple of times. *(The salad may seem wet but the rice will absorb vinaigrette as it sits.)* If you don't plan to serve the salad the same day, cover and refrigerate.

Anchovies give a richness and depth of flavor to this salad. Great source of omega-3 oils, too. The best I've had is an 8.4-ounce bottle of *Scalia* anchovies packed in extra virgin olive oil and imported from Italy. The *King Oscar* brand has been dependable, but anchovies can vary pretty wildly in quality. Even if the thought of anchovies makes you squirm, please at least try adding two of the little fellows, mashed thoroughly with a fork, to the dressing of this salad.

Other Grains

Buckwheat (Kasha)

Buckwheat is not actually in the cereal family — the buckwheat groat is technically a fruit that belongs to the same family as rhubarb. My favorite form of buckwheat is called *kasha*, whole toasted buckwheat groats. I love the deliciously aggressive flavor and aroma of hot cooked kasha. Leftover buckwheat is a hot commodity in our refrigerator, either for a between-meal snack or in bread dough. (See recipe for *Millet Bread* on page 170.)

(Makes about 2 cups)

> 1 cup water
> ¼ teaspoon salt
> 1 teaspoon butter
> ½ cup toasted buckwheat

- Bring water to the boil in a small saucepan, and then stir in salt, butter, and roasted buckwheat. Turn heat down very low, cover pan, and simmer 15 minutes.

- Remove from heat and set aside, covered, for about 5 minutes. Serve as is, or with honey and milk. Store in the refrigerator and eat cold or hot.

Note:
➢ Uncooked buckwheat has a benign crunch and can be added to muesli or granola.

Barley (Whole)

Barley is a great source of soluble fiber, lowering blood sugar, insulin, and cholesterol. It may also have a significant cancer-fighting effect through its beta-glucan content. Because of its assertive personality it is not used as much as the easygoing and all-purpose brown rice, but it is worth getting to know.

Whole barley (also called 'whole hulled' barley) is the form we recommend using. It generally takes a good hour to cook, and even then one would never accuse it of being tender. (Pearled barley is by far the most common form of barley – its hull and bran have been polished off, so it takes about half the time to cook.)

It is often suggested that one soak the barley overnight, and also to dry roast the grains to improve the favor. As usual, I choose the simplest route and just simmer barley in plenty of water for about an hour.

(Makes about 3 cups)

> 6 cups water
> 1 cup *whole* barley (not pearled)
> 1 teaspoon salt

- Bring water to the boil in a 4-quart saucepan. Add salt and barley. Turn heat down to allow a steady simmer, and cook for 1 hour, at least.

- Check a few grains for doneness. If they are the least bit rubbery, simmer for another 10 minutes before testing again.

- Drain barley, saving liquid for soup stock. Use as a brown rice substitute (try with recipes on page 126), or in place of quinoa in the salad on page 134.

Millet

Millet has a mild but curious flavor and is rich in protein. Its grains are yellow and tiny and round, but swell amazingly when cooked. (Be sure to buy hull-less millet.) Properly cooked millet should be almost fluffy and expand to four times the original quantity, but I have found it to be a bit tricky to cook. My experience with buying millet is that a large number of grains are still encased in their shiny little hulls so they are still a bit crunchy even after being cooked. Should you find yourself with a soggy pot of millet, save it for the *Millet Bread* on page 170. Millet can often substitute for rice, or as a hot cereal for breakfast with a bit of butter and salt and/or honey and milk. I love millet in any form.

(Makes about 1½ cups)

> ½ cup millet
> 1¼ cups water
> ¼ teaspoon salt
> (1 teaspoon or so of butter)

- Place millet in a 1½-quart pot or sturdy skillet (one that has a lid) over medium-high heat. In a few minutes, or as soon as the grains begin to pop and smoke, begin to shake the pan every few seconds. In about 1 – 2 more minutes the grains begin to look and smell toasty. *(Note; This toasting process is optional but it improves the flavor of the millet.)*

- So, with the skillet still on the heat, add the water salt, and butter, and bring to the boil. Turn the heat down low, cover the pan, and cook millet for about 15 – 20 minutes.

- Remove from heat and set aside, still covered, for about 5 minutes.

Note:

➢ For 3 – 4 cups of cooked millet the following method of cooking works well. Add a cup of millet (toasted according to preceding directions) to 6 cups of boiling water and a teaspoon of salt. Reduce heat to low, and simmer for about 20 minutes. Pour into a sieve and drain thoroughly, then fluff with a fork.

Quinoa

Quinoa comes with a natural coating that acts as its own built-in insect repellent. It can give the quinoa a bitter taste so it needs to be rinsed before it's cooked. Although most quinoa is apparently pre-washed, I give it a rinse, just in case.

(Makes about 3 cups)

> 1 cup quinoa, rinsed
> 1½ cups water
> ½ teaspoon salt

- Rinse quinoa in a sieve, swishing the grains back and forth in a mixing bowl of water. Make sure the sieve is fine enough — quinoa can sneak through some pretty small holes. Set aside to drain. Remember to measure the quinoa *before* you rinse it — it swells.

- Bring water and salt to a boil in a 1½-quart pot (one that has a lid) and add rinsed quinoa. Bring back to a boil, then reduce to a simmer, cover, and cook for about 20 minutes. The water should be absorbed and quinoa should be tender.

- Remove quinoa from the heat. Fluff grains by tossing gently with a fork or rubber spatula, then cover and set aside for 5 – 10 minutes.

Quinoa Salad
with Corn & Radish

Quinoa (*KEEN-wah*) is a South American grain that looks like ivory-colored millet. (Actually, it isn't strictly a grain; it's the fruit of an herb.) It is particularly high in protein and a marvelous alternative to brown rice, especially since it cooks in about half the time. (Quinoa is interchangeable with brown rice in recipes like *Green Eggs and Rice* and makes a fine substitute for bulgur in *tabbouleh*.)
Quinoa pairs nicely with corn, and radishes give crunch, color, and pep all in one. This salad is especially suited to the assertive texture of barley (see page 132).

(Serves about 4 – 6)

> 2½ cups *cooked* quinoa (*See directions on previous page.*)
>
> 1 cup frozen petite corn
> 1 bunch radishes, trimmed, cleaned, and in ¼-inch dice (1 – 1 ½ cups)
> ½ cup finely sliced green onion
> ½ cup walnuts, broken in pieces (toasted, if possible)
>
> 2 tablespoons lemon or lime juice or cider vinegar
> 2 tablespoons olive oil
> 1 teaspoon freshly crushed garlic
> ½ teaspoon ground cumin
> ½ teaspoon salt
> ½ teaspoon freshly ground pepper
> ½ cup chopped fresh cilantro

- Place frozen corn in a strainer or colander and thaw by running briefly under hot water while shaking the corn gently. Make sure corn is thoroughly drained by tossing in a colander lined with paper towels.

- Combine lemon juice, oil, garlic, cumin, and salt and pepper in a mixing bowl and add corn, radishes, green onions, walnuts, cooked quinoa, and cilantro, and toss to blend thoroughly. Serve at any temperature. Keeps nicely in the refrigerator for several days.

Note:
➢ Mother prefers this salad without corn, which works fine. Mild white onion can substitute for green, but the salad does need some touch of green, whether green onion or cilantro.

Tabbouleh
Lebanese wheat salad

Tabbouleh (tah-BOO-lee) is made with *bulgur,* which is whole wheat that has been steamed or parboiled before being dried and chopped. Bulgur is not interchangeable with raw cracked wheat — bulgur has a different flavor and absorbs water much more quickly. Authentic Lebanese *tabbouleh* usually calls for *equal amounts* of bulgur and minced parsley as well as fresh mint, just for a start. I've often had to make it without any parsley at all, and with finely diced sweet white onion instead of green, but follow your conscience.

(Serves about 6)

1 cup uncooked bulgur, fine or medium grind
1 cup boiling water

¼ cup lemon juice
¼ cup extra virgin olive oil
¾ teaspoon salt
½ teaspoon freshly-ground pepper
½ - 1 cup thinly-sliced green onions (about 3 – 6)
2 – 4 fresh tomatoes, ¼-inch dice (at least 2 cups)
½ - 1 cup minced fresh parsley
1 can (14 ounces) chickpeas, thoroughly drained (see note)

- Place bulgur in a small bowl (clear 4-cup Pyrex measuring jug works well) and add boiling water. (Just hot water isn't good enough.) Set aside for 30 minutes; the bulgur will absorb the water, soften, and swell to about 2 cups.

- Combine lemon juice, oil, and salt and pepper in a mixing bowl and add softened bulgur, onions, tomato, parsley, and chickpeas. Toss to blend thoroughly. Serve at room temperature or chilled. Keeps nicely in the refrigerator for several days.

Note:

➢ If I have any cucumber on hand, I like to add 2 cups in ¼-inch dice.

➢ If you choose to include chickpeas, try this treatment: heat a tablespoon of olive oil in a skillet over medium heat and add the chickpeas, shaking the pan to settle them into a single layer. Sprinkle with ¼ teaspoon of salt and a grinding of pepper and cook them until they start to turn a toasty brown, giving the pan a shake now and then. Chickpeas fixed this way are tasty on their own *or* in *tabbouleh.*

Polenta

You may have read that polenta is just the Italian word for cornmeal. That could be confusing, given the range of what is called cornmeal. Cornmeal can be almost flour-like or impossibly gritty, and often a mixture of the two. It can be bland or dominating, organic or degerminated, stone-ground or commercially processed. So, know your cornmeal.

True *polenta* is the coarse golden stuff used for the Italian dish by the same name. It is actually degerminated, so is not strictly a whole grain. You can find polenta as well as whole grain stone ground cornmeal (medium grind) in the bulk food sections of natural food stores and in supermarkets packaged by Bob's Red Mill.

- Polenta can generally be used as you would pasta or rice, or even mashed potatoes, and it has the perfect personality to partner rich and garlicky meat or bean stews like chili, or vegetable stews like *ratatouille*. Polenta loves strong flavors.

- Polenta can be austere (with just the necessary salt) or decadent (with some injudicious additions of butter and cheese). You can stir in any cheese, fresh herbs, sliced green onions, diced green chilies, frozen or canned corn, or just plain butter, salt, and pepper. Consult your refrigerator for ideas.

- Cooked polenta firms so quickly that it can be frustrating to work with for the busy cook who has a tight meal-prep schedule. When polenta is hot, it's soft and easy to serve in a luscious heap on the plate. But — wait ten minutes and you will be serving odd-shaped chunks. One solution is to keep it hot in a double boiler. My usual strategy is to scrape the still-hot polenta mixture into a clear Pyrex loaf pan from which it can be served in neat slices. If you have made it in advance you can just refrigerate it, and then decide how you want to serve it another day. (Polenta can be turned out of its serving dish after it cools for 15 minutes or so, especially if you rinse the bowl beforehand.)

- Cooked polenta may be stored in the refrigerator, covered, for several days. Reheat in a 350-degree oven, covered with foil, for about 30 minutes. Or gently heat thick slices in a nonstick skillet, covered. A really delicious treat is slices of polenta fried in olive oil until beginning to turn brown.

- You can cook polenta in water, milk, stock, or a combination of any of those. Even the proportion of polenta to liquid is flexible – but the most common proportions are one part of polenta to four parts of water. The higher the ratio of water, the softer the polenta will be. Recipes for grilled or fried polenta would usually call for a lower ratio of water, like one-to-three.

- There are two cooking methods I use: cooked on the stovetop or baked in the oven. (You can also use the microwave method for polenta in 15 minutes, but I don't. Oven baked polenta is as easy as I ever need. *And* there is no polenta cooked onto the bottom of the pot, which generally happens when I cook polenta on the stovetop.

- (… but if you have a pot with a layer of polenta cooked onto the bottom, let it soak in cold water overnight. It should be easy to scrape off in the morning.)

Basic Polenta
Stovetop method, plain

Contrary to rumor this dish does not need constant stirring. It is perfectly happy to be stirred at your convenience while you are working on other things. *(However, I would not recommend cooking polenta on the stovetop if you can cook it in the oven as described on the next page. There is no substitute for the bake-and-busy-yourself-elsewhere method.)* Using a heavy pot is helpful, but a layer of polenta stuck to the bottom will be easier to scrape off after an overnight soaking in cold water. (For more about polenta see previous page.) This is one of my favorite and most versatile dishes to have as leftovers, especially with the additions mentioned in the following recipe for oven baked polenta.

(Serves 4 – 6)

> 6 cups water
> 2 teaspoons salt
> 1½ cups polenta
> 1 – 2 tablespoons butter

Have available the dish in which you want to store or serve the cooked polenta before it cools.

- Bring water to a boil, add salt, and then slowly and steadily pour in the polenta, at the same time stirring with a wooden spoon or a whisk to prevent lumping. Turn the heat down to low and simmer polenta for 30 – 45 minutes, sprinting over to the stove every few minutes or so to stir it. If you find it beginning to stick because you forgot to stir, just patiently scrape the bottom of the pan with your wooden spoon or whisk until all or most of the roughness is gone. If you catch it too late it doesn't really matter — it will soak off later. The longer you cook it, the thicker it will become.

- When polenta is cooked (grains should be soft, with no core) which should take at least 30 minutes and preferably longer for the best results, stir in butter.

- Scrape into a serving dish while hot and freshly cooked and serve right away, *or* if you're making the polenta in advance, transfer to a loaf pan and smooth the top. It will become firm quickly. If you would like to keep the polenta soft and scoop-able for a couple of hours, transfer to a double boiler over simmering water or cover and place in a 200-degree oven.

Easy Polenta
Oven Baked

This is the method I use the most for cooking polenta. Done in the oven, it's a low maintenance dish, and — best of all — the polenta never sticks to the bottom.

(Serves about 4)

> 5 cups hot-to-boiling water
> 2 teaspoons salt
> 1½ cups polenta
> 1 – 2 tablespoons butter

Preheat oven to 325 degrees.

- Place hot water in a 2-quart oven-safe dish (like Pyrex). Whisk in polenta, salt, and butter and place uncovered in oven. Ignore polenta for 30 minutes, and then remove from oven and whisk to blend fast-cooking edges with liquid center. *Be very careful* – being splashed with molten polenta can ruin your night. Scrape sides of dish and return to the oven for another 15 – 30 minutes: the longer time may increase succulence. (If you are making *Easy, Cheesy Polenta*, now is the time to stir in the sliced green onion or fresh herbs, and the grated cheese.)

- Scrape polenta while hot into a serving dish or Pyrex loaf pan. Serve hot, warm, or reheated. *(The polenta will take on the form of the dish you use, and a loaf shape is convenient for slicing and heating or frying leftovers.)*

Easy, Cheesy Polenta

➤ With the addition of cheddar or Monterey jack cheese and sliced green onions or diced chiles, polenta is especially suited to bright Mexican flavors and goes well with either chili on pages 121 – 122. Add **1½ — 2 cups grated cheese** and about **1 cup thinly sliced green onion** or **1 can (3½ ounces) whole mild chiles, diced**. (I suggest buying canned whole chiles and dicing them yourself – the ready-diced chilies sometimes have too much skin and stem in them.)

➤ For a Mediterranean accent, stir in **¼ cup chopped fresh basil** or **2 tablespoons minced fresh rosemary** with **½ cup of freshly grated Parmesan**. This version is a natural partner for any kind of rich meat or vegetable stew, including the *ratatouille* on page 104.

Polenta with Vegetables
Oven Baked

This is a way to turn polenta into a one-dish meal, with diced vegetables and cheese cooked directly into the polenta in a succulently textured casserole. The directions seem almost too simple, but it really works.

(Serves 4)

> 1 cup polenta
> 3½ cups hot water
> 2 tablespoons butter
> 2 teaspoons salt
> 1 medium onion in ½-inch dice (about 2 cups)
> 2 slim zucchini in ½-inch dice (about 2 cups)
> 2 medium tomatoes in ½-inch dice (about 2 cups)
>
> ½ cup freshly grated Parmesan
> *or* 6 ounces *sharp* cheddar cheese, grated (about 1½ cups)

Preheat oven to 350 degrees.

- Whisk polenta with the hot water, butter, and salt in a 1½- or 2-quart ovenproof casserole. Add diced vegetables and stir to distribute as evenly as possible. Place uncovered in the oven and ignore it for 40 minutes.

- Remove polenta from the oven. Fold grated cheese into polenta and vegetables to gently but thoroughly blend. Smooth the top and clean up the sides before returning to the oven. Bake for another 20 minutes or until vegetables are soft and the polenta has absorbed the liquid. Let polenta firm up for 5 – 10 minutes before serving.

Note:

➢ As simple as this recipe is, it can't be rushed. Try it when you have the time to allow it at least the full hour of cooking.

Black Bean Polenta

This one-dish meal delivers beans, grains, and vegetables in one fell swoop. It can be made easily in less than an hour, keeps for days in the refrigerator, re-heats by the slice as needed, and, except for the green onions, requires only ingredients you could easily keep on hand in your cupboard. You can adjust the level of heat in *Black Bean Polenta* by way of the salsa or chilies, and you can certainly adjust the amount of cheese, beans, or any other ingredient.

(Serves 4 – 6)

6 cups water
2 teaspoons salt
1½ cup polenta

16 ounces *sharp* cheddar cheese, grated and divided in half
1 bunch green onions, sliced thinly (about 1 – 1½ cups)
1½ cups salsa, bottled or fresh, mild or hot, drained of excess liquid
1 can (7 ounces) mild whole green chilies, diced
2 cans (14 ounces each) black beans, drained and roughly mashed

Preheat oven to 400 degrees. Oil a shallow casserole dish, about 9 x 11 inches.

- Bring water to a boil in a 4-quart heavy-bottomed pot, add salt, then slowly and steadily pour in the polenta while stirring constantly with a whisk to prevent lumping. Reduce heat to low and simmer polenta for 30 minutes, stirring frequently and scraping the bottom of the pan regularly to prevent sticking. The cooked polenta grains should be soft, with no noticeable core.

- Meanwhile, assemble grated cheese, green onions, salsa, chilies, and beans. Lay out oiled casserole dish. When polenta is cooked, stir in the sliced green onions, and 2 cups of the grated cheese. Mix very well, making sure to reach the polenta at the very bottom, and then remove pot from heat.

- Scrape half of the polenta mixture into the casserole and spread evenly. *(The remaining polenta will begin to firm as it cools, so work briskly at this point.)* Spread with salsa, then black beans, then chilies, then the remainder of the grated cheese. *(If the black beans are too thick to spread easily you can loosen their texture by mixing with the chopped chilies.)* Cover with the rest of the polenta mixture, and smooth the top.

- *If you are not going to serve it the same day, set aside to cool completely, then cover and chill.* To serve, bring to room temperature and heat uncovered at 400 degrees for about 30 – 40 minutes, or until hot in the middle. It will be easier to slice and serve if you allow it to sit for about 10 minutes.

7 *More* Main Dish Recipes

Canned Tuna
Tuna Favorites
Two Main Course Soups
Recipes With and Without Meat

Canned Tuna

There are good reasons to eat more tuna, or any high-fat fish, for that matter — wild salmon, sardines, anchovies, and so on. Deep-sea fish like these are rich in omega-3 fatty acids and are also a valuable source of fat-soluble vitamins A and D. Canned tuna can be incorporated into all kinds of cooked and uncooked dishes, and its availability makes it practical to keep a good supply in your cupboard. It's a particularly easy way to lift your fish consumption and answer last-minute dinner questions at the same time. (See recipe for *Tuna Salad* on page 64, as well as several tuna based main dishes on the following pages.)

Plain or fancy?
When it comes to canned tuna, I favor fancy. Good tuna, whether imported from Italy or from somewhere in the Pacific Northwest of the U.S., is worthy of being the centerpiece of a meal you would serve to anybody. The variety of canned tuna on the supermarket shelves has increased considerably since the Mediterranean approach to eating has become newsworthy. The price for a six ounce can of tuna ranges from under one dollar to around ten dollars and there is a tremendous variation in quality, but you should be able to find a moderately priced one that you like.

Solid or chunk?
Solid tuna is always my choice. I always prefer to deal with as intact a fillet as possible, to serve whole or to flake myself, depending on my purposes. Chunk tuna costs less than solid, and tends to be stronger tasting and softer textured. It can even be a bit mushy, and it is harder to squeeze the liquid out when one is making something like tuna salad.

Light or white?
"Light" tuna (from yellowfin tuna, for example) probably contains less mercury than "white" tuna (from albacore) and has been found to have higher levels of omega-3 fatty acids. Albacore is the mildest tasting of the tunas. If color or subtlety of flavor is an issue, or if you are serving tuna to a wary eater, solid white is probably the best bet.

In oil or water? Or its own juice?
Our first choice is tuna packed in its own juice. Our second choice is tuna packed in extra virgin olive oil. If neither is available, we would choose tuna packed in water. If you are planning to drain tuna before using, as in the tuna salad on page 64, for instance, it may be best to buy tuna packed in water. Tuna packed in olive oil may leach a high proportion of the important omega-3 fatty acids into the oil, so you don't want to discard the oil. (There are recipes that can incorporate the tuna and the olive oil it is packed in, like *Tuna & Broccoli Pasta* and *Tuna & White Bean Salad*.)

Mercury contamination
The issue of mercury contamination in fish could be summarized this way: smaller, younger fish have the lowest mercury levels. Highest mercury levels are found in large fish like swordfish and shark, which eat other fish and live long enough to build up significant mercury. Moderate levels are found in the large albacore tuna most commonly used in canned white tuna. The general recommendation is two servings (12 ounces total) of canned tuna per week, with only one of the servings to be albacore. 'Light' tuna may not need to be limited. For more on this issue try the following website: www.epa.gov/waterscience/fish

Tuna and White Bean Salad
with Fresh Fennel

Fennel is not always easy to find but is deliciously crispy and with a delicate licorice flavor. If I can't find nice young fennel I don't make this salad: the tops should be fluffy and delicate, the bulb smallish and rounded for the best crunch. Instead of fennel you could use celery, preferably cut in long, slim diagonal slices.

(Serves 4)

> 1 can (7.5 ounces) solid light tuna packed in its own juice (*see **Note***)
> ***or*** 1 can (6 ounces) solid light tuna packed in olive oil
> 1 can (15 ounces) great northern or cannellini beans
> 1 fennel bulb
> ½ cup onion in ¼-inch dice
>
> ¼ cup lemon juice and/or cider vinegar
> 2 tablespoons extra virgin olive oil
> 1 teaspoon freshly crushed garlic
> ½ teaspoon salt
> ½ teaspoon freshly ground pepper

- Open can of tuna but *do not drain*. Tip tuna and oily juices into a small bowl and break up into pieces with a fork. Set aside.

- Drain and rinse beans and set aside to drain thoroughly.

- Trim root end of fennel bulb, and slice off everything just above the bulb. Trim feathery parts of the stalks; mince and set aside. If the stalks are tender and tasty, slice thinly on the diagonal. Quarter bulb lengthwise and remove any tough layers and core. Cut in ¼-inch (or thinner) slices: you will probably have about 2 cups. Set aside.

- Dice onion and combine with lemon juice, olive oil, garlic, salt, and pepper in a medium to large bowl. Add sliced fennel and beans and toss thoroughly. Add tuna and toss gently.

Note:
> ➢ I try to use the best tuna for this dish. My current favorite is Newman's Fish Company's *Oregon Albacore Tuna* that comes packed in its own juices in 7½-ounce cans. I save the juice (about ¼ cup) for the next time I make chowder or *Tuna Tetrazzini*.

Tuna and Broccoli Pasta

This is delightfully simple in ingredients and construction, with no cooking beyond boiling a pot of pasta water. This is a great way to cook broccoli, by the way. Critical to the looks and taste of this meal, though, is not allowing the broccoli to overcook. Undercooking is safer.

(Serves 4 – 6)

> 12 ounces *whole-grain* pasta spirals (brown rice, whole wheat, etc)
> 6 – 8 cups of broccoli florets (about 2 – 3 heads)
> 2 cans (6 ounces each) solid light tuna *in olive oil*
> 2 tablespoons lemon juice or cider vinegar
> 1 – 2 teaspoons freshly crushed garlic
> 1 teaspoon salt
> 1 teaspoon freshly ground pepper
> 1 cup freshly grated Parmesan

- Set a big pot (8-quart is a nice size) of water on the stove to boil with 1 tablespoon salt.

- Prepare broccoli florets: rinse about 3 heads of broccoli and slice off just the actual florets from each. *(I find it easiest to hold the stalk in one hand with the broccoli head against the cutting board.)* Divide larger florets into bite-sized mouthfuls. You can save the stems for another meal, or peel and slice in ¼-inch slices and add to florets.

- Empty cans of tuna with their olive oil into a small bowl and break up tuna into bite-sized chunks. Add lemon juice or vinegar, garlic, and the teaspoon of salt and pepper, and blend gently to avoid mushing tuna. *(If you choose a tuna packed in water, drain thoroughly, discarding the liquid, and then add ½ cup extra virgin olive oil.)*

- Add pasta to the pot of boiling water. Cook pasta for about 8 – 10 minutes, or until pasta is just *barely* done. Crank the heat up to high and add the broccoli. Watch for water to come back to a boil, and then remove in about 30 seconds, while broccoli is still vibrant green and tender-crisp. The delicate florets mush quickly.

- Empty the pot into a strainer and drain for about 5 seconds, tossing gently in strainer a couple of times. Tip drained pasta and broccoli into a large bowl, add the tuna mixture and grated Parmesan. Mix thoroughly, but lightly and serve hot or warm.

Tuna Tetrazzini

This is a good way to introduce pasta alternatives to your family (or yourself) and to increase your consumption of tuna fish and omega-3 fatty acids. You may raise your eyebrows at all the dicing but try it first. Remember that this is a one-dish meal so it's a good idea to add *more* vegetables, not less. Chopped cooked broccoli is another good addition. The diced red bell pepper is helpful for color, but any bell pepper is good. *Tuna Tetrazzini* can be made a day or so in advance, or eaten a day or so later as leftovers. Cooked brown rice can replace the pasta.

(Serves 4 – 6 as main course)

> 12 ounces *whole-grain* pasta spirals (brown rice, whole wheat, etc)
> 2 cans (6 ounces each) solid light tuna *in olive oil*
> 1 medium-large onion in ¼ inch dice (2 – 3 cups)
> 2 – 3 stalks celery in ¼-inch dice
> 1 sweet red bell pepper in ¼-inch dice
> ¼ cup all purpose flour
> 2½ – 3 cups milk/chicken stock
> 1 teaspoon salt
> ½ teaspoon freshly ground pepper
> ¼ teaspoon dried thyme, rubbed fine
> ½ teaspoon Tabasco sauce
> 2 tablespoons fresh lemon juice and chopped zest from 1 lemon
> 8 ounces *sharp* cheddar cheese, grated (about 2 cups)

Preheat oven to 400 degrees. Oil a 2-quart casserole dish.

- Drain about 2 tablespoons of olive oil from each can of tuna and set aside. Tip remaining tuna with oil into large mixing bowl and break tuna into even-sized flakes.

- Cook pasta according to instructions and drain. Add pasta to tuna in bowl.

- In pasta cooking pot, heat the 4 tablespoons of reserved olive oil. Sauté onion and celery for about 15 minutes or until tender. Stir in diced red bell pepper.

- Sprinkle flour over sautéed vegetables and stir over a medium-low heat for about 2 minutes. Blend half of the milk/stock into the mixture. When it's smoothly blended add remaining liquid. Return to the heat, bring to a simmer, and cook about 10 minutes, stirring often. (Sauce will thicken slightly.)

- Add remaining ingredients to sauce and blend. Combine with pasta and tuna mixture and mix thoroughly but gently. Scrape into an oiled 2-quart casserole dish. Bake uncovered at 400 degrees for 30 minutes or until hot through.

Tuna (or Salmon) Cakes

This is a good way to bring canned tuna or salmon — or any leftover cooked fish — to the dinner table while shamelessly exploiting the weakness most of us have for hot fried things. These are golden brown and crispy, speckled with green onion, and lively tasting. You could serve them as appetizers if you made them smaller.

(Serves 3 – 4)

>   2 cans (6 ounces) solid light tuna
>   *or* – 1 can (14 – 15 ounces) salmon
>   *or* – about 2 cups flaked leftover cooked salmon or other fish
>   2 eggs
>   1 tablespoon lemon juice
>   ½ cup thinly sliced green onion (3 – 4)
>   ¼ teaspoon salt (more if using fresh fish)
>   ¼ teaspoon freshly ground pepper
>   ½ teaspoon Tabasco sauce
>   ½ cup old-fashioned rolled oats

Preheat oven to 200 degrees (for keeping fish cakes warm).

- Drain canned fish and break up with a fork. *If using canned salmon you can include skin and bones. Save drained liquid for Crowded Chowder on page 148. If you use tuna packed in olive oil, save oil for another fish friendly recipe – for example, in place of the olive oil in Crowded Chowder.*

- In a mixing bowl, beat eggs briefly with a fork and add lemon juice, green onion, seasoning, and oats. Add to fish and mix gently but thoroughly.

- Using a ¼-cup measure, scoop mixture into about 6 – 8 portions and form into patties. A spoon and a fork make good tools for this job. *(You can form the patties in advance and lay them between plastic wrap misted with non-stick spray until ready to cook.)*

- Heat 2 – 3 tablespoon of olive oil in a non-stick skillet over medium heat. Fry patties in 1 – 2 batches, about 3 – 5 minutes on the first side and 3 minutes on the second, or until browned and crisp. Transfer to a plate in the oven to keep warm. Serve with a side of *Rich Yogurt Aioli* mixed with some minced green tops of green onions, if possible.

Note:
➤ If you tend to look sideways at canned salmon, try canned red Alaskan sockeye. It's beautiful stuff, and worth the extra expense if it means you eat more salmon.

Kedgeree
Tuna and Rice: Variation on an Anglo-Indian Classic

Kedgeree (pronounced *kedger–EE)* is a simple but rich and complex tasting meal you can stir up quickly on the stovetop, calling for ingredients you probably have on hand anyway. The traditional kedgeree calls for smoked haddock and chopped hard-boiled egg and *certainly* doesn't mention canned tuna, but this rendition is practical and delectable. Don't be intimidated by the generous (and untraditional) amounts of celery and onion: they provide balance and freshness and help turn kedgeree into a complete meal. If you have all the ingredients measured and waiting, this can be started within 15 minutes of serving.

(Serves 4 as main dish)

> ¼ cup olive oil
> 2 cups thinly sliced celery, including leaves
> 2 cups diced onion (a medium-big onion)
> 1 teaspoon crushed fresh garlic
> 1 teaspoon curry powder
> 1 teaspoon salt
> 1 teaspoon freshly ground black pepper
> 4 cups cooked brown rice
> 12 ounces solid light tuna, drained and flaked (see page 142)
> ¼ cup lemon juice
> (½ cup minced fresh parsley, if you have it)

- Heat oil in a deep 10-inch skillet and sauté celery and onion for 10 minutes or until barely tender. Add garlic, curry powder, salt, and pepper, and sauté for another minute.

- Add rice, tuna, lemon juice, and parsley, and toss gently, breaking up any lumps of rice, until mixed thoroughly and heated through.

Note:
➤ The traditional chopped hard-boiled eggs are actually an addition I like. Flaked smoked salmon substitutes nicely for the tuna. Another compatible and traditional addition is peas. If you choose to add peas, thaw 2 cups of frozen petite peas (or a 10-ounce box) in a sieve under hot running water, drain well, and add to the kedgeree with rice and tuna. (Make sure the peas taste good before you add them.) Or just serve them on the side, which certainly helps make for a pretty plate of food, especially if you don't have any parsley to add to the kedgeree.

Crowded Chowder

This creamy crowded chowder, or a variation thereof, is in the top five of the world's ten most useful recipes. This recipe can just as easily be transformed into clam chowder or vegetable chowder (see **Note**). Leftover cooked salmon added at the end makes a delicious variation, and barbecued salmon gives a nice smoky taste. This is a good time to use leftover olive oil from any tuna you have drained.

(Serves about 6 as a main course)

> ¼ cup extra virgin olive oil
> ¼ teaspoon crushed red chilies
> 1 medium-large onion (at least 3 cups diced)
> 2 cups diced celery, including tender leaves
> 2 carrots in ¼-inch dice (about 1½ cups)
> 1 teaspoon curry powder
> 1 tablespoon freshly crushed garlic
> 2 medium potatoes in ¼-inch dice (about 3 cups diced)
> 2 tablespoons all purpose flour
> 6 cups water (see **Note**)
> ½ teaspoon dried thyme
> 1 teaspoon dried oregano
> 2 teaspoons salt
> 1 teaspoon freshly-ground pepper
> 2 lbs fresh fish fillets, sliced in ½ x 1 inch chunks (*See Note)*
> 1 can (12 ounce) evaporated whole milk (See **Note**)
> (½ cup minced fresh parsley or finely sliced green ends of green onions)

- Heat a heavy pot (about 5-quart) over medium heat and add oil. When oil is hot, add crushed chilies, onions, celery, carrot, and curry powder, and sauté until vegetables are barely tender, about 10 – 15 minutes, depending on the size of the pot and the amount of vegetables. Stir in garlic and potatoes and sauté for another minute or two.

- Sprinkle flour over the sautéed vegetables and cook for a couple of minutes, stirring and scraping the bottom of the pan to keep the mixture from sticking. Then blend in 2 cups of the water, mixing thoroughly to make sure all of the floury vegetable mixture is incorporated before you add the rest of the liquid.

- Add remaining water, thyme, oregano, salt, and pepper. Simmer for about 20 – 30 minutes or until potatoes are tender. (The soup should taste pretty lively at this point; the milk will mute the flavor.)

- Stir milk and fish pieces into soup, and cook soup just under a bare simmer (no bubbling) for about 5 – 10 minutes. Add the minced parsley or sliced green onion tops and serve it forth.

Note:

➢ Halibut is my fish of choice, especially if I am making the chowder for people I don't know. It is usually expensive, but dependable in texture (not too firm and not too soft) and with a mild flavor.

➢ The richer the milk, the less you need. I like the convenience of evaporated whole milk: a 12-ounce can is 1½ cups. Speaking of liquids, any combination of water and/or fish or chicken stock for the liquid will work, and replacing a cup or two of the water with white wine is a fine idea.

➢ For **vegetable chowder**, just skip the fish and increase the vegetables or include more variety, if you like. Broccoli florets are a great addition, and so is chopped spinach. Some people like to add corn. For **clam chowder**, add perhaps a 10-ounce can of whole baby clams and a can or two of 6½-ounce minced clams. For liquid you can use clam juice, stock, or water.

To Poach Halibut

If you happen to be using halibut steaks for some reason, or a fillet of halibut with skin attached, and you don't feel like messing with raw fish, try my alternative. I like the effect of the broken up and naturally flaked fish, and this poaching method gives me some nice fish stock for the chowder.

- Bring 6 cups of water and a teaspoon of salt to a boil in a 3-quart pot and put the fish in the water. *(I rinse the fillets first, especially if there is skin attached, but I don't bother to remove skin and bones from the fish; the skin adds flavor to the stock, and the bones are much easier to see or feel and remove from the cooked fish.)* Reduce heat and simmer for about 7 minutes or until fish turns opaque at its thickest point. It need only be barely cooked.

- Lift the fish out with a slotted spoon and set aside. When cool enough to handle, remove any skin and bones. I also remove any dark-colored flesh which I find it is usually too fishy-tasting. Break the cooled cooked fish into large flakes.

Tom Kah Gai
a Thai Chicken Soup, loosely translated

This is a liberal interpretation of a classic Thai soup. Composition and presentation vary wildly from restaurant to restaurant and among recipes, but Tom Kah Gai is usually a thin but potent soup exploding with flavors of chilies, ginger, lime, and fresh cilantro, mellowed with coconut milk and crowded with chicken and mushrooms.

At least three authentic elements are missing from this recipe: kaffir lime leaves, lemongrass, and galangal, all of which are available in the produce sections of some specialty stores. The intention here is to offer a recipe that anyone can make after a brief stop at the supermarket on the way home from work. (Some authorities find it acceptable to replace galangal with fresh ginger, but consider the lime leaves and lemongrass to be non-negotiable. You decide.)

For maximum impact, this soup should be served shortly after adding the mushrooms, green onions, chicken, and cilantro. The mushrooms should be creamy and fresh looking and the green onions and cilantro need to be bright green and fresh tasting. It is possible to serve this soup within an hour of actually starting to make it.

(Serves about 6)

> 4 cups chicken stock (1 quart or 3 cans (14 ounces each))
> ½ - ¾ teaspoon crushed dried red chili flakes or fresh minced chilies
> 2 tablespoons curry powder
> 2 tablespoons finely minced fresh ginger
> 2 tablespoons freshly crushed garlic
> 2 tablespoons honey
> ½ cup fresh lime juice
> ¼ cup Thai fish sauce
> 1 teaspoon salt
>
> 2 cans (14 ounces each) coconut milk
> 2 packets sliced mushrooms (8 ounces each)
> 12 green onions (about 2 bunches)
> 1½ lbs thinly-sliced chicken breast or thighs, raw
>   *or* about 4 cups of cooked chicken in delicate bite-sized shreds
> lime zest from juiced limes (see page 36 for more on zest)
> ½ – 1 cup chopped fresh cilantro

- Heat chicken stock in a 5-quart pot over medium heat. While stock is heating, add chili flakes, curry, ginger, garlic, honey, lime juice, fish sauce, and salt. (Add the lime zest at the end. It gets tired and khaki colored when cooked the whole time.) Simmer for about 15 minutes.

- Add coconut milk and bring to a simmer again. Add sliced mushrooms and sliced chicken. The thin slices of chicken will cook very quickly, so only allow the soup to come back to a gentle simmer. Add green onions and lime zest. *If you use already cooked chicken, stir it in now.*

- Finally, stir fresh cilantro through soup. Serve with a steaming pot of brown jasmine or basmati rice. To use a Thai expression, *yum.*

Notes:

➢ This recipe is mild by Thai standards, but you can fix that easily enough by adjusting the chili factor. If you are chili savvy you could use fresh Thai chilies. I have also often used Thai red chili paste for flavor and heat. Sample paste for firepower by mixing a smidgen with a bit of soup liquid. A few whole fresh red chilies floating around have a certain dramatic appeal, and anyone who likes it hot can catch one and release it in their own bowl.

➢ I prefer chicken thigh meat even though it is certainly fussy to trim and slice. Chicken breasts are easiest. Another option is simply to use the meat liberated from a chicken you have cooked yourself.

➢ I have even made this soup replacing the chicken with fresh halibut. All liked it and some loved it, but the chicken always gets the most votes.

➢ Thai fish sauce is available in most supermarkets, and is an important ingredient here. (However, I have successfully substituted a tablespoon of mashed anchovies, or about 3.) In fact, every ingredient is critical in this soup. It needs every element present to do it justice.

Coconut Milk

Canned coconut milk is available under many labels almost anywhere for a wide range of prices. Before you decide on any brand, always read the ingredient label and shake the can to make sure the contents haven't solidified. As usual, it's a good idea to buy this sort of product from a busy store. The brand I like has only coconut milk with xanthan gum and soy lecithin as natural emulsifiers.

For an absolutely decadent coconut milk of your own: combine 3 cups dried unsweetened shredded coconut with 3 cups of 2 percent milk in a saucepan and bring slowly to a simmer, watching that it doesn't scorch while your back is turned. Remove from the heat and cool for about 30 minutes. Blend in small batches in a blender at high speed for about 30 seconds. Squeeze each batch in 2 layers of cheesecloth or a tea towel, extracting every bit of milk you can.

Southwest Couscous Salad
with Chicken and Jicama

This salad is wonderfully easy to make, lively and rich tasting, good warm or cold, and makes for popular leftovers. Couscous is not a grain, so this is essentially a pasta salad. Whole-wheat couscous is not as easy to find as the regular couscous, but it is available in both bulk and packaged forms. Jicama (*HEE-kuh-muh*) is a vegetable that looks like a tan oversized turnip, has the crisp texture of a water chestnut, and a flavor that is both slightly sweet and starchy. Choose a jicama weighing about 1½-lb (they tend to range between 1 – 3-lbs) with smooth, hard skin.

(Serves about 6)

> 1 box (10 ounces) or 1½ cups *whole-wheat* couscous
> 2½ cups water and/or chicken broth (see directions)
> ¾ teaspoon salt
>
> 2 lbs skinless boneless chicken breasts or thighs
> 1 bunch green onions, sliced (or about 1½ cups)
> 1 medium jicama, peeled and sliced into matchsticks (or about 3 cups)
> ½ cup chopped fresh cilantro
> 1 cup *Southwest Dressing* (recipe below)

Southwest Dressing
⅓ cup lemon juice
2 teaspoons freshly crushed garlic
2 teaspoons mild chili powder
2 teaspoons ground cumin
1½ teaspoon salt
¾ teaspoon Tabasco sauce
⅔ cup extra virgin olive oil

To Prepare Couscous
- *Note: For the proportion of water to couscous, follow directions on the box. Some brands of couscous are 12 ounces or 2 cups couscous, so be aware.* In a saucepan with a lid bring 2½ cups chicken broth/water and salt to a boil. If you use the chicken poaching liquid (details next page), you won't need to add any more salt.)

- Stir in whole-wheat couscous and bring back to the boil. Allow to boil for 30 seconds, and then remove from heat. Cover pan and set aside for 10 minutes.

- Remove lid and fluff couscous with a fork. Set aside.

To Poach Chicken

When I start with raw chicken, I usually poach it this way. It's easy, and the chicken meat ends up tender and moist. I prefer the richer meat of thighs, but the chicken breasts are easier to work with if your timing is tight. You can use the poaching liquid to cook the couscous.

- Pour 3 cups of chicken broth (or broth and water mixed) and a teaspoon of salt into a 1½-quart pot with a tight-fitting lid. Bring liquid to a boil, then reduce heat and add chicken, arranging it to submerge as much of the meat as possible.

- Bring broth back to a simmer, and gently simmer chicken for 15 minutes. Remove from heat and cover pot, and let chicken finish cooking in the hot broth for another 10 minutes.

- Transfer chicken to a bowl and set aside until meat cools enough to handle. *(If you're cooking chicken in advance, return cooled chicken to poaching liquid to keep it moist.)* Reserve 2½ cups of the poaching liquid for cooking the couscous. If necessary, add water to make correct amount.

- Cut cooked chicken into thick slices (about 1 inch) and tear slices into bite-sized pieces. Set aside: you should have about 4 cups.

To Prepare Dressing
- For dressing, combine all ingredients except oil and cilantro in a 2-cup Pyrex jug and whisk thoroughly. Add oil in a thin stream, whisking as you pour. Stir in cilantro. If possible, allow dressing to sit for an hour at room temperature.

To Assemble Salad
- For jicama with tough brown skin, strip off with paring knife and then peel once more with regular peeler. To slice into matchsticks, halve or quarter jicama and slice into ⅛-inch slices. Cut slices into ⅛-inch sticks about 2 inches long. You should have about 3 cups.

- Place chicken pieces, sliced green onion, jicama matchsticks, and chopped cilantro in a large mixing bowl and add couscous. Pour dressing over the top and toss to blend thoroughly. Serve at any temperature.

Roasted Chicken Thighs

Buy them with their skin on to protect the meat during cooking, and remember that leftover chicken is very useful. This is just about the simplest and quickest treatment of chicken I know.

(Serves about 4 – 6, depending on thigh size)

> 8 chicken thighs, with skin
> salt
> freshly ground pepper

Preheat oven to 400 degrees.

- Trim excess fat and skin overhang from chicken thighs and save for stock. (See *Simple Stock* below.)

- Lay thighs skin side down in an 8 x 10-inch casserole dish and sprinkle undersides with salt and pepper. Then turn the thighs over so the skin side is up and sprinkle with more salt and pepper. (Mother says a sprinkling of paprika is important for color, and she's right. *If* you have some paprika.)

- Roast in the upper third of the oven for about 45 minutes at 400 degrees.

Note:
- A mixture of a teaspoon each of freshly crushed garlic, olive oil, and kosher salt (coarser than regular salt and available in supermarkets) is pretty delicious rubbed into the underside of the thighs.   Or you can combine a teaspoon of salt with a tablespoon each of grainy European-style mustard and honey in the casserole dish, and roll the chicken thighs to thoroughly coat before roasting.

Simple chicken stock

Collect the bones and skin (including raw skin and fat trimmings as mentioned above) in a container and store it in the refrigerator until you can boil it all up for stock. Just transfer the bones, etc., to a pot, cover with water, and then bring to a boil. Reduce heat and simmer uncovered for a couple of hours. Strain and cool stock, then chill. The fat will solidify on top and seal off the stock from the air. The fat is easiest to remove when very cold. You can store the stock in the refrigerator for a few days or in the freezer for up to several months. Boil for at least 5 minutes before using.

Just Plain Old Roast Chicken

This is one of those recipes that aren't really recipes, but could be classified under *Things Mother Taught Me*. When it comes to roasting chickens, one is faced with all kinds of questions. Low and slow? Hot and fast? A combination? Truss? Baste? (… and if so, with what?) Covered or uncovered or both? With or without a thermometer? Who cares? Just do what Mother did.

> chicken, 4 — 5-pound, a drug-free, free-range clean-living bird
> olive oil
> salt and freshly ground pepper
> onion (optional)
> celery tops (optional)
> lemon (optional)
> garlic (optional)

Preheat oven to 425 degrees. Find a pot with lid that will fit your chicken: I use a 3-quart enameled cast iron pot or a 5-quart Dutch oven.

- Check the cavity of the chicken. If there is a neck, toss it back into the cavity. If there is a bag of giblets, rip it open. There are usually a couple of funny little things that I believe are the heart and gizzard and which I throw in with the neck. If the liver looks nice and fresh I sauté it briskly in butter, then grind some salt and pepper over it and eat it while it's hot. Mm-mm.

- If you choose to rinse the chicken, pat it dry with paper towels. Rub a teaspoon of olive oil around inside the pot before putting the chicken in. Stuff chicken with a squeezed lemon, if you have one (save the juice for something else), a quartered onion (no need to peel it, but strip off any loose brown papery skin), a couple of leafy celery tops, and some garlic cloves, not necessarily peeled but lightly smashed. Coat visible surfaces of chicken with olive oil, then dust generously with freshly ground pepper and salt.

- Cover pot, place in oven, ***reduce heat to 400 degrees***, and roast for about 1½ hours. Check for doneness by wiggling a drumstick; if it moves with any reluctance, or tends to bounce firmly back to its original position, cook it for another ½ hour or so. If the drumstick moves easily in the joint, the chicken is cooked. (If the drumstick comes away in your hand — well, it's probably overcooked, and therefore more meltingly delicious, according to Mother.)

- Give the cooked chicken 15 minutes to brood before serving. (Save carcass for *Simple Chicken Stock* on previous page.) Leftover cooked chicken is useful for *Chicken Potpie* (page 69), *Southwest Couscous Salad* (page 152), and *Tom Kah Gai* (page 150).

Meat Loaf

A rich and redolent meat loaf is a truly great dish. It is also a sensible way to serve meat when you don't know exactly how many you are serving, or when. Meat loaf can be mixed ahead of time and stored in the refrigerator, and preferably brought to room temperature before cooking. A well-constructed meat loaf even waits cheerfully *after* it's cooked without losing its appeal. Leftovers are useful, too. There is the legendary meat loaf sandwich, or you can chop it up and use it in soup, or in chili (page 122), or with tomato sauce (page 70) to serve over polenta (page 137-8), brown rice (page 125), or whole grain noodles.

(Serves 4 – 6)

> 1½ lbs finest quality ground beef, not too lean
> 1 medium onion, finely chopped (about 2 cups)
> 2 tablespoons extra virgin olive oil
> 2 eggs
> ¼ cup yogurt
> 2 tablespoons Dijon-style or whole grain mustard
> 1 teaspoon freshly crushed garlic
> 1 teaspoon salt
> 1 teaspoon freshly ground pepper
> ¾ cup old-fashioned rolled oats

Preheat oven to 350 degrees

- Heat olive oil in 10-inch skillet over medium heat. Sauté onion for 10-15 minutes or until tender. Set aside.

- Meanwhile, combine eggs with yogurt, mustard, garlic, salt, and pepper and whisk until well blended. Add rolled oats and sautéed onions and mix well. Add ground meat and blend thoroughly.

- *Traditional:* Pack meat loaf mixture lightly in a 9x5-inch loaf pan and bake in 350-degree oven for about 1¼ hours.

- *Alternative:* Use a spatula to pat meat mixture into a vaguely loaf-shaped lump while it is still in the mixing bowl, and then tip it into a shallow 1½-quart oven-to-table casserole and finish shaping the meat into a free-form loaf (using the spatula). Bake in a 350-degree oven for about 1¼ hours.

Note:
➤ Meat loaf is not an inherently glamorous thing, so a topping of *Tomato Sauce* (page 70) before serving is a particularly good idea. It pairs well with the meat, and one could consider the sauce an extra serving of vegetables.

Zucchini Frittata

The *frittata* is basically an omelet with the filling and eggs combined, so there is obviously lots of room for experimentation here. The possibilities range from complex to simple and this recipe is *very* simple. The seasoning is understated, so this dish goes down nicely anytime from breakfast to midnight snack.

(Serves about 2 – 4)

> 4 eggs
> 3 slim zucchini grated on medium grater or about 4 cups
> ¼ cup freshly grated Parmesan or crumbled feta cheese
> ½ teaspoon salt
> ½ teaspoon freshly ground pepper
> 1 tablespoon extra-virgin olive oil

- Crack eggs into a mixing bowl and beat with a fork, just enough to blend. Add grated zucchini, cheese, and seasoning, and mix well. *(If you grate the zucchini ahead of time, toss with a teaspoon of salt and set aside in a sieve for 30 minutes. Press out excess liquid before adding to egg mixture, and reduce salt to ¼ teaspoon.)*

- Heat oil in a 10 – 12-inch non-stick skillet over medium high heat until a drop of the frittata mixture sizzles wildly. Give mixture a final stir and pour it into the skillet, spreading it evenly. Reduce heat to medium-low and cook until mixture is almost set, about 10 – 15 minutes, shaking pan from time to time in the first few minutes to prevent sticking. (The smaller sized pan will make a thicker frittata, which will take longer to set.) The frittata will be wet on top.

- To finish cooking, place pan under broiler for about 3 minutes **or** cut frittata in quarters and flip carefully. Or if you're feeling deft, place a plate over the skillet and, holding plate and skillet tightly together with hot pads, invert so frittata falls onto plate, and then slide frittata back into hot skillet to finish cooking the top. I don't recommend doing this the first time with an audience.

Notes:

➤ A favorite variation of mine is made with spinach. Prepare a 10 ounce packet of frozen chopped spinach using the directions on page 76, draining it of about ¼ cup of liquid. Use it instead of the zucchini in the recipe above. It's a great emergency meal because I always have eggs and frozen spinach on hand.

➤ A frittata made with leftover cooked vegetables can be wonderful. Potato or broccoli, for example, and thinly sliced green onions for freshness.

Spinach and Cheese Crepes
with Tomato Sauce

This is a vegetarian dish in three parts, all of which may be made days ahead, if necessary, and call for no last minute shopping. Good for potlucks and those suppers for tired and hungry houseguests who arrive a couple of hours later than they're supposed to. One filled crepe topped with the bright sauce makes a first course that doubles as a vegetable and can boost a simple meal. Two crepes make a main course finished with an easy salad. They also reheat nicely the next day.

(Serves 6 with 2 filled crepes apiece)

Crepes:
Crepes are a wonderful addition to any cook's repertoire, and they even freeze well.

(Makes about 16 x 6-inch crepes.)

> 4 eggs
> 1 cup milk
> 2 tablespoons extra virgin olive oil
> ½ teaspoon salt
> 1 tablespoon sugar
> 1 cup whole wheat flour (preferably pastry flour)

For crepe batter:
- Combine ingredients in a food processor or blender and process until smooth, or beat eggs in a 4-cup measuring jug, add remaining ingredients, and blend until smooth with an immersion blender or whisk. (The whisk method is adequate, but will not give you a completely smooth batter.) Set batter aside for 1 – 2 hours if you can; this technically relaxes the gluten and makes a more tender crepe. *If you store the batter overnight in the refrigerator, it will separate; just stir to a smooth consistency again.* While cooking crepes, stir batter regularly.

To cook crepes:
- Heat crepe pan, or a 6 - 7 inch skillet with sloping sides, over moderate-high heat. When drops of water sizzle in the pan, it is ready. Wipe with oil-soaked paper towel. Pour batter into pan from a spoon or scoop holding about 3 tablespoons, holding pan handle in your other hand and swirling pan quickly to cover the bottom evenly with batter. Keep swirling pan until batter no longer runs and set pan back on heat.

- When the crepe's surface is dry and the underside is a lacy golden-brown it is ready to flip: this will probably take about 20 – 30 seconds. (One clue that it is ready to flip is a slight darkening of the very edge.) After flipping, cook for another 10 seconds and then flip again onto a plate covered with a paper towel. (The second side will be pale and freckled.)

- Stack crepes as you cook them. You will notice there are enough crepes to allow for some disasters or passers-by or whatever. *The crepes may be made up to a week in advance and stored in the refrigerator sealed in plastic.*

Spinach and Cheese Filling:
   1 box (10 ounces) frozen chopped spinach, thawed and drained
   2 eggs
   1 teaspoon freshly crushed garlic
   1 teaspoon salt
   ½ teaspoon freshly ground pepper
   8 ounces mozzarella cheese, grated (about 2½ cups)
   1 cup freshly grated Parmesan

For spinach and cheese mixture:
- Thaw and drain spinach. *(Either leave frozen spinach in a bowl in the refrigerator overnight, or at room temperature for a few hours, or into a covered skillet over a low heat for about 10 – 15 minutes, breaking up spinach as it thaws. Drain off excess liquid in a sieve, pressing spinach with a spatula; you should be able to extract ½ cup.)*

- Whisk eggs in a medium bowl and add spinach, garlic, seasoning, and cheeses, mixing very thoroughly.

To assemble crepes:
- Butter or oil shallow casserole dish, about 8 x 12-inch.

- Lay 12 crepes out on counter, pale freckled side up. Divide filling between crepes, about ¼ cup on each. Spread filling across the lower three-quarters of each crepe and roll up.

- Place in baking dish and cook, covered loosely with foil, at 400 degrees for about 30 minutes. *(If crepes were made ahead and chilled, bring to room temperature before baking.)* Serve with **Tomato Sauce** (page 70).

Note:
➢ You can also spread the spinach and cheese filling on strips of cooked whole-wheat lasagna, then roll them up, crowd them in the casserole, and cover with the tomato sauce.

Macaroni and Cheese

It's easy to justify a meal of macaroni and cheese if you don't compromise on the ingredients. Happily, this recipe doesn't *taste* uncompromising. As for the onions, remember that diced onion, when sauteed according to the directions below, will melt down to half its original volume and will virtually disappear into the macaroni and cheese. The "don't ask, don't tell" policy works well here.

(Serves 4)

> 3 cups **cooked** *whole-grain* macaroni (brown rice, whole wheat, etc)
> 2 tablespoons olive oil
> 1 medium onion, in ¼-inch dice (about 2 cups)
> 4 eggs
> 1 can (12 ounces) evaporated *whole* milk (1½ cups)
> 8 ounces *sharp* cheddar cheese, grated (about 4 cups)
> 1 teaspoon salt
> ½ teaspoon Tabasco sauce

Preheat oven to 300 degrees.

- Heat olive oil in 10-inch pot. *(I like to use the heavy-bottomed pasta pot; I just tip the cooked pasta into the colander to drain, then put the pot back on the stove and add the oil.)* Sauté onion for 10 – 15 minutes or until very tender.

- Whisk eggs in a 2-quart mixing bowl. Add milk, cheese, and seasoning, and blend thoroughly. Combine with cooked macaroni and onion.

- Scrape into an oiled 2-quart casserole dish. *(You will have about that much macaroni and cheese mixture.)* Bake uncovered at 300 degrees for 45 – 60 minutes or until set.

Note:

➢ A dish like this begs to be customized, but keep it real. Use real cheese, not "lite" or processed, with real flavor, if possible. A cup of grated feta cheese is one of our favorite additions, if I have any left from the last time I made *Greek Salad* (page 93.) And if you don't use evaporated *whole* milk, use milk with a respectable butterfat content, like whole milk.

➢ Brown rice macaroni is softer and milder than whole-wheat pasta, so is probably the more acceptable substitute for regular white pasta.

8   Bread and Baking

Breadmaking:
Eight common questions

One problem is that it's *too* easy to make bread; that's why so many of us make bread without really understanding how bread is made. Then, when our plump and soaring loaf emerges from the oven pocked and sullen, it's just one more unsolved mystery that knocks another leg out from under our confidence. The point is, once you understand the few basic principles governing the action of yeast and gluten, you'll never again be bullied by breadmaking or all the silly misconceptions about it.

Water, yeast, and flour; there you have the framework on which hang all yeast-risen breads. Mixed together in a bowl, the water moistens the wheat proteins to develop the gluten, which during the stirring and kneading is stretched and toughened to form an elastic network of little pockets (a sort of honeycomb effect) able to trap the gases produced by the fermenting yeast.

So the bread rises. The only way it won't rise is if the yeast is dead, or we kill it. Now, yeast is sensitive, but it's not fragile, and will usually survive in spite of us. Once you master a simple loaf and understand how and why it works, you'll know when to ignore unnecessary and sometimes crazy recipe instructions.

From there it takes only practice and an awareness of the effect of other ingredients — like salt, sweetening, and fat — on the teamwork of gluten and yeast. Following are the most-asked questions about making bread, with answers that I hope will simplify the process for you.

How important is water temperature?
Just don't scare the yeast! It doesn't like hot water or cold water. Yeast is inactive when cold, sluggish when cool, thriving when warm, hysterical when hot, and dead when the temperature hits 140 degrees. The ideal temperature for activating dry yeast is about 110 degrees. Anything within the range of warm is fine. Bread recipes often urge you to use a thermometer (I never have), but as long as yeast has such a casual approach to the warm water issue, you may as well.

What kind of yeast?
The active dry yeast granules are easier to find, use, and store than the fresh compressed yeast (which is usually sold in little cakes in the refrigeration department). Any brand of active dry yeast is fine. If you find yourself with past-dated yeast, test it before you toss it – it's probably fine. The common supermarket brands come in 4 ounce jars or ¼ ounce packets: unless you plan to make only three loaves of bread a year, the jars are more economical. But by far the best deal is pre-packed bulk baking yeast from a good natural food store. As for something called "rapid-rise" yeast, I've used it interchangeably with regular yeast. (This all may sound haphazard but that's one of the charming aspects of bread making. A bit of yeast either way will not raise the eyebrows of any dough.)

How much yeast?
Yeast is not like baking powder. Yeast cells are alive and grow by multiplying: given enough time, a half-teaspoon of yeast is able to aerate a batch of dough just as well as a tablespoon of yeast. This is an especially important point to make in view of the fact that you may come across recipes that call for *two packages* (almost 2 tablespoons) of yeast, even for a standard batch of white

bread. Obviously more yeast works faster and makes both the recipe-writer and the baker feel safe, but once you get used to tipping in that amount of yeast, you're more likely to feel doubtful when a perfectly sane recipe calls for one third of that amount. Excess yeast rushes the dough's fermentation along, as well as causing the loaf to dry faster.

Whole grain dough can use more yeast and doesn't benefit from long or multiple risings. (Technically, dough that is allowed a leisurely rising period undergoes a ripening process which develops its natural acidity: this is one of the keys to those crusty, fragrant artisan breads in paper bags we pay so much for.)

Does it matter what kind of flour I use?
You bet it does. For yeast raised breads you should be using high-gluten flour made from what is called "hard" (high protein) wheat. Look for something called *stone ground whole wheat bread flour.* My choice is *Bob's Red Mill* stone ground whole-wheat bread flour, which is ground and packaged here in Oregon and easy to find in most supermarkets. Whether you buy flour packaged or from the bulk food department, choose a food store with high standards and a brisk turnover. (See *Favorite Portland Sources* on page 33.)

The critical factor is gluten, the protein in wheat which becomes elastic when moistened, and which is what makes yeast breads possible. Yeast works relatively slowly and depends on the strength of the gluten to trap and hold the gases it produces. (Pastry flour, however, is made with "soft" low-gluten wheat and is best for quick breads like scones and muffins which call for a fast acting rising agent like baking

powder. If your loaf seems too crumbly, make sure you're not using pastry flour.) If you're using high-gluten flour, you should never need to add gluten flour (which is pure, powdered gluten), even in 100 percent whole-wheat bread. Once you have handled the springy, exuberant dough made from high-gluten flour, you won't give up until you find it.

How do I know when I've added enough flour?
Never take the flour quantities in recipes too seriously. Flours absorb at different rates and people measure different ways. Once dough is too stiff to stir, add no more than one or two tablespoons of flour at one time. It doesn't matter how much flour the recipe calls for — let the dough have the last word. Dough should feel soft, but bouncy. (The bounce comes from well-developed gluten, which is the result of adequate kneading.) It may take a good bit of practice, though, to feel the bounce in sticky whole-wheat dough.

A "wet" dough is inherently less stable than a drier dough, and if left to rise too long before baking will tend to collapse more easily in the oven, coming out dimpled and flat or misshapen on top. However, it will certainly have a better flavor and moister texture than the loaf with more flour and a nice rounded crust. The trick is to find the right balance, and that comes with practice.

Can I over-knead dough?
Probably not, unless you're using a food processor or some other mechanical kneader. Kneading manually, your arms would drop off before the dough was even tired. (In fact, dough made from high-gluten flour begs to be kneaded much longer than most of us are willing.) The trick is to avoid adding too much flour to the dough during kneading because of the temptation to try to

remove the stickiness from the dough. Too much flour makes dense, dry, bland bread.

Can I make good bread without fat, sugar, or salt?

Certainly without fat or sugar (consider the traditional baguette, for example), but salt in bread can be a rather emotional issue. Except in commercial baking salt's role in dough development is insignificant, but it is critical as a flavor enhancer. Leave it out at your own risk.

Sweetening is not necessary for the dough at any stage, but it will make the dough rise faster by exciting the yeast. Honey is my preferred sweetener, and is a major ingredient in the versions of my *Whole-wheat & Honey Loaf* recipes that follow. Added sweetening also makes the crust brown quicker and darker, as does fat.

Fat makes bread more tender, and even a small amount, like a tablespoon per pound of dough, can increase the final loaf volume by 20 percent. More fat, like ¼ cup or more per pound of dough will require more yeast to get the work done. Remember that milk and eggs have the effect of fat in dough. (Eggs can create a fine, close crumb, which is useful if you use bread for sandwiches.)

Can I substitute other kinds of flour instead of wheat?

Remember that most non-wheat flours have no appreciable gluten, and gluten is a critical factor in yeast-risen breads. Unless you are confident of producing a successful loaf of bread using wheat flour, you probably should put off experimenting with recipes using non-wheat flours. Also, you generally find it necessary to incorporate too much white flour, and that would seem to defeat the purpose. Keep in mind that it is hard to be sure of buying fresh flour of the less

popular — and slower selling — varieties like oat, barley, rice, and even rye flour.

Whole-wheat Breadmaking

It has always seemed curious that most recipes for what is called "whole-wheat bread" require only about half the flour to be whole wheat. Not surprising, though, because half-white dough is simply easier to handle than the stickier whole-wheat dough. However, it's confusing to call bread made with any proportion of white flour *whole* wheat, regardless of how enriched, unbleached, organic, and untainted by genetic modification it is. There are times, though, when the addition of white flour is especially welcome for texture and handling, and examples of this are my recipes for pita pockets, focaccia, and pizza (pages 174-78).

100 percent whole-wheat dough is trickier to handle because whole-wheat flour absorbs more liquid than white flour, and takes longer to absorb the liquid. The dough is stickier, so we tend to either add too much flour or knead too briefly (thus under-working the gluten). The easier option is to find a way to knead it apart from your hands. These days we have options like electric mixers, bread machines, and food processors, which make the job simple. My preference is for the dough cycle of a bread machine — I find it the easiest way to deal with the needs of whole-wheat dough.

Make the same loaf again and again until you feel comfortable enough to adjust the ingredients and methods to suit yourself. Starting on page 166 are my recipes. These include examples of three different methods to mix the dough by hand, bread machine, and food processor.

Tips and Rules of Thumb

- Becoming a confident bread-maker is easy if you make bread often in small batches.

- When making bread by hand, always start with the liquids in the bowl, and then add the flour. The flour, not the liquid, should be the variable. (An exception is when using a food processor. See page 174.)

- You never need to sift flour in bread making, but before measuring flour from the bag it's a good idea to stir it first with a fork to fluff it up. You'll find that measuring will be more consistent once compacted flour is loosened up.

- The best way to measure flour is always to spoon or pour flour from the bag into your measuring cup. Flour can be packed firmly or loosely, and if you reach in with a measuring cup and scoop out flour, this variable can obviously throw off your proportions.

- As a rule of thumb, you will need *about* 2¼ cups of whole-wheat flour or 2¾ cups of white flour for every cup of liquid, but always let your dough decide. Whole-wheat flour absorbs more liquid, *and at a slower rate*, than white flour.

- Remember to handle dough briskly and authoritatively. When dough senses uncertainty, it sticks to the hands. It's also handy to know that dough will not stick to wet hands.

- Oiled plastic wrap over rising dough is easy to remove later, and will keep the dough moist and skin-free. Spray the plastic briefly with non-stick cooking spray, which is convenient and efficient for bread pans, too.

- To clean a doughy counter, scrape with a dough scraper first. And to clean a bowl or bread machine bucket, scrape out as much dough as you can, then use cool water, never hot.

- *Do not store bread in the refrigerator*, even if your mother always did. Bread turns stale faster in the refrigerator than at room temperature. But it is critical to cool a loaf completely before storing in a plastic bag — any moisture from condensation will mold bread quickly, especially in warm temperatures. Double-wrap and freeze extra bread.

- If you're new to bread making, keep things simple at first. Start with a basic, useful recipe, and then experiment within the recipe. Note what happens when you add more or less flour, more or less sweetening or fat, milk instead of water, less yeast with longer rising times, and so on. It's the best way to learn how to control the texture, moistness, crust, flavor, and shape of your bread, and with the least chance of failure.

- Always eat your failures while they're still warm.

Little Whole-Wheat & Honey Loaf
Wooden spoon method

Making a small loaf like this is the best way to learn to make a good loaf of 100 percent whole-wheat bread, in my opinion. It is pretty easy to mix by hand and makes a fairly manageable lump of dough: if you mess it up somehow, it's not critical. However, I wouldn't recommend making a loaf this small once you get comfortable with the breadmaking process. It makes more sense to put the effort into a larger loaf (See *Whole-Wheat Family Loaf*) and freeze several slices for future need. I suggest you slice it thin for sandwiches and thicker for toast.

If you would rather ease more gradually into an all-whole-wheat loaf, replace the last cup of whole-wheat flour with unbleached white bread flour. As for the honey, we like the level of sweetness in this loaf but it can naturally be adjusted to suit you. (It is important to remember that honey counts as a liquid, so the recipe will take less flour.)

(8 x 4-inch loaf)

> 1¼ cups warm water
> 1 tablespoon active dry yeast
> 1½ teaspoons salt
> 2 tablespoons oil
> ¼ cup honey
> 2½ - 3 cups stone-ground whole-wheat bread flour

- Sprinkle yeast over warm water in mixing bowl and set aside about 3 minutes to soften. Add 1½ cups of flour and stir until smooth. The mixture should feel like *very* thick batter. *(If not, add flour 2 tablespoons at a time until it feels very thick but still beatable.)* Beat vigorously by hand - a wooden spoon works best - for about 150 strokes. *(Switching hands keeps your arm from having to stop to rest. Feels clumsy but it works.)* Scrape sides of bowl, cover with plastic wrap, and let dough (technically what recipes would call a "sponge") rise for about an hour, or until at least doubled.

- Add salt, oil, honey, and ½ cup of flour and stir until smooth. Beat for 50 strokes. Stir in another ½ cup of flour, blending until smooth. Stir spiritedly for 100 strokes, if possible. *(The stirring develops the gluten and reduces your kneading time later.)* If the dough is still slack enough to be stirred, work in more flour a tablespoon or two at a time until dough becomes too stiff to stir. Scrape sides of bowl clean, making sure all loose flour is blended into dough. Cover with plastic wrap, and set aside to rise for about an hour or until doubled.

- Using a rubber spatula, deflate dough and gather into a sticky ball. Sprinkle with a tablespoon of flour and scrape out onto a floured patch of countertop.

Knead the dough for a minute or two, dusting the counter with only as much flour as you absolutely need. The dough should be soft and tacky; until you get used to handling whole-wheat dough, you may find your palms constantly gathering a layer of dough during kneading.

- Pat dough into a flattened oval cushion on the flour-dusted counter, roll it up into a fat sausage about 8 inches long, then tuck it into an oiled 8 x 4-inch loaf pan. Pat the dough down evenly and cover with oiled plastic wrap. ***Preheat oven to 400 degrees.*** Allow dough to double, which should take about 30 – 45 minutes, depending on the warmth of your kitchen.

- Place in the lower third of your oven (or directly on preheated baking stone), reduce heat 375 degrees and bake for 30 minutes. The bottom crust should be a toasty golden-brown, and have a hollow-sounding *thok* when you knock it, rather than *thud*.

- Don't try to slice off more than the crust in the first half-hour of cooling. Allow it to cool for *at least* a couple of hours before sealing in a clean plastic bag. And don't store it in the refrigerator!

Note:

➢ The amount of flour you add will determine the height and roundness of the crust as well as the moistness of the bread, but don't forget that a dramatically soaring loaf probably is a symptom of too much flour. The secret to moist, well-textured *wholly* whole-wheat bread is well-kneaded yet sticky dough, but it's hard to knead sticky dough for long without adding too much flour. One answer is to give the dough a good thrashing while it is still slack enough to be stirred, but there's no escaping the fact that hand-mixing whole-wheat dough does require significant arm-work.

➢ The temperature of your kitchen and the time of year can make a significant difference in the time your dough takes to rise. (The final rise generally takes less than 30 minutes in my kitchen.) Keep an eye on it, and begin preheating your oven as soon as you have set the loaf aside to rise. If you let the dough over-rise, the shape of the top crust will not be as nice and the bread will tend to be very weak in the middle.

Whole-Wheat and Honey Family Loaf
Using the bread machine to mix dough

Bread machines are hard working helpers with impressive white uniforms but no brains. They are tireless, unquestioning, cheerful in the face of the wettest dough, and easy to clean. However, because you need a brain to deal with the variables that affect the loaf's moistness and the timing of the final rising and baking, that part of the process is their weakness. Brainlessness notwithstanding, bread machines do a splendid job of mixing and kneading and are worth their expense as a dough-making machine. The gentle, thorough, supervision-free kneading of dough too sticky to knead by hand is one way to perfect 100 percent whole-wheat bread.

Also, bread machines have managed to do what no amount of written reassurance could; they have proved that bread making is a simple science. You combine the flour, water, and yeast, and the machine simply baby-sits, applying prescribed doses of a little paddling here, a little nap there, and gentle heat as needed. Eventually, a loaf is hatched. Technology trampling art? No, it's just an uncluttered view of the essence of the bread-making process.

(If you're shopping for one, avoid bread machines that take themselves too seriously; you need a sturdy machine that starts when you push the button — unless you like the delayed start feature — and can handle two pounds of dough.)

(9 x 5-inch loaf)

>2 cups warm water
>2½ teaspoons (or 1 packet) active dry yeast
>about 3 cups stone-ground whole-wheat bread flour
>
>2 tablespoons extra virgin olive oil
>½ cup honey
>2½ teaspoons salt
>about 2 cups stone-ground whole-wheat bread flour

- Place warm water in bucket of bread machine and sprinkle yeast into water. Allow a few minutes for yeast to soften, and then add 3 cups of flour. *(Measure the flour by pouring or spooning flour into the measuring cup.)* Set bread machine on dough cycle and start. Check after 10 minutes, and scrape down sides with a spatula. You should have a mixture that looks like very thick batter but not yet beginning to gather into dough. *(This mixture of water, yeast, and flour is called a "sponge", which is the perfect environment for the development of yeast and gluten. If it doesn't look thick enough, add flour ¼ cup at a time.)* Allow machine to complete the kneading stage of the dough cycle, after which the machine rests and the rising cycle begins.

- When the sponge has had 30 minutes to raise, during which time it has probably tripled in volume, push *stop* button. Start dough cycle again, and with a rubber spatula scrape down the sponge from the sides of the bucket. Add oil, honey, salt, and 2 cups of whole-wheat flour.

- Check after 10 minutes, scraping clean the sides of the bucket again. When mixed, the dough should be able to form a soft ball that pulls away from the sides of the bucket, tending to climb slightly upward rather than slop around in a relaxed mass as it is kneaded. If dough forms a ball that looks patchy and dry, add 1-2 tablespoons of water. If you think dough might be too wet, be very cautious about adding flour. However, if dough really seems too sloppy and only forms a half-hearted sort of ball, add flour cautiously, a tablespoon or two at a time. *Avoid adding any more flour than necessary. It's safer to err on the moist side with 100 percent whole-wheat dough.* Allow the dough to continue through kneading cycle, and then 20 minutes of rising cycle.

- Start kneading cycle again. Meanwhile, mist a 9 x 5-inch bread pan with non-stick spray and set aside. Position oven racks so that there is room for loaf on the bottom shelf. If you have a baking stone, place it on bottom rack.

- When dough is kneaded down into a ball again, shake and scrape dough out of bucket onto a floured patch of countertop. It will feel warm from the bread machine. Knead the dough briefly to form it into a ball of sorts; the point is not to knead more flour into the dough, but to keep adequate flour between the dough and your hands and the counter. The dough needs no more kneading, obviously, but only shaping. Pat into a flattened oval cushion, roll up into a fat sausage about the length of the pan, and lift it quickly into the pan. *(If the dough is very soft it pays to handle it briskly.)*

- Pat the dough down evenly and cover with oiled plastic wrap. Take a good look at it so you have an idea what it should look like when doubled. **Preheat oven to 400 degrees**.

- Check dough after 30 minutes. *(It should only take that long because the dough's warmth from the machine's kneading process accelerates the rising.)* If you think it has doubled, go ahead and put it in the oven. It's easy to let the dough rise too far, which means the bread will have an airy, weak center.

- Place loaf on the lowest rack in the oven (or directly on a preheated baking stone) and reduce heat to 375 degrees. Bake for 40 minutes. Allow loaf to cool completely (about 3 hours) before sealing in a clean plastic bag. Store at room temperature, and slice as you need it.

Millet Bread
Master Recipe # 1: Using Cooked Grain Cereal

Using cooked whole grains in whole wheat bread is a great idea. It makes not only more nutrient-dense bread, but also bread full of character that stays moist longer. This recipe and the two following use different methods, but they all try to incorporate generous doses of whole grains. The idea is to achieve bread with delightful character while avoiding anything reminiscent of baked porridge. If you decide to experiment, I suggest being conservative at first, especially if you're working with dense-textured mixtures.

Speaking of porridge, the following recipes offer some fine ways to use leftover cooked cereal. You can mix boiling water with cooked grain straight out of the refrigerator, for instance, and then add the yeast when the mixture cools to a yeast-friendly temperature.

In this recipe I call for cooked millet, a grain I don't tend to use often. My personal favorite is cooked kasha (toasted buckwheat). Both grains are covered on pages 132-33. You can substitute any cooked whole grain cereal like cracked wheat, bulgur, or cracked rye. If you're using a denser porridge like cooked corn meal (or polenta), or any sort of leftover cooked oatmeal, start with 1 cup.

Although the amount of cooked millet I call for here is 2 cups, it's fairly fluffy. Unless it's soggy or gritty or mushy or crumbly or lumpy, which is a very good reason to make this bread.

(Makes 8 x 4-inch loaf)

> ½ cup milk
> ½ cup hot water
> 1 tablespoon active dry yeast
> 2 cups *cooked* millet, warm or room temperature
> 2½ – 3 cups stone ground whole-wheat bread flour, divided
> 1 tablespoon oil
> ¼ cup honey
> 1½ teaspoons salt

- In a mixing bowl, combine cold milk and hot water to make a warm liquid. Sprinkle yeast over the top and allow to soften for about 5 minutes. Add cooked millet and 1 cup of whole-wheat flour and stir until smooth. Add another ½ cup of whole-wheat flour. The mixture should be like very thick batter, but stirable. Stir briskly for about 100 – 200 strokes. Scrape sides of bowl clean, then cover with plastic wrap and set aside for 30 – 45 minutes or until at least doubled.

- Add oil, honey, salt, and ½ cup of flour. Stir until smooth, and then blend in another ¼ cup of flour and stir vigorously for at least 50 strokes. Thoroughly mix in another ¼ cup of flour. *(Keep bottom and sides of the bowl scraped to avoid ending up with dried shreds of dough hanging around the outskirts.)* By now the dough will probably be too stiff to stir but too sticky to knead.

- Sprinkle a tablespoon of flour over the dough, gather into a lump, and then turn it out onto a flour-dusted patch of countertop. The dough should be soft and sticky at this point, so just begin by folding part of the dough's floury bottom up and over onto its top. Do this until the sticky surface of the dough is more or less tucked inside the floury surface pulled up from the bottom.

- Continue with this same up-from-the-bottom-and-over-the-top motion, but start giving the dough a quarter-turn between each fold-over motion. Dust the counter, not the dough, as you notice it sticking. As the dough becomes easier to handle, try to develop a rhythm to your kneading: fold over, push down, quarter turn, fold over, push down, quarter turn. Handle dough lightly and briskly, giving it less opportunity to stick to your hands.

- Knead for at least 5 minutes, adding only as much extra flour as you need to keep the dough from clutching your palms or grabbing the counter. You should not be trying to remove the dough's stickiness. Your goal is soft but springy dough with no lumps or wet patches.

- Put dough into the cleaned, lightly oiled mixing bowl, cover with plastic wrap, and set aside to rise for 30 – 60 minutes. The dough should double.

- Mist an 8 x 4-inch loaf pan with non-stick spray. ***Preheat oven to 400 degrees***. Scrape risen dough out of the bowl onto a lightly floured patch of countertop, and knead again for a few minutes. *(The dough might feel sloppy at first but will quickly tighten as the gluten springs back into action, so resist the impulse to add any more flour than you have to.)*

- Pat dough into a plump oval cushion about 8 inches long, fold in half, and tuck into loaf pan. Cover with oiled plastic wrap and let rise for 30 – 45 minutes or until doubled.

- Reduce heat to 375 degrees and bake for 35 minutes. (The crust will brown quickly because of the milk in the loaf.)

Brown Rice Bread
Master Recipe # 2: Using Cooked Whole Grain

Cooked rice makes moist and nubbly bread that is substantial, yet mild mannered. Its slightly chewy texture makes especially good toast. You can use any well-cooked whole grain or any sort of rice with this method, but I like my version below the best. If I haven't any freshly-cooked rice (see page 125), I steam leftover rice in a steamer basket over boiling water for about 10 minutes.

(Makes 9 x 5-inch loaf)

> 1 cup warm water
> 1 tablespoon active dry yeast
> ⅓ cup honey
> 2 cups hot cooked brown rice
> 3 cups stone ground whole wheat bread flour, divided
> 1½ teaspoons salt

- Mix together warm water and yeast in a measuring jug and set aside for at least 5 minutes. Add honey.

- Combine *2 cups* whole-wheat flour and salt with hot cooked rice in a mixing bowl. Blend thoroughly. (It will feel like a bowl of floury rubbery pellets.) Scrape the sides of the bowl clean.

- Add yeast and honey mixture to the warm rice and flour. Mix well, and then stir vigorously with a wooden spoon for about 100 strokes. Add another ½ cup and stir for another 100 strokes. *(This is an important step in developing the gluten. It's not as hard as it sounds if you switch arms after each 50 strokes or so.)* Work another ½ cup of flour into the dough. When the flour is thoroughly blended in, scrape the sides of the bowl and cover with plastic. Let rise 1 hour, or until at least doubled.

- Scrape risen dough away from sides of bowl and into a lump. Sprinkle with ¼-cup flour and tip out onto floured counter. Have handy more flour for dusting counter. The dough should be too soft and sticky to handle easily, but you only have to handle the dough enough to prepare dough for shaping. Form dough into loaf and place into an oiled 9 x 5-inch loaf pan. Cover with oiled plastic wrap.

- ***Preheat oven to 450 degrees and place rack in lower third of oven.*** Let dough rise for 30 – 60 minutes or until not quite doubled. Bake at 450 degrees in the lower third of oven for 15 minutes, and then reduce the temperature to 350 degrees and bake for another 20 minutes. Remove from pan and put back into oven on its side for another 10 minutes.

Bulgur and Oat Bread
Using Quick-Cooking Whole Grain

This is a full-bodied and mildly chewy little loaf. If you don't like the taste of molasses, substitute honey. Even mild molasses has a dominating presence, but it's compatible with these grains. If you have blackstrap molasses, use just one tablespoon with two of honey.

⅓ cup medium or fine bulgur
1 cup boiling water
⅓ cup rolled oats

¼ cup warm water
2 teaspoons active dry yeast
1 tablespoon oil
2 tablespoons mild molasses
1 tablespoon honey
1 teaspoon salt
1½ cups stone ground whole wheat bread flour

- Put the bulgur into a medium-sized mixing bowl (like 2-quart size) and add boiling water. Sprinkle the oats over the top, then cover and set aside for 30 minutes, or until the bulgur is completely soft and mixture is just warm. Meanwhile, stir yeast into warm water and set aside for 5 minutes to soften.

- Add oil, molasses, honey, and salt to grain mixture and blend well. Add yeast mixture and 1 cup whole-wheat flour and mix well. Stir vigorously with a wooden spoon for a minute or two, if you can. Scrape sides of bowl and gather dough into a lump, then cover with plastic wrap and leave for about 1 hour or until doubled.

- ***Mist a regular pie pan or baking sheet with non-stick spray.*** Scrape dough into a lump again. Sprinkle it with 2 tablespoons of flour, then tip the floury lump onto the counter and knead for a few minutes. Dust counter with flour as needed but don't try to get rid of the dough's stickiness. You only have to knead dough just enough to shape it into a plump little loaf, either oval or round. Place in pan and cover with oiled plastic wrap. ***Preheat oven to 375 degrees and place rack in lower third of oven.***

- Let loaf rise for about an hour or until it has almost doubled. If you want it to look fancy, brush with a bit of beaten egg white and sprinkle with rolled oats. Bake at 375 degrees for 35 minutes.

Pita Bread
By processor

Pita, or pocket, bread is the fastest bread to make that I know of, whether by food processor or by wooden spoon. With the processor you can make the dough at 5 p.m., and have the pockets out of the oven and ready to eat by 6 p.m. The best part is watching the pockets puffing up in the oven; they always look like they're in such a hurry. And if you are in a hurry, it's comforting to have the bread rushing right along with you.

These directions for making dough using the food processor method can be applied to any recipe of this general size. The standard 7-cup processor can easily handle this amount of dough, which is about 1½ pounds. Consider using a plastic blade, if you have one: the metal blade works better but it is too easy to cut yourself when extracting it from the dough.

> You will find this recipe, through Step #6, used as a Master Recipe for preparing the dough for the *Focaccia* and *Pizza Margherita* recipe further on.

(Makes 9 7-inch pita pockets)

> 1½ cups warm water
> 1 tablespoon (or 1 packet) active dry yeast
>
> 2 cups whole wheat flour
> 2 cups unbleached white bread flour, plus extra if needed (see Step 2)
> 2 teaspoons salt
>
> 2 tablespoons olive oil
> 2 tablespoons honey

1) Pour warm water into a 2-cup measuring jug (with pouring spout) and stir in yeast. Set aside for about 5 minutes for yeast to soften.

2) Measure whole wheat and white flour and salt into the processor bowl, and process a few seconds to mix.

3) Add oil and honey to yeast and water mixture. With processor running, pour yeast mixture slowly (but within 5 seconds) through food chute. Within another 5 seconds the dough should lump together and begin to revolve under the cover. Let it revolve about 10 times, then stop the machine and let the dough rest 5 minutes or so. (See **Note** following recipe.)

4) After dough has rested, turn on machine and let ball of dough rotate under the cover again another 30 times. *The kneading process should not last longer than 60 seconds altogether.* Cover processor bowl with plastic wrap and set aside for about 30 – 45 minutes or until doubled.

5) Turn on machine and process dough for about 5 – 10 seconds, just enough to gather it back into a lump. Scrape dough out of processor and turn out onto lightly floured surface.

6) **Preheat oven to 500 degrees and set rack in top third of oven.** Knead dough briefly to shape into a ball and divide ball in thirds, and then divide each third into 3 pieces. Beginning with 3 pieces, form each into a ball, as if you were making rolls. When you have finished with the third ball, return to the first. Flatten it with your hand, then use a rolling pin to roll it out into a circle about 7 inches across. When you have rolled out the first 3 this way, place them on the baking sheet and let rest 10 minutes. (No need to cover them for this length of time.)

7) Bake at 500 degrees for 4 - 5 minutes. *(If your oven has a window, you will notice that in about 3 minutes the pita pockets will be swelling up and practically standing on their tiptoes.)* Because of the high temperature, whip them out as soon as you think they're ready, which may be after 4 minutes in your oven. Cool them on a rack between the folds of a clean tea towel.

8) Needless to say, repeat the process with the remaining pieces of dough.

Note:
(Step 3)
If the dough stubbornly remains a thick batter instead of forming a roughly cohesive lump, add white flour while the machine is running, a tablespoon or two at a time, until a rough ball forms. As usual, add flour cautiously; everything happens pretty fast, and dough that is choking up the blade one moment may be riding friskily around in a ball on the blade the next, with the addition of a scant tablespoon of flour. If the dough is too dry, add water while machine is running, 1 tablespoon every few seconds, until ball forms. Let ball rotate under cover about 5 times before stopping machine.

Focaccia
Italian flatbread with olive oil and seasoning

Focaccia was originally just the homemade version of pizza. The name comes from the Latin word *focus* (the hearth), which is where women baked bread at home. Traditionally it was simple; pizza dough topped with olive oil and salt, and maybe garlic and fresh herbs like rosemary or sage. Naturally it's been worked over thoroughly in this country and often turns up looking like a sort of deep-dish pizza. And that's fine, I hasten to add, but I prefer my version. If I want pizza, I make pizza. If I want focaccia, I make this.

This is wonderfully versatile bread; you can serve it either as an appetizer or at the table as you would any bread — except it doesn't need butter, so you don't need butter or butter knives at the table, and you don't have people waiting for the butter to be passed. You can make it thick or thin. You can serve it in wedges or squares, or just tear off chunks, which has a certain reckless earthiness. You can also split it and use it for sandwiches.

I like a thinnish focaccia with a simple olive oil, salt, pepper, and herb topping. It's tempting to add fresh crushed or minced garlic, but burned bitter bits of garlic on the cooked focaccia are not nice. It's a hot oven, and any shred of garlic that pokes its head up is, literally, toast. However, there are *endless* variations with both dough and toppings.

(Makes enough focaccia to serve about 6 - 8 rational people)

Dough:
Follow directions for the preceding *Pita by Processor* through Step #6.
OR
Use the following directions for making the dough with your bread machine, or mix dough by hand using the directions on page 166.

1½ cups warm water
1 tablespoon (or 1 packet) active dry yeast
2 teaspoons salt
2 tablespoons olive oil
2 tablespoons honey
1¾ cups whole wheat flour
1¾ cups unbleached white bread flour

(Note: The secret to achieving a chewy, moist, airy focaccia is wet but well-worked dough. Don't add any unnecessary flour.)

Topping:
½ cup extra virgin olive oil
1 tablespoon fresh rosemary, chopped (Don't use dried.)
kosher (coarse) salt
freshly ground pepper

Bread machine method
- Place warm water in bucket of bread machine and sprinkle yeast into water. Allow a few minutes for yeast to soften, and then add whole-wheat flour and 1 cup of white flour. *(Remember to measure the flour by pouring or spooning flour into the measuring cup.)* Set bread machine on dough cycle and start. In 10 minutes add salt, oil, honey, and remaining white flour. Scrape down sides with a spatula. You should have a soft dough. Allow machine to complete the kneading stage of the dough cycle. When dough has completed most of the raising stage, or when dough at least doubles in volume, push *stop* button and remove bucket from machine. Tip dough directly into prepared pan.

Preheat oven to 450 degrees and place rack on lowest position.

- Place 2 tablespoons olive oil in 13-inch pizza pan or a 9 x 12-inch pan and spread to edges with fingers. Scrape dough out of bucket (or food processor) into pan and pat out to edges as evenly as possible. *If the dough acts stubborn, ignore it for 5 minutes and it will relax.* Set aside to rise until about doubled. *(It's harder to judge with bread as flat as focaccia, but it takes about ½ hour in my kitchen.)*

- Using the tips of your fingers, firmly poke the surface of the dough, pushing your fingers right through the dough until it is covered with deep dimples an inch or two apart. Use a pastry brush to spread the remaining oil over the dough. *(This is not the time to be squeamish; the olive oil is a critical element of the focaccia, and the finished bread should taste rich enough to banish any heretical suggestions - or even **thoughts** - of butter.)* Sprinkle with the herbs, kosher salt, and freshly ground pepper.

- Bake at 450 degrees on the lowest rack or baking stone for about 15 minutes.

Pizza Margherita

Opening up the subject of pizza is scary. It's not only vast, but it's cluttered and altogether subjective, and trying to pin down definitive recipes and methods is impossible. In colloquial Italian, *pizza* just means a pie of any kind – and apparently was made in some form or other all over Europe long before tomatoes were even cultivated there. For that matter, the *Armenians* claim to have invented the pizza! What most of us know for certain is what we happen to like on a pizza, and that's as deep as some of us are interested in digging.

This version was apparently born in Naples in 1889, created and named for Queen Margherita. The crust is thin and crisp, the topping simple and fresh. (For the record, neither whole-wheat flour nor garlic belongs in the original recipe; the poor queen was born well before the benefits of fiber and garlic were understood.)

(Makes 2x 12-inch pizzas)

Pizza Dough:
Follow directions for the preceding *Pita by Processor* through Step #6.
(or mix dough by hand using the directions on page 166.)

Topping:
2 lbs tomatoes, approximately (preferably Roma – more flesh, less core)
¼ cup torn-up fresh basil leaves
¼ cup olive oil
2 tablespoons minced fresh garlic
½-lb whole milk mozzarella, sliced
kosher salt and freshly ground pepper

Preheat oven to 500 degrees and place rack in lowest position. *(If you have a baking stone that doesn't live full time in your oven, place it on the lowest rack before turning on the oven.)*

- Quarter tomatoes and scoop out seed clusters with your thumb. *(Don't discard! Eat or save for soup or something.)* Remove bits of core, which in Roma tomatoes are pretty inoffensive. Dice in ¼ -inch chunks and combine with basil, olive oil, and garlic. Slice mozzarella.

- Divide dough in half and form each half into a smooth ball. Roll out first half to a 12-inch circle on well-floured surface. Transfer to baking sheet sprinkled with cornmeal or misted with non-stick spray. Spread with half of tomato mixture, arrange half of sliced mozzarella over the top, and sprinkle with salt and freshly ground pepper.

- Bake for about 10 - 12 minutes or until edges and bottom crust are at least golden. Prepare second pizza the same way.

Scottish Oatcakes

These oatcakes are not for wimps. Neither cracker nor cookie, these are stalwart, simple, rich little repositories of cardio-friendly fiber. I love them. To me these are as good as cookies, yet a person can feel almost self-righteous eating them. They keep well for at least a week, in my opinion, but they're best freshly baked. I serve oatcakes as snacks anytime or with morning or afternoon tea with a chunk of extra *sharp* cheddar cheese on the side. (I always keep a few packets of Bob's Red Mill Scottish oatmeal on hand.)

(Makes about 18 1½-inch oatcakes)

> 1½ cups Scottish oatmeal
> ½ cup whole wheat pastry flour
> 2 tablespoon sugar or honey
> ½ teaspoon salt
> ½ teaspoon baking powder
>
> ¼ cup melted butter
> ⅓ cup boiling water
>
> (extra ¼ cup Scottish oats for sprinkling on counter)

Preheat oven to 325 degrees.

- In a mixing bowl combine Scottish oatmeal, flour, salt, and baking powder.

- Combine melted butter, honey, and boiling water and add to oatmeal mixture, blending thoroughly. The mixture will be moist and sticky. Set aside for 5 minutes while some of the liquid is absorbed.

- Sprinkle countertop thickly with extra Scottish oats and pat out oat mixture. Using a rolling pin dusted with flour, roll out mixture to ⅛ inch thick. Cut out rounds or diamonds or whatever shapes you prefer, and place on an ungreased baking sheet. (You can crowd them.)

- Bake in the middle of a 325-degree oven for 30 – 40 minutes, or until oatcakes are lightly golden. (*Note:* a slight difference in thickness or an oven that runs hotter than average can make a significant difference in timing.) I like them good and crispy, but you can experiment by removing a couple after 20 minutes and comparing them to the toastier ones that stay in the oven the extra 10 - 20 minutes.

About Muffins

People generally seem to like muffins, and they're relatively simple and quick to make. The only type of muffin worth making, though, is one that delivers a hefty dose of fiber and the minimum of refined sugar and flour. Fiber-rich muffins can serve a useful purpose when you're dealing with people who haven't made the transition to a better diet, philosophically or otherwise.

But expectations are key. Anyone who is used to muffins that are like large, fluffy cupcakes is going to be horribly disappointed in the sort of muffins we're talking about here. Whole grain muffins can be pretty dense and tend to make a bit of a statement. Unless a person is used to eating unrefined high-fiber carbohydrates, or is open-minded about the subject, think of something else to spend your time making. Whole-wheat bread may be a better choice, sidestepping the whole expectation issue.

Some muffin tips:

- These muffins are 100 percent whole grain. You can adjust the level of whole-wheat flour and bran to suit, but *at the least* you can start with 50 percent whole wheat without any problem from picky eaters who may be used to muffins made with white flour. You can gradually increase the proportion of whole-wheat flour over time to an unsuspecting audience.

- Muffins are especially quick to make if you happen to have nuts prepared in advance. (Some of us have a strong preference for nuts in muffins.)

- I have never noticed a difference in muffins whose wet and dry ingredients have been mixed "only until just blended" and muffins whose ingredients have been "thoroughly mixed". I choose to thoroughly mix.

- When you're using whole-wheat flour the batter may seem too runny right after it's mixed. I find that if I let it sit while I clean up the kitchen, it not only thickens, but the muffins rise better in the oven. This is especially useful to know when you have forgotten to preheat the oven.

- I bake muffins at 400 degrees, and I don't wait for them to brown. I want a moist muffin, and whole grain muffins can be dry, if you're not careful. Naturally, though, your oven may behave differently than mine: you can test a muffin by breaking it in half immediately after pulling the tin out of the oven, and if it's still a bit wet in the center, bake the rest for another 2 – 4 minutes. Keep in mind, however, that a muffin hot from the oven can *seem* undercooked but will firm up as it cools.

- Using the general proportions in these recipes you can easily create your own variations. There are so many options, it's dizzying. Don't forget, though, that muffins generally should still be classified as high-fiber cake and not your daily bread.

Serious Muffins
with Flaxseed Meal and Carrot

It should be understood that this is not your average superficial, giddy sort of muffin. This is a muffin of substance and conviction. The recipe was adapted from the version printed on the flaxseed meal package from Bob's Red Mill of Milwaukie, Oregon. Natural food stores and some supermarkets carry flaxseed meal — and it should be refrigerated. In any case, you *can* buy whole flaxseeds and grind your own meal in a coffee grinder dedicated to that purpose.

(Makes 12 muffins, ½-cup size)

> ¾ cup flaxseed meal
> 1¼ cup whole wheat pastry flour
> 2 teaspoons baking powder
> 2 teaspoons baking soda
> 1 teaspoon salt
> 1 teaspoon cinnamon
> ¼ teaspoon ground cloves
> 1 cup chopped walnuts
> 1 cup golden raisins
>
> 2 eggs
> ¾ cup milk
> ¾ cup brown sugar
> 2 raw carrots, finely grated (about 2 cups)

Pre-heat oven to 400 degrees. Oil muffin tins and set aside.

- Combine dry ingredients and mix thoroughly. (A dry wire whisk works well.) Stir in nuts and raisins and set aside.

- In a mixing bowl or an 8-cup Pyrex jug, whisk eggs. Add milk and sugar, and mix well.

- Grate carrot on fine holes of grater (the ⅛ inch teardrop-shaped holes). Add to egg mixture and blend well.

- Tip dry ingredients into wet and blend thoroughly. Set batter aside while you clean up your mess. Scoop into muffin tins – I like using a ⅓-cup measure. You can fill muffin cups at least ¾-full. Bake in center of 400-degree oven for about 20 minutes. Using a butter knife, ease muffins from tins and cool on wire rack.

Banana Bran Muffins

Most homes seem to have bananas, and most bananas are over-ripe at some time in their lives. This is where muffins come in. For those of us who feel vaguely guilty about our frank distaste for eating bananas straight, especially when the banana is such a practical and well-meaning fruit, there is a tremendous sense of satisfaction in being able to use *three bananas* in one recipe.

(Makes 12 muffins, ½-cup size)

1 cup wheat bran or oat bran
1¼ cup stone-ground whole wheat pastry flour
2 teaspoons baking powder
1 teaspoon baking soda
1 teaspoon salt
1½ teaspoons cinnamon
1 cup chopped pecans or walnuts

2 eggs
¾ cup milk
½ cup brown sugar
¼ cup extra virgin olive oil
2 – 3 ripe bananas, or about 1¾ cups, diced and roughly mashed

Pre-heat oven to 400 degrees. Oil muffin tins and set aside.

- Combine dry ingredients and mix thoroughly. (A dry wire whisk works well.) Add nuts and set aside.

- In a mixing bowl or 8-cup Pyrex jug, whisk eggs. Add milk, sugar, oil, and banana. *If you dice the bananas first and then only roughly mash them, you will end up with nice little bits of creamy banana in the cooked muffins.* Mix well.

- Tip dry ingredients into wet and blend thoroughly. The mixture may seem too wet; let it sit and rest while you clean up your mess and wash the dishes. Scoop mixture into muffin tins (I like to use a ⅓-cup measure for this), filling them about ¾ full.

- Bake in center of 400-degree oven for about 20 minutes. Using a butter knife, ease muffins from tins and cool on wire rack.

Extreme Muffins
Wheat-free

These are favorites of mine partly because they are so unconventional and partly because they are so sensible. A muffin this sensible has an uphill battle in the taste department but these are good. They are also short and stubby with a flat top and tender crumb. They are wheat-free and gluten-free, and call for oat bran instead of any kind of flour. They are sweetened with maple syrup instead of sugar, have yogurt instead of milk, and include fresh apple, dried prunes, and olive oil. These muffins rise very little in the oven.

(Makes 12 – 15 muffins, ½-cup size)

2 cups oat bran
2 teaspoons baking powder
1 teaspoon baking soda
1 teaspoon salt
2 teaspoons cinnamon

2 eggs
½ cup yogurt
½ cup maple syrup
¼ cup olive oil
zest (the orange part of the peel) from 1 orange, minced (or 1 tablespoon)

1 apple, peeled and grated (about 1- 1½ cups)
1 cup chopped dried pitted prunes (¼-inch pieces)

Pre-heat oven to 400 degrees. Oil muffin tins and set aside.

- Combine dry ingredients and mix thoroughly. Set aside.

- In a mixing bowl or an 8-cup Pyrex jug, whisk together egg, yogurt, maple syrup, oil, and orange zest. Stir in grated apple and prunes.

- Tip dry ingredients into wet and blend thoroughly. The mixture will probably be quite wet; set it aside while you clean up your muffin mess and the mixture will thicken and make a slightly more rounded muffin.

- Spoon into the oiled muffin tins. *Muffin cups should be no more than ⅔ full: if the muffins rise above the level of the cups, they will spread out, not up.*

- Bake in center of 400-degree oven for about 20 minutes. Using a butter knife, ease muffins from tins and cool on wire rack.

Almond Tea Cakes
Wheat-free

In this recipe, ground almonds replace flour. These are rich, sweet, and nutty-textured – perfect for the times you want a bit more than a cookie, but something less than dessert.

(Makes 12 tea cakes, ½-cup size)

> 2½ cups ground almonds
> 1 teaspoon cinnamon
> ½ teaspoon baking soda
> ½ teaspoon salt
>
> 2 eggs
> ¼ cup melted butter
> ½ cup honey

Pre-heat oven to 375 degrees. Line 12 ½-cup muffin tins with paper liners and set aside.

- Combine ground almonds with cinnamon, soda, and salt, and mix very well.

- Combine eggs, butter, and honey, and beat together with electric beaters or a whisk.

- Add almond mixture to egg mixture and blend thoroughly. Line muffin cups with paper liners, and fill half full with mixture. Bake in lower third of oven for 15-20 minutes.

Oatmeal Cookies

WARNING **:** We strongly recommend that any cookies should be an occasional treat or something to make when company is coming. Cookie jars don't belong in the home of responsible adults. But if you *do* make cookies, don't lose sight of their mission, which is to brighten the eyes and delight the soul.

(Makes about 18 3-inch cookies)

> 1 cup (½-lb or 2 sticks) butter
> 1 cup brown sugar, packed (see ***Note*** below)
> 2 eggs
>
> 1 cup whole wheat pastry flour
> 1½ teaspoons cinnamon
> 1 teaspoon baking soda
> ½ teaspoon salt
>
> 3 cups old-fashioned rolled oats
> 1 cup chopped walnuts or pecans
> 1 cup raisins

Preheat oven to 350 degrees and set rack in middle of oven.

- Beat together butter and sugar until creamy, and then beat in eggs.

- Mix together flour, cinnamon, baking soda, and salt. (Make sure the baking soda has no little lumps.) Stir into the butter mixture until well blended.

- Combine rolled oats, raisins, and nuts in a mixing bowl. (I prefer a large bowl – the oats tend to be a bit frisky during the mixing.) Add butter/flour mixture and blend thoroughly.

- Using 2 spoons, drop lumps of cookie dough 1½ inches apart on an ungreased baking sheet. (I press them out a bit – I don't like them too thick in the middle.) Bake in 350-degree oven for about 18 minutes or until golden brown.

Note:

➢ This recipe produces an oatmeal cookie that I consider all-purpose. More sugar will produce a crispier version and less sugar will produce a more cakey texture that I don't like. You can customize your cookies to suit the occasion; if you need a more traditional oatmeal cookie, add ¼ - ½ cup of white sugar.

Coconut Macaroons

Macaroons are a marvelous answer to excess egg whites. These particular coconut macaroons are disgracefully simple to make, they store well, and they freeze beautifully, too. (In fact, I have served them directly from the freezer.) You can generally find dried unsweetened shredded coconut in the bulk food section of natural food stores or packaged by Bob's Red Mill.

(Makes about 2 dozen)

>2 egg whites (scant ⅓ cup)
>½ cup white sugar
>1 teaspoon pure almond extract
>¼ teaspoon salt
>2 cups dried unsweetened shredded coconut

Preheat oven to 350 degrees. Set rack in middle of oven. Mist baking sheet with non-stick spray.

- Whisk egg whites, sugar, extract, and salt in a mixing bowl until well blended. Add coconut and mix thoroughly. The mixture will be thick and sticky, and not especially cohesive. Using 2 spoons, form walnut-sized blobs about an inch apart on the oiled baking sheet. (Stir mixture if it sits for a while, as the egg white tends to settle.)

- Bake at 350 degrees in the middle of the oven for 20 minutes, or until macaroons are golden top and bottom. Transfer from baking sheet to cooling rack with a thin-edged metal spatula. Store in covered container for a week, or store for a few months in the freezer, very well sealed.

Note:
- ➢ You can fool around with proportions to suit your taste or circumstances. Macaroons made with a wetter mixture will spread slightly as they cook, be chewier, and will last longer. (I've kept them successfully for 2 weeks.)

- ➢ For **Almond Macaroons**, replace all or part of the coconut with toasted ground almonds. (See directions for toasting slivered almonds on page 128.) Depending on the proportion of almonds to egg white, the cookies may spread a bit: place them at least 1½ inches apart on the baking sheet. Otherwise, the other ingredients and instructions are the same. I love these cookies but they can be too hard for some. It is safer to err on the side of too wet for this batter; if crunchiness is a problem, a thinner cookie is better.

Hot Chocolate (Cocoa)
Basic model

Here is a recipe for a simple mug of hot chocolate. Ordinary pure unsweetened cocoa from most suppliers is perfectly suitable and satisfying: there is no need to use one of the premium products, even if it is grown on a private plantation in a remote corner of South America. When choosing one just be sure you are starting with pure cocoa — sweetened cocoa mixes are mostly sugar. Where we live, plain unsweetened Hershey's cocoa is a good choice, and available in most supermarkets. "Dutch process" cocoa may not be as good a choice due to the damage the process does to the phenolic nutrients. Remember to check the baking section if you can't find what you want on the beverage shelves.

(Makes 1 mug, or about 1¼ cups)

1 cup whole milk
2 tablespoons pure unsweetened cocoa powder, like Hershey's
¼ cup boiling water
1 – 2 teaspoons honey, or to taste
⅛ teaspoon salt

- Heat milk over medium heat in a little saucepan (1-quart size is perfect for this amount of milk) until it is steaming energetically *but not bubbling.* It's a good idea to set a timer for 5 minutes: by then the milk should be steaming. If you let the milk boil it will develop a skin and an overcooked flavor.

- Meanwhile, combine cocoa, water, honey, and salt, and blend with a spoon or a little whisk until cocoa lumps are gone.

- Add chocolate mixture to hot milk and whisk vigorously. Pour into a warmed mug. Drink immediately or thereabouts.

Note:
➢ Salt enhances most food, sweet or savory. It also has a way of reducing the need for as much sweetening.

➢ Vanilla essence is a traditional addition to cocoa, but a good-quality pure vanilla is more expensive than its effect is worth, in this opinion. Orange extract is delicious to some.

➢ Honey is the best choice for a sweetener but it has more flavor than sugar. Use a very mild-tasting variety like clover honey.

Index

Recipe Index
General Index

Recipe Index

Dressings, Dips, Spreads, and Sides

Sauces & Miscellaneous

Vegetables

Frozen Vegetables

Vegetable Sides

Vegetable Salads

Vegetable Soups

Main Course Soups

Beans

Grains

Brown Rice Recipes

Other Grain Recipes

Main Dishes

Baking

Yeast Breads

Quick breads & Cookies

General Index

Good Food, Great Medicine - A Homemade Cookbook
Third Printing
by Mea Hassell and Miles Hassell, M.D.

Ordering Information
Please fill out this form, choose a payment option and return to our office via mail or fax:

Mail:
Miles Hassell, M.D.
Attn: Cookbook
9155 SW Barnes, Suite 302
Portland, OR 97225

Fax:
(503) 291-1079

Please print

Date:	
Name:	
Street:	
City:	
State:	
Zip code:	
Telephone:	
E-mail address:	

Good Food, Great Medicine	Quantity	Cost	Total
I will pick up my order		$ 20.00	$
Please mail my order to the address listed above		$ 25.00	$
	Total Amount Enclosed		$

Payment options (choose one):
○ I want to pay by check or money order (*payment enclosed - payable to: Miles Hassell, M.D.*)
○ I want to pay by Visa or MasterCard
Name as it appears on card:
Card number:
Expiration date: